LECTIONARY SCRIPTURE NOTES

FOR SERIES B

Norman A. Beck

CSS Publishing Co., Inc.
Lima, Ohio

LECTIONARY SCRIPTURE NOTES FOR SERIES B

FIRST EDITION
Copyright @ 2011 by
Norman A. Beck

ISBN-13: 978-0-7880-2636-2
ISBN-10: 0-7880-2636-4

PRINTED IN USA

EDITOR'S NOTE

Prior to 1969, most of the congregations in the denominations of Christians that use pre-selected texts from Scripture as readings during their worship services utilized a one year cycle of texts. In response to a directive from Vatican II that a more comprehensive lectionary be made available, a three year series (cycle) of texts, *Lectionary for Mass*, was developed and was published in 1969, so that approximately 12-15% of the Bible over a three-year period rather than perhaps 4-5% of the Bible repeated each year would be read and heard within the worshiping congregations for those who attended at least once each week. Most Lutheran groups soon approved use of the Roman Catholic three-year lectionary, which they adapted slightly so as not to use readings from the so-called Old Testament Apocrypha. Other Christian groups, initially Episcopal, United Church of Christ, Presbyterian, Disciples of Christ, United Methodist, and United Church of Canada, developed a lectionary based on the Roman Catholic three-year cycle and differing somewhat from the Lutheran selections by selecting consecutive readings in certain instances, especially in their use of texts from the Older Testament.

During the years between 1983 and 1992 a larger group of Christian denominations, attempting to achieve greater uniformity in their selections, produced first The Common Lectionary, and then The Revised Common Lectionary. The work of lectionary revision continues. Particular attention and sensitivity is needed during this task of revision to avoid use of texts that present all Pharisees and in some instances all Jews negatively. For easy access to a discussion of this, please see my article "Removing Anti-Jewish Polemic from our Christian Lectionaries: A Proposal," http://jcrelations. net/en/?item=737 (also in a Spanish translation).

The book you are holding provides guidelines and resources for homilies and sermons, worship planning, and Scripture study based on the texts in Year B (Cycle B) in *The Revised Common Lectionary: Consultation on Common Texts* (Nashville: Abington, 1992). Leaders in worship and worship planning and other members of Christian congregations and communities will find this book to be helpful for use as individuals and in study groups as they prepare for more meaningful worship experiences each weekend.

BACKGROUND INFORMATION

This resource provides guidelines for preaching, worship planning, and Scripture study based on the texts in Year B in *The Revised Common Lectionary: Consultation on Common Texts* (Nashville: Abingdon, 1992). It is a revised and updated replacement for Norman A. Beck, *Scripture Notes B* (Lima, Ohio: CSS Publishing, 1984).

Unique to this resource is its sensitivity to the lectionary selections that include negative statements about Jews in general and about Pharisees in particular. For additional information regarding these negative statements, please see my article, "Removing Anti-Jewish Polemic from our Christian Lectionaries: A Proposal," http://jcrelations. net/en/?item=737. For a more comprehensive study of the negative statements about Jews in our texts, see my *Mature Christianity in the 21st Century: The Recognition and Repudiation of the Anti-Jewish Polemic of the New Testament* (New York: Crossroad, 1994). For translations of the Greek New Testament into modern English that are sensitive to the negative statements about Jews, see the Contemporary English Version of the Holy Bible published by the American Bible Society in 1995 and my *The New Testament: A New Translation and Redaction* (Lima, Ohio: Fairway Press, 2001). The latter work includes as an Appendix, A New Four Year Lectionary, in which, instead of the texts within The Revised Common Lectionary that are negative about Jews, much more edifying texts are provided, Gospel selections for Year 1 are from the Gospel According to Mark, and Gospel selections for Year 4 are from the Fourth Gospel.

Gospel Selections in Year B

The majority of the Gospel selections in Year B of The Revised Common Lectionary are from the Gospel According to Mark. After many centuries in which this shortest of the

5

Four Gospels was given relatively little attention, Mark re-emerged during the nineteenth and twentieth centuries as the favorite among many biblical scholars because it is now generally considered to have been the earliest of the Four Gospels to have been written and the closest in many respects to the Jesus of history, the primary founder of the Christian faith.

Most of "The Gospel of Jesus Christ," the title given to this document in Mark 1:1, may have been written within an extended eschatological community of followers of Jesus in rural and small town southern Syria followers who were refugees of war during the time of the Jewish revolt against Roman occupation force rule in Galilee and Judea in 67 CE, as suggested by Howard Clark Kee in *Community of the New Age: Studies in Mark's Gospel* (Philadelphia: Westminster, 1977). In this document, perhaps written initially by John Mark, which the author and the Markan community members at that time may have thought would be the only Gospel of Jesus Christ that would be compiled, sayings of Jesus remembered and stories developed about Jesus, together with bits and pieces of the Jewish Scriptures that we as Christians call the "Old Testament," were shaped into a connected narrative in order to express what the inspired author and the people of the Markan community of faith believed about God, Jesus, the world, and themselves.

Segments of the Markan Gospel had almost certainly been used prior to the time of the writing of this "Gospel of Jesus Christ," much as we today use segments of it and of other biblical texts as the primary basis for our Christian message and teaching. When the first forty years after the crucifixion of Jesus had passed without the expected culmination of the present age, it is likely that, as most of the members of this extended eschatological community moved to urban areas to seek day labor in the market places of cities, they took with them copies of their precious Markan document. In Antioch and in Ephesus other followers of Jesus, also inspired by God, revised and added to early copies of this "Gospel of Jesus Christ" to produce what would later be called "The Gospel According to Matthew" and "The Gospel According to Luke."

"The Gospel of Jesus Christ," the first of the Synoptic Gospels and the most creative in its development of the gospel genre, continued to be used in Rome and elsewhere within the emerging Church, but it did not regain its pre-eminence until nineteenth and twentieth century New Testament studies recovered evidence of the priority of this story within the Four Gospels collection.

THE GOSPEL SELECTIONS IN SERIES B
The Revised Common Lectionary

The Gospel selections in Series B are the most diverse of the three Series A, B, and C. Although approximately 60% of the Gospel selections in Series B in the Revised Common Lectionary are from the Gospel According to Mark, many are from John and a few are from Luke and Matthew. Since the majority of the Gospel selections during Series B are from Mark, we consider the Church Year of Series B to be the year of Mark. Because Mark, however, unlike Matthew and Luke, does not have extensive introductory "infancy narratives" and, unlike Matthew, Luke, and John, in the most ancient manuscripts available to us does not have reflective "resurrection appearance" accounts, selections from Mark in Series B of this lectionary are supplemented by using many texts from the other Gospels. There is no year of John in these series. Nevertheless, there are many more texts from John in Series B, the year of Mark; than in Series A, the year of Matthew; and Series C, the year of Luke. This pattern was established within the Roman Catholic Church in its Lectionary for Mass in 1969 as authorized by Vatican II, adapted with numerous changes by Lutheran and various other Christian groups after 1969, and modified somewhat more during the early 1990s as *The Revised Common Lectionary* (Nashville: Abingdon, 1992).

As is well known, the so-called "historic pericopes," widely used prior to the late 1960s, were one-year cycles of texts, repeated every year. The Roman Catholic Lectionary for Mass established a three-year cycle, which has been dominant since that time. There have been a few four-year cycle lectionaries produced, most notably A Four Year Lectionary developed in the British Isles and published by the Canterbury Press in Norwich, England, in 1990, and my own more accessible "A New Four Year Lectionary," published as an Appendix in my *The New Testament: A New Translation and Redaction* (Lima, Ohio: Fairway Press, 2001).

After many centuries in which the shortest of the Four Gospels was given relatively little attention in the Church, Mark has become during the past few centuries the favorite Gospel among many biblical scholars. The reason for this is that most of us consider Mark to have been the earliest of the Four Gospels to have been written and the closest in many respects to the Jesus of history.

The location and the situation in the lives of followers of Jesus in which Mark was developed and written have been of great interest with many possibilities suggested. Because there is evidence of Mark being used in Rome during the latter decades of the first century and during the second more extensively than in any other area, Rome is the choice of many scholars. Galilee and Syria are preferred by others. My own personal preference is heavily influenced by the suggestion of Howard Clark Kee in his *Community of the New Age: Studies in Mark's Gospel* (Philadelphia: Westminster, 1977), that most of "The Gospel of Jesus Christ," the title given to this document in Mark 1:1, may have been written within an extended eschatological community of followers of Jesus in rural and small town southern Syria during the time soon after the Jewish revolt in Galilee and Judea against Roman occupational force rule.

The situation in the lives of followers of Jesus in which Mark was developed and written is perhaps more important than the location and is certainly closely related to it. The references in Mark to Jesus' activities in the regions of Tyre, Sidon, Caesarea Philippi, and the Decapolis, in which Jesus interacted with persons of other than Jewish backgrounds, fed multitudes of hungry followers, and heard Peter's statement that Jesus is the Christ support Kee's contention that much of the development of Mark may have occurred in those regions. Along with information supplied by Flavius

9

Josephus, a scenario can be constructed in which many followers of Jesus in Galilee and in Judea fled from those areas and became refugees of war in the regions of Tyre, Sidon, Caesarea Philippi, and the Decapolis when battle-tested Roman legions regained control of Galilee and Judea in the year 67 CE. Although most of these followers of Jesus would not have participated in the Jewish nationalistic revolt of 66 CE, they were well aware that when the Romans regained control of rebellious areas, the Romans decimated the population in those areas, killing some and selling many on the Roman slave markets without bothering to ask which persons had participated in the rebellion. The areas of Tyre, Sidon, Caesarea Philippi, and the Decapolis formed a semi-circle around Galilee, outside the areas of rebellion, but close enough to Galilee that if these followers of Jesus heard that Jesus had come back to Galilee, they would overcome their fear of the Romans and within a day's time would be able to rush back to be with Jesus.

The numbers whom it is said in Mark 6 and in Mark 8 that Jesus fed, approximately 5,000 men plus women and children of Jewish background in Mark 6 and approximately 4,000 men plus women and children of non-Jewish background in Mark 8, suggest that these refugees of war who were followers of Jesus may have numbered 25,000-30,000. Since they would have very few monetary resources and would be competing for day labor opportunities with even larger numbers of Jewish refugees of war who were not followers of Jesus, their position would soon become perilous. A decision would have been made to migrate to the north to the area of Antioch, a trade center with a large population and more opportunities for being hired as day laborers in the market areas of that city. It would have been known that there were significant numbers of other followers of Jesus in Antioch who would help as much as possible. There would also be other people there who might join with them as followers of

Jesus. There was a major problem of language, however. The messages about Jesus that they shared orally were expressed in Galilean Aramaic. The prevailing language in Antioch and in the eastern areas of the Roman Empire was koiné Greek.

If John Mark, who having grown up in Jerusalem would have had adequate proficiency in the Greek language, who had been a young adolescent who perhaps had become a follower of Jesus when Jesus came to Jerusalem for that final week of Jesus' life, had camped with Jesus and the somewhat older male followers of Jesus from Galilee each night on the Mount of Olives, and later had heard from Peter and others much more about Jesus' life and message, was among these refugees, he would be the best person to be asked or to offer to put the message about Jesus into written form in koiné Greek. The content of what later would be called the Gospel According to Mark indicates that John Mark, or whoever else may have participated in the composition of the document, used sayings of Jesus and stories about Jesus as the Christ, the Son of God, who was empowered by the Spirit of God to perform miraculous events, together with bits and pieces of the Jewish Scriptures, and shaped them into a connected narrative to express what the people of this refugee community of faith believed about God, about Jesus, about the world, and about themselves. This "Gospel of Jesus Christ, the Son of God" (Mark 1:1) was given a plot, suspense, development of characters, point of view, with intended readers, ideal readers, and other features that we can identify. It was a very significant accomplishment, compiled with much "inspired creativity."

Some of the resources utilized in writing what was labeled a "gospel" in its initial sentence may have been formulated and used in both oral and written form in Galilee and in Judea prior to the Jewish revolt, portions may have been written during the weeks and months of refugee community existence in rural and small town southern Syria, and other portions may have been written in Antioch during the siege and fall of Jerusalem. A few other words and details may have been added later when the document was used in Rome.

While at the time of its composition, the writer and the community for which this Gospel was written probably thought that it would be the only Gospel of Jesus Christ to be compiled, subsequent events resulted in the formulation of the other two Synoptic Gospels and, somewhat separately, the Fourth Gospel. Because of the size of the refugee community of followers of Jesus who migrated to Antioch and because of competition for day labor in the marketplaces of Antioch, it is probable that a second difficult decision had to be made. A portion of the community would have to migrate farther from its base in Galilee and Judea. Several weeks walking across Asia Minor would take that portion of the community to the large city of Ephesus on the Adriatic Sea, where with fewer refugees of war better opportunities for day labor would be available. It was known that relatively more affluent communities of followers of Jesus primarily of non-Jewish origin, a result of the labors of the Apostle Paul and others, already present in the Roman province of Asia would help them with initial food and shelter as they had been helped by followers of Jesus in Antioch. The group that moved on to Ephesus may have included John Mark and without doubt carried a copy of the "Gospel of Jesus Christ" with them.

Still later, it seems likely that a few of the most adventurous among the extended Markan community group in Ephesus traveled by sea to Rome itself, where there were followers of Jesus meeting on the first day of each week in various homes and where there were the greatest opportunities for economic advancement. They too would have taken with them a precious copy of the "Gospel of Jesus Christ." John Mark was most likely within this small group. A few others may have taken a copy of the "Gospel of Jesus Christ" with them to seek employment in the prosperous city of Alexandria in Egypt.

In each of these locations, as additional hand copies of the Markan Gospel were produced, intentional as well as inadvertent changes and alterations would have occurred in the document. After perhaps twelve to fifteen years of usage in Antioch, a team of redactors, some of whom were still very Jewish in their thinking and others, frustrated after repeated attempts to convince Jews, especially Pharisees, in that region to join in the beliefs and practices of the Markan followers of Jesus, modified and added sayings and teachings of Jesus and about Jesus to their copies of the Markan document. Thus they produced a first draft of what would later become and be called the Gospel According to Matthew. Spending so much of their time in the market areas of this major trade route city of northern Syria, they would have been influenced by wisdom traditions, including ideas passed by one group of traders to another from areas as far distant as South and even East Asia, ideas associated with the Zoroastrians in Persia (the Magi of the Matthew 2:1-12 account), Hindus in India, and even Buddhists in Southeast Asia (evident in portions of Matthew 6:25-34). Some of these sayings attributed to Jesus and/or from Jesus may have existed in oral or written form as Logia associated with the disciple Matthew and in what scholars in Germany and elsewhere centuries later would classify as "Q" selections.

It would be expected that on one of the occasions when members from the group in Antioch traveled across Asia Minor to Ephesus they would have taken with them a copy of their first draft of Matthew to share with their close friends and relatives in the communities in the area of Ephesus. Someone in the communities in Ephesus, thoroughly familiar with the Greek vocabulary and style of the Septuagint translation of the Hebrew Scriptures but not with the geography of Galilee and of Judea, would soon after that with inspired creativity produce what that redactor claimed in a preface that we designate as Luke 1:1-4 to be a superior and more orderly account than either the "Gospel of Jesus Christ" (Mark) or the initial draft of the document that had been produced by the "committee" of redactors in Antioch. This writer utilized much more of the literary style and many more ideas from the Septuagint than were used by the Matthean redactors. A copy of what later would be labeled the Gospel According to Luke would then be taken back to Antioch. Changes that partially harmonized these two documents would then begin and would continue for centuries, as text studies of the Gospels indicates. The members of the extended Markan communities in the areas around Antioch would prefer their Matthean redaction. Those in the area of Ephesus would prefer their Lukan document. In both areas, usage of the earlier "Gospel of Jesus Christ" declined as usage of their own favorite redaction increased.

The smaller numbers in the extended Markan communities in Rome and in Alexandria probably did not produce major redactions as was being done in Antioch and in Ephesus. Somewhat isolated geographically from the larger extended Markan community groups, they merely made minor modifications of their copies of the Markan Gospel and continued to use and to prefer them, even when eventually copies of the Matthean and Lukan redactions became available. This scenario, although certainly only one possibility among many, provides an explanation of how the Gospel of Jesus Christ was taken to Rome and why it rather than Matthew and Luke continued to be the most significant Gospel in Rome for many decades. It also provides explanations of many of the similarities and of many of the differences within our copies of the Synoptic Gospels.

The "Gospel of Jesus Christ," the first of the Four Gospels and the most creative in its development of the gospel genre, continued to be used within many areas of the developing

Christian Church, and 100 years after its composition it was among the twenty documents that comprised the Christian canon at that time. It did not, however, regain its pre-eminence until modern New Testament studies developed evidence of its priority among the Four Gospels.

SEASON OF ADVENT
FIRST SUNDAY OF ADVENT

"Come back, O Lord! Return to us! Split the heavens open wide and come down the way you used to come!" With these words, paraphrased and summarized from the Isaiah tradition, the inspired leaders of the Isaiah tradition called out to the Lord at the end of the period of Israelite exile and during the long, difficult decades of their struggle to restore Jerusalem.

"Stir up your power, O Lord, and come to save us! Restore us! Let your face shine so that we can see it and be saved!" The words of the psalmist are appropriate for any people in need at any time and place. The opening words of the traditional Prayer for the Day for this Sunday, "Stir up your power, O Lord, and come!" would serve very well as the theme for the message in all four of the texts for this day.

Each time I go with students in my New Testament Studies and History of Religions classes at Texas Lutheran University to worship God among Hindus at the Hindu Temple of San Antonio, with Buddhists at the Thai Buddhist Wat Dhammabucha, with Jews at Temple Beth-El in San Antonio, and with Muslims at the Islamic Center of San Antonio and we are warmly welcomed, I think about possibilities and situations in which we might invite Hindus, Buddhists, Jews, and Muslims to worship God among us in our Lutheran Christian services. Of all of the seasons of the Church Year, I think that the four Sundays of Advent are the best choices, especially this First Sunday of Advent with the texts selected for this day.

In the Old Testament texts for the First Sunday of Advent in Series B of this lectionary (Isaiah 64:1-9 and Psalm 80:1-7, 17-19) the Lord God is called upon to come into the current situation of distress and need within this and every time and space and to do what the Lord is reported to have done in the past. Hindus, Buddhists, Jews, and Muslims can all resonate with these texts together with us. Within the New Testament accounts for this day, on the other hand, the emphasis is placed upon the end of time, the end of the age, the coming Day of the Lord. Here the message is to wait patiently, prepared for the revealing of our Lord Jesus Christ, being sustained guiltless on that day (1 Corinthians 1:3-9), watching at the door, sleeplessly, on a 24-hour seven-day alert (Mark 13:24-37). Hindus can relate well to this, but these particularities cannot be easily embraced by Buddhists, Jews, and Muslims. Nevertheless, pastors who have a sound theology of creation and who have familiarity with the experiences of Buddhists, Jews, and Muslims can structure the message on this occasion in ways that would be welcoming to Buddhists, Jews, and Muslims. That is a challenge we should accept, especially during the Sundays of Advent. An adequate message should include both universalities and particularities. That is what we are called to do.

We note that in the Isaiah 64:1-9 and Psalm 80:1-7, 17-19 texts the Lord God is addressed. In 1 Corinthians 1:3-9 and in Mark 13:24-37 followers of Jesus are addressed. In the Older Testament texts the Lord is called upon to save us here. In the Newer Testament texts the expectation is that the Lord Jesus Christ will come to take us from here. Let us, then, look briefly at each of these four texts.

Isaiah 64:1-9

This selection is a portion of the psalm of intercession that runs from Isaiah 63:7—64:12. A reading and an analysis of this entire song will help us to regain something of the context of this portion and of the vivid images within it. The selection that is our First Lesson should be read with much feeling! The lector for the day should be encouraged to read this text vibrantly. It is our task as those who proclaim the Word to recapture and to recapitulate the same vibrant feeling in the sermon or homily. We must address our needs, the needs of the people within the community of faith in which we live, just as they did in theirs.

Psalm 80:1-7, 17-19

The restoration emphasis within this great group lament suggests that this psalm may have had its *Sitz im Leben* (situation in the life of the people of that time) at the same time and perhaps at the same place as that of the Isaiah 64:1-9 song. Dare we today pray as this psalmist prayed? Can we update the psalm in some way within the proclamation of the message, substituting terminology current for our time and place while retaining the urgency of the prayer? In doing this, we will be calling upon the Lord to bless us with the strong presence of the Lord here and now in this present world of time and space.

1 Corinthians 1:3-9

The primary point of contact between this text that includes the reading of the final part of Paul's salutation and all of the thanksgiving section of this extensive letter and the other three tests appointed for this day is "as you wait eagerly for the revealing of our Lord Jesus Christ who will also establish you until the end, blameless on the Day of the Lord Jesus Christ" in 1:7b-8. It would be helpful to give 7b-8 the most emphasis during the reading of this Second Lesson for the day.

Mark 13:24-37

Our study of this Mark 13 "Little Apocalypse" supports the hypothesis that along with the other portions of the Gospel According to Mark this chapter includes reminiscences about Jesus and sayings of Jesus passed down and adapted by followers of Jesus in order to meet their own needs. As is characteristic of general apocalyptic thought prevalent among many Jews during this period, there are specific references to Daniel 9:27 and to Daniel 7:13 in Mark 13:14 and in Mark 13:26 respectively. Mark 13 reflects the urgency with which the Markan eschatological community proclaimed this message as the end of the forty-year generation since the crucifixion of Jesus approached, its conviction that the end of the age was near, and its uncertainly about the precise moment in which the end would come. Most of the Mark 13:24-37 text may have come to us relatively unchanged from the Jesus of history. The words "not even the Son" in 13:32 may, however, have replaced something such as "nor do I know" during the 35-40 years of transmission of the saying after the death of Jesus. Nevertheless, the message that is inherent in 13:32-37 is as appropriate today as it was during the first century of the common era.

The message in all four of these texts on this First Sunday of Advent in Series B is in essence therefore, "Watch and Pray! Be watching and ready for the end. At the same time be open in prayer for God's coming to us in the here and now of our present and continuing life together." We greatly need God's grace whenever God comes to us, whether it is to restore our life here (the Older Testament emphasis) or to bring it to an end and to provide a new beginning (the theme in the Newer Testament texts for this day).

SECOND SUNDAY OF ADVENT

In each of these texts God's grace is proclaimed in typical Advent season form in part as a gift already received and in part as a gift anticipated for the future. In Isaiah 40:1-11, in Psalm 85:1-2, 8-13, in 2 Peter 3:8-15a, and in Mark 1:1-8 the hearers of the message are urged to prepare the way for the Lord to come by repenting of their sins and by being open to the grace of God.

Isaiah 40:1-11

This text is a rich source for Advent hymns and for Advent messages. The message of comfort is especially beautiful when the word usually translated as "double" in 40:2 is expressed in English as "a doubling over," that is as a cancellation of the record of human sin, or in other words as "forgiveness" for all of the sins of the people of Jerusalem. The idea is that it is as if God takes a paper on which all of our sins and debts are recorded, doubles it over from the bottom of the page to the top and writes "forgiven" on the part that has been doubled over. This fits the context of verses 1 and 2 and of the nature of God as proclaimed throughout the traditions that we as Christians share with Jews and with Muslims far more closely than does the translation "double," which implies a vindictive double punishment. God is not generally presented elsewhere in our traditions as being cruelly vindictive against us in our sin, imposing a double punishment upon us as payment for our sins.

Psalm 85:1-2, 8-13

As in Isaiah 40:1-11, restoration is the theme here. Perhaps this psalm had its life situation during a period of suffering within the restoration of Jerusalem period, some time after 538 BCE. The salvation of the Lord God is said to be readily at hand for all who fear and respect the Lord. In both of these texts from the Older Testament, salvation is perceived primarily in terms of the community of believers here in the present situation rather than as individual salvation through a resurrection from the dead at the end of time.

2 Peter 3:8-15a

The grace of God in this text is seen in the delay of the coming of the "Day of God." Why has the day not come? The explanation given here is that God has waited to come so that all would have an opportunity to repent and thus avoid destruction. This document, therefore, as likely the last early Christian literature to be written that was included within the Newer Testament canon, has a message of God's grace that is especially appropriate for us today. For us, too, the "day" has been delayed. What reasons do we give for this prolonged delay? What is our proper response to this delay from the perspective of our faith and of our lives?

Mark 1:1-8

Here God's grace is expressed in a very important document with its title self-designated in its opening sentence as "The Gospel (Good News) of Jesus Christ, the Son of God." The "gospel" that Paul and others had earlier proclaimed about life and salvation portrayed in the death of Jesus so that our sins would die with him and of God raising Jesus from death to new life to be shared with all of us is expressed here in narrative form, a new genre of ministry of Jesus. The narrative begins with a brief account about John the Baptist.

We see in Mark 1:2 the initial example of a literary technique used frequently in Mark, that is, the bringing together of two or more quotations from various places within the Older Testament so that in their juxtaposition they say something more than that for which they had earlier been intended. "My messenger" in Malachi 3:1 almost certainly was a reference to the prophet Malachi, whose name itself means "the messenger of me," a messenger of God. As used in Mark 1:2, "my messenger," "the messenger of God," is a reference to John the Baptist, the precursor of Jesus as the Christ, the Son of God. The voice in the wilderness crying out "Prepare the way of the Lord" in Isaiah 40:3 was a divine voice, an oracle, a message of a prophet from a period near 538 BCE. As used in Mark 1:3, referring to John the Baptist, a prophetic voice from an earlier period is reapplied as a prophetic voice for a period more than five centuries later. The Markan narrative documented both the Malachi tradition and the Isaiah tradition as Isaiah tradition, unacceptable documentation by our literary standards, but not only acceptable but also very appropriate here, since from the perspective of this "Gospel" narrative all of the accepted Israelite tradition is understood as one as "Word of God."

The Matthean and Lukan redactors "corrected" the Markan narrative by not using the Malachi tradition portion of the quotation, and most copies of the Markan text centuries after its original composition "corrected" the Markan quotation itself by changing the words "in Isaiah the prophet" to "in the prophets." If we choose to use the earliest Markan manuscripts that are available to us, we follow the original Markan intention of attributing both quotations to Isaiah in order to make it appear that God through the "Word of God" in the Isaiah tradition was writing specifically about John the Baptist who would appear approximately 560 years later, rather than about a historical situation at the conclusion of the Israelite exilic period. This illustrates for us that the Markan narrative, the "Gospel of Jesus the Christ, the Son of God," is primarily a theological document; not an attempt to relate or to portray history.

Information is now accessible to us from the study of Jewish literature that John the Baptist was not the first or the only person during his time to proclaim and to perform a "baptism for the forgiveness of sins" within a gathered eschatological community. We recognize also the theological "exaggeration" inherent in Mark that "all of the people of the Judean countryside and all of the people of Jerusalem were going out to him and were being baptized by him." We see that these are primarily theological statements in the narrative, not primarily historical statements. By becoming aware of this at the beginning of the Markan narrative, we are enabled to have a better understanding of the nature of the "Gospel of Jesus Christ." The clothing and behavior of John identify him as a classic prophet, a prophet outside the central religious and political sanctuaries, similar to great "peripheral" Israelite prophets of the past such as Amos and Jeremiah. (See Robert R. Wilson, *Prophecy and Society in Ancient Israel* (Fortress, 1980), for a study of these "peripheral" prophets.

In the manner in which John the Baptist is said to have placed Jesus so much higher than himself, we see efforts of early followers of Jesus to incorporate followers of John the Baptist into their own communities. Finally, the Mark 1:1-8 text indicates, as suggested above, that the grace of God is here experienced partially as a gift already received through the baptism by John for the forgiveness of sins and partially as a gift anticipated for the future. The latter is expressed in the reference in Mark 1:8 to Jesus as "the one who will baptize you in the Holy Spirit." We live today in this same relative position regarding God's grace. In part we have already received it and do receive it, and in part it is a gift still to come. That is the essence of the Advent season for us. For us, as for the members of the Markan community of faith, many of the benefits of the baptism of Jesus are still to come. The futuristic element in our Advent tradition makes the season of Advent for us each year a new exciting anticipatory experience.

THIRD SUNDAY OF ADVENT

How shall we put together a well-constructed worship service based upon Isaiah 61:1-4, 8-11 and Psalm 126 with their liberation theology for Zion, the Magnificat from Luke 1:47-55 with its emphasis on God bringing down those who are mighty and exalting those who are lowly, 1 Thessalonians 5:16-24 regarding appropriate behavior for the Thessalonians as they wait for the Day of the Lord, and John 1:6-8, 19-28 with its depiction of John the Baptist as a man sent from God to be a witness to the Light, one who was much less worthy than was Jesus? How shall we do this when in many congregations the children are already presenting their Christmas program, people want to sing the Christmas carols in church because they have been hearing them in the department stores and discount stores since long before Thanksgiving, and many families are getting ready to leave soon so that will be able to travel to other places to be together with their extended families for Christmas? Our task as worship leaders on the Third Sunday in Advent is never easy.

There is obviously a point of contact with the Second Sunday in Advent through the person of John the Baptist. One week earlier we heard about John from the perspective of the Markan narrative; now we have John from the vantage point of the Fourth Gospel. (Although we are in the Markan cycle in Series B, we shall not see Markan texts again until the First Sunday after the Epiphany, one month away. Our three-year lectionary Series B is constructed in this way because in the Markan narrative there is no annunciation to the Virgin Mary, no virgin birth from the Virgin Mary, and Mary as the human mother of Jesus worries about the safety of her son as he becomes a significant political as well as religious leader. In Mark, Jesus was "adopted" by God as the Son of God when the voice of God announced this as Jesus was being baptized by John.) The Fourth Gospel perspective of John the Baptist is also different from that of the Markan narrative in important aspects. Unlike Mark and its Synoptic parallels, the Fourth Gospel does not emphasize the Baptist's role as one who condemns those who come to him for a baptism of repentance for the forgiveness of their sins and baptizes Jesus along with many others. Perhaps this is because the Fourth Gospel tradition with its high Christology could not and would not perceive Jesus as participating in a baptism for the forgiveness of sins, even in order "to fulfill all righteousness." In the Fourth Gospel Jesus is the exalted "Lamb of God who takes away the sins of the world." If we as worship leaders gently maintain the integrity of the Advent season and utilize Advent hymns and texts within an Advent worship service, we can focus the service primarily on the John 1:6-8, 19-28 text and use the other texts chosen for this day in doing this.

One of the ways in which we can utilize these Advent texts is to use the extended comparison "just as." We see that just as John the Baptist was "sent from God" (John 1:6), we too are "sent from God." Just as John the Baptist came not as the Light but to bear witness to the Light (John 1:7-8), we have not come as the Light but to bear witness to the Light. Just as John the Baptist was not the Christ, not Elijah, nor "the Prophet" (John 1:19-21), we today are not the Christ, not Elijah, nor "the Prophet." Just as John the Baptist is presented as "the voice of one crying in the wilderness, 'Make straight the ways of the Lord' " (John 1:23), we too are voices crying in the wilderness, "Make straight the way of the Lord." Just as John the Baptist baptized with water and said that he was not worthy to untie the sandals on Jesus' feet (John 1:26-27), we today baptize with water and are not worthy to untie Jesus' sandals.

This extended comparison can and should be continued in a similar manner with the other texts chosen for this day in order to construct a cohesive message that will have an impact and be remembered, while being true to the Advent theme. Just as Mary, according to the Magnificat canticle that the inspired Lukan writer skillfully constructed on the Song of Hannah model of 1 Samuel 2:1-10, sang that her soul (her entire being) magnifies the Lord and her Spirit rejoices in God her Savior (Luke 1:47-55), we also should sing that our soul magnifies the Lord and that our Spirit rejoices in God our Savior. Just as a leader within the Isaiah tradition at the end of the Israelite period of exile in Babylon proclaimed that the Spirit of the Lord God was upon that person because the Lord had anointed that person to bring good news to the afflicted (Isaiah 61:1ff.), we too can and should proclaim that the Spirit of the Lord God is upon us. Just as the writer of Psalm 126 rejoiced with shouts of joy, we also should rejoice with shouts of joy on this Third Sunday in Advent. Just as the Apostle Paul wrote to the Thessalonians, saying, "Rejoice always, pray, and give thanks as you wait for the coming of the Lord Jesus Christ" (1 Thessalonians 5:16-24), we can and should say the same.

When we do this, we proclaim the message of these texts, we identify ourselves with the message of these texts, and we demonstrate audibly and visibly that we today are what John the Baptist, the Lukan writer, Mary, the Isaiah tradition prophet, the Israelite psalmist, and the Apostle Paul were in their times, i.e., instruments of God's grace, bearers of God's Word, people being used by God, and, just as they were, joyful to be used by God.

It will be especially effective if we use simple drama, or at least dramatic readings of these texts by a variety of people within the congregation, in presenting this message and in showing that clergy and lay people are bearers of these messages now as in the past. Biblical storytelling in which various persons memorize and tell the stories dramatically will be especially effective. A bit of sweeping dance as the stories are told will add beauty to the Advent presentation.

FOURTH SUNDAY OF ADVENT

If we concentrate on the Luke 1:26-38 Gospel account exclusively or even primarily, we will probably emphasize the person of Mary along with her relationships with God, with the angel Gabriel, and with Elizabeth. On the other hand, if we utilize all of the texts appointed for this day, we will probably in some way apply to our own life situation the Jewish and the Christian "Messianic expectations" regarding the promise of the Lord of an everlasting throne of David, a house, a kingdom that will endure forever.

It would be appropriate to take the latter of these two paths since we have most likely heard many sermons and homilies, including some of our own, in which Mary's experiences as developed within the Lukan Gospel's creative drama were further expounded from the preacher's own supply of interpersonal relationships, experiences, and inspired imagination. There is, of course, much value in continuing the Lukan Gospel's process of thorough research of the subject, the gathering of oral and written traditions, and the use of earlier biblical style in the formation of a new literary or homiletical product. The Lukan playwright used effectively the references to the angel figure Gabriel in Daniel 8:15-17 and Daniel 9:21-23 in formulating the scene that we know as Luke 1:26-38, our Gospel text for this occasion. The Lukan writer also used the same type of terminology that is included in the Zoroastrian account of how the "Holy Spirit of God" (Ahura Mazda's Spirit) had come over the mother of Zoroaster and had caused her to conceive Zoroaster without any interaction with a man. (The concept of the Spirit of God as the agency of conception of the Savior figure was also used in the Matthean tradition. Therefore, both of the Newer Testament traditions that developed a virgin conception explanation of how Jesus could be truly divine and truly human share terminology with the Zoroastrian tradition.)

By using all of the texts appointed for this day, however, we have an opportunity to explore an area with much broader implications for our own faith and lives today than that of the virgin conception accounts and to this we now turn.

2 Samuel 7:1-11, 16

This text is a very important component of the suspense-filled "Succession Document" or "Court History of David" narrative that extends from 2 Samuel 6 through 1 Kings 2. It contains the delightful pun regarding the "house" that David had wanted to build for the Lord God but instead the Lord God would build for David. The "house" that the Lord God will build for David will be a structure made not with timbers and adornments but with the lives of people, for it will be a dynasty, a Davidic dynasty intended to last forever. This is the "Messianic expectation" within the Succession Document, and it became a dominant theme in much of the Older Testament, as well as later within Judaism where it provided a new phase of the promise of land, people, nationhood, and blessing to the patriarchs that had served its purpose and would be continued by being blended into this new Messianic expectation.

We can perceive a measure of how vitally important and relevant this Messianic expectation of continuity on the "throne of David" must have been for the remnant among the exiles from Jerusalem who remained faithful to the Lord God during many decades of relocation in Babylon where many among them accepted the religion and culture of the Babylonians and worshiped Marduk, the Lord of the Babylonians. We note the importance of this Messianic expectation with its Zionist hopes for Jews who were deprived of basic human rights in country after country throughout the centuries. We see also the related use of this Messianic expectation within the developing traditions of many of the followers of Jesus, as in this Luke 1:32-33 text, and continuing for us as Christians since that time. Jews have intensely wanted continuity as a People of God and have struggled valiantly to maintain their identity as a people and as a culture. The striving for continuity of life within the "kingdom of God" has dominated and shaped oral and written traditions within apocalyptic Judaism and within apocalyptic Christianity. As Christians, we ride upon this Jewish Messianic expectations vehicle within a somewhat modified Christian model. Certainly we shall want to acknowledge with great respect the Israelite-Jewish origins of this Christian vehicle in which we ride in accordance with the Word of God in these texts selected for this day. As the Christmas season approaches, what can be more appropriate than to acknowledge this in order to inform and to sensitize our own people and help them and ourselves to appreciate the heritage that we have received from the Jewish people. If we do this, the Fourth Sunday of Advent this year will be a good time to have Jewish guests within our worship services.

Psalm 89:1-4, 19-26

In this context we concentrate on these few verses of this fascinating psalm. Psalm 89 should be taken seriously in its own setting, with its expectation that the descendants of David will be established forever, the throne of David built for all generations to come. The best of our Christian theology in harmony with the views of the Apostle Paul that he expressed in Romans 11:28b-29 has held that the gift and calling of God are irrevocable for Israel and for the church. For the sake of our Christian covenant, we must respect the irrevocable nature of the antecedent Israelite-Jewish covenant. We must realize that if we reject the antecedent Israelite-Jewish covenant, it is only right and just that someday our derivative Christian covenant may also be rejected. For more about this, please see, among others, Norbert Lohfink,

The Covenant Never Revoked: Biblical Reflections on Christian-Jewish Dialogue (New York: Paulist, 1991); Mary C. Boys, *Has God Only One Blessing? Judaism as a Source of Christian Self-Understanding* (New York: Paulist, 2000); and Mary C. Boys, "The Enduring Covenant," in *Seeing Judaism Anew: Christianity's Sacred Obligation*, ed. by Mary C. Boys (Lanham, Maryland: Rowman & Littlefield, 2005, 17-25.

Luke 1:46b-55

If this text is used on the Fourth Sunday of Advent this year, the emphasis should be focused on the final summation two verses 54 and 55 of the Magnificat in which the emphasis is on God's enduring covenant with Israel, an emphasis easily overlooked within Christian Bible studies and worship services. With the texts selected for the Third and Fourth Sundays of Advent in Series B, the emphasis is on the enduring covenants of God, which, while they may and indeed often are broken by us as people, are according to these texts, never revoked by God. Our Jewish, Christian, and Islamic traditions, at their best, are always fully aware of this and find comfort in this. What better way than this can we as Christians prepare to celebrate during the coming Christmas season!

Romans 16:25-27

May this beautiful benediction with which the Apostle Paul concluded his momentous letter to the followers of Jesus in Rome be ours also, together with the entire People of God! And with this benediction, shall we not let God define the extent of "God's People"?

Luke 1:26-38

As followers of Jesus, we have every right to claim that the Lord God has given to Jesus the "throne" of David, so long as we realize that this is a theological throne and not a political or physical throne. Other necessary qualifications are that we understand the process by which some of the followers of Jesus made this theological claim, and that we openly recognize and continue to acknowledge the continuing validity of Jewish spirituality, Jewish life and faith, and of Jewish Messianic expectations. We know that we as Christians have taken the Jewish Messianic expectations into a new extended phase and in doing this we have given to them a somewhat different Christian Messianic expectation meaning through the Christian claim that Jesus in his life fulfilled the Messianic "prophecies" of the Older Testament. But what we have done is alongside the Jewish use of these expectations and in no way replaces or excludes the ongoing and dynamic Jewish use for which Jews have the primary claim. What we as Christians have done and are doing with these Messianic expectations must be seen as in a sense secondary to the Jewish use and in continuity with and congruent to the ongoing Jewish hope and expectations. It would be most appropriate for us as Christians to remember this and to acknowledge it at all times and especially here at the conclusion of our Advent season. Then perhaps we could invite Jews to be our guests in our Christian worship services and to hear our understanding of the Messianic expectations that we share, even as we are invited to be their guests and to hear their understanding of their Messianic expectations. When we have done all of this, we are truly "ready" for Christmas and prepared to celebrate the Nativity of the Lord.

SEASON OF CHRISTMAS
NATIVITY OF THE LORD
CHRISTMAS, PROPER I (A, B, C)

Isaiah 9:2-7

The usage of religious traditions affects the form and even the content of those traditions. For example, usage of evergreen trees that are brought into our homes, stores, and churches during the season of Christmas over periods of time has affected the trees themselves. The use of such trees, especially when they are placed into stores and even into homes and churches many weeks prior to Christmas, has mandated that unless the trees are constructed out of materials that are made to look as if they were live trees cut from a forest or tree farm, even though they were not, they will deteriorate to the point that they are no longer useful objects of beauty. When automobiles began to be used not only to transport people slowly from one place to another on gravel roads, but to become portable sound systems transported at high speeds on superhighways, the form and the content of the vehicles have been changed radically. The automobiles themselves have become, in a sense, religious traditions. The time when teenagers are able to drive and to own their own cars or trucks becomes a "religious rite of passage" for them and for their families. Usage affects form and content.

Usage has affected the form and the content of Isaiah 9:2-7 dramatically and, of course, of other religious texts as well. While the precise details of the environment in which Isaiah 9:2-7 had its origins are unknown to us, it is likely that life conditions had been difficult for the Israelite people and for their nation. Now, however, there was reason to be hopeful. A young man, a descendant of King David, was being acclaimed as the new king. There was an expectation that, unlike their recent kings, this one would be wise, compassionate, strengthened by God, as concerned for them as a loving father would be, a king whose reign would be a reign of justice and of peace. Unfortunately, the hopes and the dreams of the people were never realized. Once the king had power and authority, his power and his authority were misused and lost and the people again suffered, sometimes even more than they had earlier.

As the ancient Israelites and the Jews who came after them experienced repeated injustices and hardships, their hopes for an ideal king repeatedly rose and fell. Especially when for long periods of time they had no autonomy as a nation, their hopes and expectations for their own fair and just "king" and "messiah" were embellished by their poets and heroes. The Isaiah 9:2-7 text, along with Isaiah 11:1-9 and others, are evidence of their efforts, and remain useful as expressions of Messianic expectations for Jews today. For many Orthodox Jews, expectations of the coming of a truly worthy earthly ruler sent by God continue, even after countless disappointments. For most non-Orthodox Jews, these texts are treasured as expressions of the coming Messianic Age of justice and of peace, for which they should strive.

For followers of Jesus whose efforts eventually resulted in the Christian tradition, these same texts initially provided expressions of hope that were similar to those of Jews who did not become Christians. Many of these followers of Jesus developed a belief that Jesus was the ideal Messianic King, not merely human, but also divine. Their usage of Isaiah 9:2-7, and of other Israelite-Jewish texts, affected the form and the content of the texts. Long before Handel composed his magnificent "Messiah," and certainly ever since that time, translations of Isaiah 9:2-7, and most of all of the titles given to the ideal king in the latter portion of Isaiah 9:6 were affected for Christians in ways that departed significantly from the texts and translations used by Jews. As is well known, in most of our Christian translations into the English language we see the adjectives beginning in upper case form as "Wonderful," "Counselor," or "Wonderful Counselor," as "Mighty God," "Everlasting Father," "Prince of Peace." The usage has almost indelibly affected the form and the content of Isaiah 9:2-7, for Christians differently than for Jews.

Does this mean that we should not use Isaiah 9:2-7 as it has evolved for us? Should we use instead the text in its most primitive possible form? Not at all. We should no more do that than we should use only Christmas trees cut live from the forest or make and utilize only automobiles that are like the first horseless carriages. We should use and enjoy fully the text of Isaiah 9:2-7 as we have it, while at the same time fully appreciating and respecting Jews who use it as it has been affected by their experiences.

Psalm 96

This is one of a series of psalms in which the Israelites were and Jews and Christians are called upon to worship the Lord God, the Creator and Righteous Ruler of the earth. In this beautiful psalm even the elements of nature are urged to sing praises to the Lord God. Since we as Christians perceive the Christmas season as the primary time when we give thanks to the Lord God as the Father of the one who is for us God's Son, Jesus the Christ, God in another form, it is in every way fitting that we, together with all Jews, praise the Lord God on Christmas Eve. Jews praise God in a universal sense at all times; we as Christians, especially during the Christmas season, praise God in a particular, as well as in a more general, universal sense at this time. It is essential that we emphasize that the Christmas season is first and foremost a celebration of God's unique gift to us all.

Titus 2:11-14

Although this text was written from a post Good Friday and Easter Christian perspective rather than from a festival of Christmas Christian perspective, it is also adaptable for our use here on this occasion. Its emphasis is on the grace of God and on our lives that are to be appropriate responses to God's grace. This text also from its perspective provides for us an early link to Good Friday and to Easter, which for us are only a few short months away.

Luke 2:1-14 (15-20)

This vivid Christmas drama written by the inspired author of the "Gospel According to Luke" within popular Christianity dominates all other texts. We as leaders in public worship services should, therefore, center our proclamation upon it every Christmas Eve. If we were to do otherwise, it would hardly be Christmas Eve for us and for the people worshiping God as Christians among us, so powerful has this Lukan drama become! Here and in the other instances in which the writer of Luke-Acts was not dependent upon written sources known to us, it is likely that the writer researched the subject thoroughly and then composed freely and with inspired creativity, much as we do when we prepare sermons and homilies.

We must read this text with every oral interpretation skill given to us, or perhaps, after memorizing a particular translation of the text, proclaim it with the techniques employed in dramatic biblical storytelling. We can also portray it in vivid chancel drama with parts for both children and adults and with the "holy family" of the parents of the youngest child and their infant "baby Jesus" seated in the chancel. (We did this in a young mission congregation in which I served many decades ago. During the worship service, the infant cried and the mother discreetly nursed him.) Infants and children should certainly be highlighted during the worship service on Christmas Eve.

But what in addition can we do to make this worship experience as meaningful and as memorable as possible? We all want to sing our favorite Christmas carols, hear well-rehearsed anthems from the choirs, gaze at the Christmas trees with their white lights and Styrofoam glittered symbols. How can we best explicate and apply the message of the Lukan Christmas story? What will God do within us that will be a continuation of what God has done within the Lukan writer? How shall we paraphrase the text with a bit of additional historicizing?

Then, now, and always the Lord comes within the activities of the people of God, as we see in all of the texts selected here. Should we not proclaim some specifics about how God comes as Savior, Christ, and Lord (the three designations used in the message of the angel in Luke 2:11) within the parish in which we serve? We can, also with well-researched and inspired creativity like that of the Lukan writer, proclaim something such as "During the early decades of the twenty-first century, while _____ was the President of the United States and _____ was the governor of _____, within a local congregation in (your location), the Lord God came to a woman stricken by cancer and sustained her and her family and friends in their grief. The Lord came to a young businessman who would not sacrifice his moral principles to gain an advantage over his competitor. The Lord came to an old rancher and his wife who shared some of their land with people who were unemployed, etc., and the Lord was born here, and the angels in the church choir sang, 'Glory to God in the highest, and on the earth peace and good will!' and the shepherds in the congregation told this story, and Jesus was Savior, Christ, and Lord among all of them."

Are we not the "shepherds" where we are? Can we not repeat what the "angels" have sung about what happens when the Lord comes within the activities of the people of God where we are? This can then be our most meaningful Christmas Eve message, a proclamation and application of the texts selected for this night. Perhaps it would also be a proclamation and application that Jews and Muslims, Hindus and Buddhists, and our other non-Christian guests could receive in a Christmas Eve worship service to which they were invited. They may want to be invited to this Christian mountaintop experience if they know that their religious traditions and practices are respected by us.

I cannot leave this text, most of all Luke 2:7 with its depiction of the mother of the baby Jesus wrapping him in soft material and tenderly placing him into a "manger" so that he and she could sleep, until I share with you an experience that I had during the years in which I was growing up on our small farm in Northwest Ohio. While my friends in town were playing sandlot baseball after school and later going to football, basketball, and track practices and games, I, five miles from town, was doing what my parents wanted and expected me to do, the daily chores of feeding our chickens, hogs, and calves, and helping to cut and husk corn with hand tools, drive our Farmall H tractor so that my mother could come back to our house to begin to prepare our supper and bring in our four or five cows to be milked by hand as well, which she often did so that my father and I could keep the tractor and team of horses going until dark during planting and harvesting times.

We had a calf shed, which unlike our other farm buildings, we never painted, in which as any given time, we had one or two calves. There was a narrow walkway along the north side of the shed, which we used so that we could bring straw to soak up the manure that the calves produced, hay and corn fodder for roughage, water for the calves to drink, and a small scoop of oats, which the calves relished eagerly. Apart from the larger area into which we placed the hay and the corn fodder, there were two feedboxes into which I would pour the oats. (There had to be two feedboxes for two calves. If you know anything about animals eating oats, you know why there had to be two feedboxes.)

The relation of all of this to Luke 2:7 is that these feedboxes, built into the feeding area by my grandfather, were raised from the floor perhaps 24 inches, were approximately ten inches wide and eighteen to twenty inches long, with sides perhaps five inches high so that the calves as they licked up the grains of oats would not spill them out of the manger. Many generations of calves, over a period of more than four decades had with their raspy tongues licked the boards smooth, even wearing away with their tongues over the years grooves in the soft wood between the darker bands of hard wood. These feed mangers were just the right size into which a mother could place her newborn child! We did not use these mangers for that, but in the Lukan Christmas story the Virgin Mary did. In Luke's Christmas story the mother of Jesus placed him into a feedbox like the ones into which I had poured scoops of oats for our calves. The mangers in the feedlots in Bethlehem were intended for use by the sheep and goats, but Mary used one of them into which to place the baby Jesus, while Caesar and Herod languished in their richly adorned palaces.

CHRISTMAS, PROPER II (A, B, C)

Isaiah 62:6-12

After many years during which the grain and the wine from the vineyards of Jerusalem had been given by the Lord God to the enemies of its people, the people of Israel are depicted here as streaming back to the city from the broad highway cleared of all stones and obstructions over which they were returning from their exile in Babylonia. The people who return to the city are called the "holy," because they are the people of the Lord; they are called "redeemed" because the Lord has purchased them from their captors. The people of the Lord will again eat their bread and drink their wine in the holy city.

Psalm 97

The land and its people will rejoice because the Lord God is now the King. The throne of the Lord God is built upon the foundations of righteousness and of justice. All adversaries of the Lord God are consumed by his fire. The earth trembles under his feet. Those who are righteous will welcome the coming of the Lord and give thanks to their God.

Titus 3:4-7

While in the Isaiah 62:6-12 and Psalm 97 texts, God is depicted as the Savior, active in the lives of the righteous, the people here in Titus 3:4-7 have been washed and reborn. What is new and different in this text from the Newer Testament is that God as the Holy Spirit is said to have been poured out upon the people through the activity of Jesus Christ our Savior. The Lord God is coming in new forms. As arranged in Proper II of our texts for Christmas, Titus 3:4-7 provides a transition from the idea that the Lord God comes in power and might to the belief that the Lord God comes in the birth of the baby Jesus in the Lukan Christmas story.

Luke 2:(1-7) 8-20

For this, see the notes under Luke 2:1-14 (15-20) in CHRISTMAS, PROPER 1.

CHRISTMAS, PROPER III (A, B, C)

All four of the texts chosen for our use on Christmas Day refer to the coming of the Lord God. That coming is perceived in a way that is unique to each text. The most noticeable differences are that in the two texts from the Older Testament the coming of the Lord is expressed by use of a series of anthropomorphisms (depictions of God using various features and characteristics of humans), while in the two texts from the New Testament the Lord is depicted as coming incarnate (in the actual form of a human person). Let us look more closely at each of these texts.

Perhaps the differences between these two depictions are not as large as they may at first appear to be.

Isaiah 52:7-10

This delightful portrayal of watchmen on the walls of Jerusalem singing joyously when they see the first indications of the return of the Lord God to Jerusalem is an entirely appropriate text from the Older Testament to serve as the First Lesson in Christian worship services on Christmas Day. The feet of the messenger who will be able to announce the return of the Lord God as they skip at a rapid pace over the hills approaching the city are described as beautiful, for their arrival means that the Lord God has come to the city to make it holy once more. The Lord God comes in the form of the feet of the messenger and of the voices of the watchmen. May our longing on this Christmas Day for the peace and salvation that only God can give to us be as great as that of the inspired poet of the Isaiah tradition during the period of the restoration of Jerusalem. May we, like the ancient Israelites, see the coming of the Lord in the feet of the messenger and in the voices of the watchmen among us.

Psalm 98

The primary anthropomorphism that is used in this psalm is that of a victorious military hero who becomes a king. The most notable human model for this achievement in ancient Israel was David and in our own history in the USA is George Washington. Most nations have military heroes who become political figures highly honored within the national-civil expressions of religion. Within the Old Testament use of anthropomorphisms, even when there are many references to physical characteristics such as the "right hand" and the "holy arm" of the Lord, it is not likely that a physical coming, an incarnation, a presence of God in human form is intended. Anthropomorphisms such as these are used with great frequency in the Old Testament and continue to be used widely among both Jews and Christians, as well as among many Muslims, Hindus, and others, simply because such anthropomorphisms are the most vivid way in which people can attempt to describe God and depict actions of God. The use of anthropomorphisms in the language with which we and other people express faith in God does not imply incarnation. There is no doubt, however, that the heavy use of anthropomorphisms in Israelite-Jewish sacred Scriptures and in Jewish theology contributed very significantly to the development of incarnation theology in the Christian Church and to our understanding of the meaning of Christmas.

In the final verse of Psalm 98 the entire world is called upon to sing praises to the Lord, who is depicted as the righteous, equitable judge of the entire world. For us as Christians during this Christmas season and throughout the year, it is easy to see Jesus as Lord with powers and responsibilities that are similar to those ascribed by the Israelites and Jews to Adonai as Lord.

Hebrews 1:1-4 (5-12)

The primary contrast in the initial portion of this treatise in which the writer argues that Jewish background followers of Jesus should not return to their Jewish lifestyle is between what is written here about Jesus as the Incarnate Son of God and the important but inferior prophets through whom God spoke and the angels who merely delivered messages from God. Jesus as the Son of God is said to be the heir of God, the one who will receive all that belongs to God. As in the Gospel According to John, the Prologue of which follows here as the Gospel selection for Christmas Day, Jesus is said to have been the one through whom God created the world. To Jesus is ascribed the reflection of the glory of God, the imprint of God's nature. It is claimed in this document that after Jesus had himself gone into the "Holy of Holies" and offered not the blood of sheep and of goats but his own blood upon the altar in order to purify us from our sins, Jesus took his position at the right hand of God on high. Within these few verses we have a brief abstract or synopsis of the entire Christian understanding of salvation. It is a huge, adult-size gift package under our Christmas tree! It is far more than a series of anthropomorphisms; it is fully an incarnation theology. Its high Christology is matched only in the Fourth Gospel within our New Testament and surpassed only by the Gnostic Christians for whom Jesus was perceived to have been only divine and never incarnate.

John 1:1-14

How different this hymn of acclamation of Jesus the Christ as the Logos face-to-face with God and as God is from the Lukan writer's literary drama scenes! Who would ever attempt to portray this hymn to Christ in a Sunday school or chancel Christmas drama? How many Christmas greeting cards have you seen that are based on John 1:1-14?

The reading from the Epistle to the Hebrews, however, has prepared us for this.

The most perceptive among the members of the congregations in which we serve will be aware from their study of our biblical traditions and from their participation in Christian worship that there is not one but many "Theologies" and not one but many "Christologies" within our New Testament collection of documents. We experience this most profoundly in this Series B arrangement of texts, the year of Mark, but of Mark interrupted by and interspersed with texts from John, Luke, and Matthew. It would be appropriate within the message on Christmas Day to show that we are aware of the richness of our biblical tradition in these various Christologies, as a "preview of coming attractions" during the subsequent Sundays of this year of Series B. It would be helpful to share that for the Apostle Paul, divine powers were bestowed upon Jesus by God the Father through Jesus' death and resurrection. For the Markan writer, God "adopted" Jesus and gave to Jesus powers as God's Son at the time of the Baptism of Jesus by John the Baptist. For the Matthean and Lukan redactors, God made Jesus the Son of God by means of Jesus being conceived within the reproductive system of a virgin woman by the power of the Spirit of God. Here in the Gospel According to John, as well as in the Epistle to the Hebrews, God had apparently made Jesus divine "before the foundations of the earth were laid," and Jesus had participated fully or perhaps even with no involvement by God as God the Father in the creative process. We see, therefore, as we proclaim the Christmas message on Christmas Day using Hebrews 1:1-4 (5-12) and John 1:1-14 that we are at the extreme outer edge of the Christologies presented within our New Testament documents, Christologies in which there is no "baby Jesus" and, therefore, actually no "Christmas" as such at all!

FIRST SUNDAY AFTER CHRISTMAS DAY

As we prepare for this occasion, we realize that in our contemporary culture the first Sunday after Christmas has become for many people a quiet time within a vacation period, a time often characterized by family gatherings, enjoyment of Christmas gifts, dried-out Christmas trees with drooping ornaments, pro-football, low church attendance, and perhaps Student Recognition Sunday. The texts selected for this day, however, are full of vibrancy and creativity, worthy of putting life and vitality into this ecclesiastically quiet time. May the Spirit of God come to us through these texts so that we too may speak creatively and vibrantly to others on this day!

Isaiah 61:10—62:3

Every word of this portion of the Isaiah tradition is Good News. Even though never in the history of Jerusalem have conditions been as favorable or the status of its people as glorious as depicted here, we can understand how important it was for those who were inspired to develop the Isaiah traditions to use exaggeration in their attempts to provide encouragement for the people. The people in Jerusalem at that time needed salvation and peace, and we need salvation and peace. We, like they, need "Good News." Perhaps we have been too restrained, too lacking in exuberance in our proclamation of salvation on this Sunday after Christmas. Since we believe that God was active in the life of Jesus in a decisive way, let us proclaim that joyously and eloquently, as salvation is proclaimed to us in this text.

Psalm 148

All people, all creatures, even all components and elements of nature are called upon here to praise the Lord. This praise is to be joined with the praise of the Lord and of the name of the Lord by all of God's angels and heavenly host. Certainly this psalm must be read and sung with great feeling and joy.

Galatians 4:4-7

Within the many letters of Paul included in our New Testament this text is most distinctively a Christmas message. The "Good News" in this text is that God has provided salvation for those who live in accordance with the guidance compiled in the Torah and for those who are not Jews but have been adopted as God's people, so that they, along with the Jews, can call God their God, and so that, like Jesus, they can call God "Abba." In this text Paul proclaims that those of us who are Gentiles are also, in Christ Jesus, by God's grace heirs of the good things that God has prepared. We are heirs of God's grace alongside of the Jews, not better than they are, but by God's grace equal to them. This is Paul's "Good News" here and in Romans 11, and it should be proclaimed as such to Christians and to Jews today. Unfortunately, this Good News of Paul's Christmas message has been largely obscured throughout most of the history of the Church by a different message, a message of Christian exclusivism and claims of Christian superiority.

Luke 2:22-40

Within these two brief scenes depicting the aged Simeon in 2:25-35 and the aged Anna in 2:36-38 the Lukan writer with inspired creativity showed the baby Jesus as the one through whom salvation would come to all people to be a light to be revealed to the nations and glory to God's people Israel. In this way the Lukan writer demonstrated that now that Jesus had come, "aged" Israel should recognize its Messiah and as a form of spirituality "aged" Israel should "depart in peace." By means of these little scenes the Lukan writer predicted *ex eventu* that Jesus would face opposition and that his violent death would cause indescribable grief to his mother. As elsewhere in Luke-Acts, the literary models here were the Scriptures of the Israelite people. Even Jesus is presented in 2:40 through use of the wisdom models readily available in the Joseph story in Genesis 37-50 and in the Daniel document. As a result, we see literary drama at its best. We are able to visualize every detail, even without the benefit of actors and stage. Apart from the subtle polemic here against Judaism — which we do not need nor should we employ — these verses beautifully portray elements that are most helpful to our Christian piety, especially during this Christmas season. We can, of course, merely perceive these stories about Simeon and Anna as documentary reports provided to the Lukan writer by Jesus' mother late in her life. Or we can note that by means of these vivid scenes the Lukan writer creatively supplied some "movies" from Jesus' childhood that would otherwise not be available to followers of Jesus late during the first century when many of them were beginning to wonder what had happened during Jesus' infancy and childhood.

Certainly we will want to lead all who hear our words on this day to thank and praise God joyfully and creatively. May the Spirit of God give to us the same kind of revelation and inspiration provided to those who wrote and compiled these biblical texts!

JANUARY 1 — HOLY NAME OF JESUS (A, B, C) (MARY, MOTHER OF GOD)

The name by which a person is addressed is important. The name of a person, even the name of a thing, such as the name given to a file in a computer, provides a means of access to the person and to the thing. The name may also identify a particular characteristic of a person. Parents in Native American tribes, for example, usually waited to give a name to a baby until a particular characteristic of the baby could be identified. Infants are taught to respond when the name given to them by their parents is spoken.

The names by which God is identified and addressed are obviously especially important. God is depicted in many languages by words that suggest transcendence. Political and religious groups often develop personal names for God to designate God specifically for their group, that is, for God as their Lord or "Boss," their on the job supervisor who teaches them their tasks, guides and disciplines them, and requires respect and loyalty from them.

The personal name for God that was developed in ancient Israel and is used by Jews is said in the Exodus 3 "burning bush" account to be the designation for "being" or "essence." Written using four Hebrew consonants, the so-called divine tetragrammaton, it is read but not spoken, lest it might be made common or profaned. Because it is considered to be so holy, a substitute, Adonai, which in the Aramaic language means "Lord," is used by many Jews. Orthodox Jews generally do not even use the substitute word Adonai, but instead the Hebrew word HaShem, *Ha* being Hebrew for "the" and *Shem* being Hebrew for "Name." They will say, HaShem says, meaning "The Name" says. Most Orthodox Jews, when writing the general word for Deity in English, "God," write it with consonants only and not the vowel, as "G-d." They do this not only out of profound respect, but also so that any material on which the complete word "God" is written will not be erased or trashed.

Most of the texts selected for our worship services on January 1 when this day of observed as "The Holy Name of Jesus" day include emphasis on the Name. The Name of God is highlighted at the conclusion of the Aaronic Benediction in Numbers 6:22-27 and in Psalm 8, verses 1 and 9. The Name of Jesus is of utmost importance in Philippians 2:9-10 and in Luke 2:21. Galatians 4:4-7 has no mention of the Name, but when the Apostle Paul wrote in 4:4 that "when the fullness of time had come, God sent God's Son, born from a woman, born under the Torah" (my translation in *The New Testament: A New Translation and Redaction* [Lima, Ohio: Fairway Press, 2001]), indirectly Paul mentioned the mother of Jesus. Mary is prominent, of course, in the Luke 2:15-21 Gospel account selected for this day.

Before we look briefly at each of the four texts selected for use on this day, it may be helpful to sketch a variety of emphases on Mary within the Christian Church today.

For some Christians, Mary as the mother of Jesus is mentioned when the Lukan Christmas story is read, but she is mostly only a silent figure in the manger scene. She appears again at the cross of Jesus but again is basically a silent figure. She is respected but not highlighted. For these Christians, especially within groups in which the Apostles' Creed and the Nicene Creed are not used, there is little emphasis on her as "the Virgin Mary."

For other Christians, those who use the Apostles' Creed and the Nicene Creed in most of their major corporate worship services, references to Jesus' mother as "the Virgin Mary" are frequent, but these Christians do not consider it to be necessary or appropriate to address her in prayer. She is called "the Virgin Mary" because that is designated as her name in the Luke 1-2 accounts. She is honored throughout the Church Year but is basically also a silent figure.

For large numbers of Christians, she is not only "the Virgin Mary"; she is referred to and prayers are addressed to her as "Mother of God." This was a result of theological development after the New Testament documents had been formed but relatively early within the history of Christianity. The line of reasoning was that "Jesus is God." Mary is "the mother of Jesus." Therefore, Mary is the "Mother of God." Women especially, but men also, among these Christians find it helpful and easier in many respects to pray to her with certain requests than to Jesus as the Christ. She is perceived as having a mother's understanding of Jesus and of them. She is their mother. For these Christians, it is a natural and somewhat necessary theological development to believe that Mary had not and does not sin, since Jesus would not have been born to a sinful mother. She also must have originated, theologically, from an immaculate conception. Additionally, it came to be believed that she had never died and that she had been taken into heaven to be with God and with her Son Jesus without experiencing death. We experience death because we sin. If Mary has never sinned, death is not needed for her. Also, there was no interruption, therefore, in her hearing and responding to the prayers of the faithful.

Finally, there are millions of Christians, going beyond the third group in their Mariology, who now perceive Mary as not only the mother of Jesus, the Virgin Mary, and Mary as Mother of God, but also Co-Redemptrix with Jesus, with power along with Jesus to grant forgiveness of sins. These Christians reason that Mary suffered horribly along with her Son Jesus as he was nailed to the cross, as he died on the cross, and as she held his lifeless body after his death. She shares, therefore, with him as a dispenser of his redeeming grace. For Christians in the third and fourth of these groups, theological development continues; it did not cease after the New Testament documents were accepted as canonical. All of our Scripture is Tradition, but not all of our Tradition is Scripture. The Word of God is dynamic, not static. God continues to inspire us, to reveal God's Self to us.

Numbers 6:22-27

It is entirely appropriate that we read this text with its familiar Aaronic Benediction on this day. This helps us to realize that this is actually an Israelite benediction that we happen to use in the Church along with many other "gems" from the Old Testament that we claim as our own. For us, of course, as we use this benediction in our Christian worship setting, the "Lord" is not primarily the Lord God of the ancient Israelites. For us, the "Lord" is our Lord Jesus Christ, the Son of God, our Savior and Redeemer. Many among us are able to believe that there is one Lord and God, Savior and Redeemer, of us all, certainly of all Jews and Christians, as well as of all Muslims, Hindus, etc., and that we merely experience God in different ways.

Psalm 8

O Lord, our Lord, how awesome is your Name throughout the earth! Just as this psalm begins and ends with this acclamation, so also we should acclaim God at the beginning and at the ending of each day. We cannot overuse this acclamation and this psalm. No matter how heavily we use this acclamation and this psalm, when we focus on the Name, the words will always be dynamic for us.

Galatians 4:4-7

In this text Paul expressed no rejection of the Jews who remain Jews. Instead, he wrote that followers of Jesus are adopted into the family of God, to live together with the Jews, those who are not merely adopted but are biological members of God's family. Paul wrote that followers of Jesus are redeemed just as Israelites-Jews are redeemed and are now heirs together with them. God's inheritance is not limited. Our shares in it are not decreased, no matter how many people share in it.

Philippians 2:5-11

In this beautiful "hymn," whether quoted from another source by Paul or composed by him, what is written in Isaiah 45:23 about the Lord God as the one to whom every knee will bend and every tongue profess is applied to Jesus as the Risen Christ. Here Jesus as the Risen Christ is Lord, to "the glory of God the Father." With this text, we as Christians are distinguished from Jews, but we are also united with Jews. In the end, there will be one Lord and God for us all. In the end, all will be one.

Luke 2:15-21

In this text we have a presentation of the "holy family." We see Mary and Joseph and we see the baby Jesus lying asleep in the feedbox where Mary has placed him. Later, theologically, Joseph as the father has to fade away and the "Holy Family" becomes God the Father, the Virgin Mary the Mother, and the Risen Christ the Son. In this text Mary ponders in her heart what the shepherds reported that the angels had said, and we ponder with Mary the Holy Name of Jesus and the significance of all of this for us today.

JANUARY 1 —
WHEN OBSERVED AS NEW YEAR'S DAY (A, B, C)

Even though from the perspective of the Christian Church Year we have already observed New Year's Day approximately one month ago on the First Sunday of Advent, we can be grateful if people will come together to worship God on the first day of our secular calendar year. It is good to see that for some people worship of God in Christian community on the first day of the secular year is more meaningful than "celebrating" with alcoholic drinks and watching football games. It is interesting to see the texts selected for us as we prepare this worship service, since the American secular year is obviously not noted in our biblical tradition. They provide for us a challenging set of choices rather than a unified theme.

Ecclesiastes 3:1-13

This popular selection from the Qoheleth supplies for us on this day a collection of philosophical reflections over contrasting activities in our lives. It concludes with the observation that it is a gift from God that our eating, our drinking, and our occupations, even if tedious, should be enjoyable to us.

The wisdom tradition here has some similarities to Eastern philosophy, to Oriental wisdom, especially to the Taoist concept of yin/yang, the combination of opposites to attain completeness. As we have completed one secular year and as we begin another, it can be comforting to realize that although much of what occurred for us during the previous year was beyond our control, we can believe that, in spite of it all, God wants us to enjoy life and wants us to believe in God and to believe that, ultimately, God is in control of our lives and of our destiny.

Psalm 8

Psalm 8 in this context is a reminder to us that God, awesome as God is for us, has given tremendous responsibilities to us to care for the creatures of this world. As we ponder this, perhaps making some serious New Year's resolutions with regard to our God-given responsibilities to care for this world and its creatures and for our own bodies as individuals and as groups of Christians in communities of faith would be appropriate. If we make resolutions, we should keep them.

Revelation 21:1-6a

Although we are not on this day in a new heaven or on a new earth, we are beginning a new secular year and the old year has passed away. The sea, however, is still with us and is rising! On this New Year's Day and every day God is the Alpha and the Omega for us, present from the beginning to the ending of our lives.

There is an expression of faith in this text that God will be with us at every moment in our new year to "wipe away every tear" that may come into our eyes. We should be ready and prepared to see the hand of God in whatever form that hand may be expressed for us during the coming year.

Matthew 25:31-46

The clear emphasis in this text upon judgment of people by the Risen Christ based on works of mercy and of kindness that they may or may not have done may appear to be in stark contrast to the insistence by the Apostle Paul that we are being judged by God and saved from eternal suffering and death by the undeserved grace of God, not based on our own good works. Certainly different and even contrasting emphases can be and are present in our biblical collection of documents. Also, it is helpful to see contrasting teaching as present in creative tension within our Scriptures.

A key factor in this Matthew 25:31-46 text, however, is that it is "all the nations" that are said to be judged by the Risen Christ as the "Son of Man" here in 25:32, not the People of God, not those who believe and trust in God. Perhaps the people who do not believe in God and who do not trust in God are considered here in this text to be judged by criteria that are different from the criteria under which we are to be judged. In any event, during the coming year as in the past, eternal judgment is the work of the eternal God, not of mortal humankind.

SECOND SUNDAY AFTER CHRISTMAS DAY
(A, B, C)

Jeremiah 31:7-14

This thoroughly optimistic text is a reminder to us that the concept "salvation" in much of the Old Testament is primarily corporate and this-worldly and in most of the New Testament is primarily individualistic and is often otherworldly. By accepting both the Older and the Newer as its biblical canon, the early Church assured itself of a well-balanced and well-rounded salvation concept. Our teaching and our proclamation should reflect this balance, not overemphasizing the individualistic and otherworldly. When the corporate and this-worldly aspects of salvation are underemphasized and neglected, as they have been for so many centuries in most of the Church and still are in significant segments of it, oppression inevitably results and social justice is neither valued nor considered to be important for the Church. Instead, the Church offers only "pie in the sky by and by" and persons and groups of people who understand the necessity for social justice look with contempt upon the Church or at least consider it to be irrelevant.

Both corporate and this-worldly and individualistic and otherworldly, salvation is a gift from God for us. Life is itself a gift from God. Although we are individuals, we are members of the Church, the corporate body of Christ.

Sirach 24:1-12

This extensive personification and praise of Wisdom introduces the second half of the document known and used in major portions of the Christian Church as "The Wisdom of Jesus the Son of Sirach," "Ecclesiasticus" (the Church's book), or simply as "Sirach." After emanating from the "mouth of the Most High," Wisdom is said in this text to have permeated the world before being commanded by the Creator to dwell in Israel.

Psalm 147:12-20

As in so many of the songs in the Psalter, praise of the Lord (Adonai) is the dominant theme here. It is possible that there are three extended "verses" (1-6, 7-11, and 12-20) in this psalm as we have it today, much as we may have hymns with three verses in our hymnals. The third verse selected here (12-20) was probably at one time separate from verses 1-6 and 7-11, as it is in the Septuagint (Greek) and in the Vulgate (Latin) major translations of the Hebrew Bible. The emphasis in verses 12-20 on the Lord sending out the Word of the Lord (v. 18), declaring the Word of the Lord to Jacob (v. 19), and the statement that the Word of the Lord runs swiftly (v. 15) explains the reason for the selection of this portion to be placed between the personification of Wisdom in Sirach 24:1-12 and the personification of the Word of the Lord in Jesus perceived as the Christ in John 1:1-18, the pre-existent Logos (Word) who became flesh and "camped" among us full of grace and truth.

Wisdom of Solomon 10:15-21

In this other major wisdom document that, together with Sirach, is sacred Scripture for most Christians, Wisdom is personified and acclaimed throughout its first ten chapters. In this segment, as in the portion from Sirach 24:1-12, Wisdom is said to have provided guidance for and become a blessing for Israel. It is written that Wisdom entered into Moses and led the former slaves through the Red Sea to freedom. We can believe that just as God via Wisdom provided salvation for Israel, God via the Word (the Logos) Jesus the Christ, provided salvation for the members of the Johannine community and offers salvation to the world.

Ephesians 1:3-14

The key words that connect this text selected from the "blessing" portion of this epistle to the Johannine Prologue (1:1-18) are Grace in verse 6 and the Word of Truth in verse 13. It should be noted that in Greek the entire "blessing" section of this epistle (vv. 3-14) is one extended sentence. When we translate this sentence into the English language for readers of modern English, we have to divide it into at least six sentences. Greek readers from the period of classical Greek and from what is for us the "biblical" period enjoyed well-constructed, "edifice" sentences; most modern readers of English want their sentences in simple, small bites.

John 1:(1-9) 10-18

Since the references to the witness of John the Baptist interrupt the flow of thought of the Prologue even though they link the Prologue to the materials in the Gospel proper that begin with 1:19, on this particular occasion on the Second Sunday after Christmas Day when the Word, the Logos, is emphasized, it would be appropriate to focus our attention on the portions of the Prologue (1:1-5, 9-14, 16-18) apart from the references to John the Baptist that we see in 1:6-8 and 15. The main and perhaps original portions of the Prologue (1:1-5, 9-14, and 16-18) express one of the highest Christologies that were included within the New Testament canon.

Here in Jesus, the pre-existent Logos, divine grace is said to be so abundant that it is literally "grace piled on top of grace." Here the only begotten God the Son, who is in the close presence of God the Father, has "exegeted" (from the final verb in v. 18) God, has brought God out so that those who follow him will be able to see the meaning of God, God whom no human has ever seen at any time.

Particularly if we have used John 1:1-14 as the Gospel text on Christmas Day, we should put our emphasis on 1:16-

18 on this present occasion. A biblically based message from this text on the Second Sunday after Christmas Day will demonstrate from Jesus as Jesus is revealed to us in the New Testament and from our experiences within the Church as it should be as the "Body of Christ" what it means to us to receive God's "grace piled on top of God's grace." Our message will also show how the Jesus of history in his life brought out for others to see the meaning of God whom no human being has ever seen at any time. It will be God who graciously forgives and Jesus who goes to the cross for us whom we, therefore, will proclaim and will depict with our lives. This will mean offering ourselves for others. It will mean giving up our life by trusting and believing in God who is the one who gives "grace piled on top of grace." Our words will be effective if our lives demonstrate these things.

SEASON OF EPIPHANY (ORDINARY TIME)
EPIPHANY OF THE LORD (A, B, C)

We have a responsibility in our ministry to observe and to preserve the festival of the Epiphany in some way each year, not only on the years in which January 6 happens to be a Sunday. The Sundays after the Epiphany will not have much special meaning unless we observe Epiphany itself in some way that will bring it to the attention of the members of the congregation. If we do not have a worship service within our usual setting, perhaps we could gather a group of young people — or people of all ages — and go Epiphany caroling to members of the congregation and community who are older, are shut-in, or otherwise are special in some way. This activity would also be a reminder to us that a substantial portion of the Church, i.e., the Eastern Orthodox tradition, observes January 6 as the Festival of the birth of the Christ. A carol singing would also highlight the beautiful Epiphany hymns on the Day of Epiphany.

If an Epiphany carol singing event is not chosen, some other unusual worship setting produced by the Worship Committee of the congregation could be most meaningful for those who plan it and participate in it. For example, worship could be in a public place to illustrate that this is the festival of revealing Christ to the "nations." It could be held in a circle on the floor or within a circle of chairs. The setting should be appropriate for a relatively small number of participants, and the setting as well as the message should be memorable. With a little imagination and some preparation, a group of youth or adults could act out each of the four texts in simple drama form, not necessarily with a narrator and following the dialogue verbatim, but with a measure of creative inspired imagination not unlike that displayed by the writer of the Matthaen tradition that became Matthew 2:1-

12. The accounts could also be memorized by four different persons and presented in the form of biblical storytelling.

Isaiah 60:1-6

This is a truly beautiful text, especially when we consider its original "life situation." Certainly the people who first shared this message had vivid memories of the darkness that they, their parents, and grandparents had experienced through defeat, the destruction of Jerusalem, and decades of exile in Babylon. Now they dared to hope and to dream of a glorious future when the glory of the Lord God would shine again on them and when people from all nations would come to that light. In their minds they pictured the return of parents with young children coming to Jerusalem from every direction. They visualized also pilgrims and foreigners bearing gifts that — in contrast with the total losses suffered during deportation and the flight of refugees — would restore the economy of their city. They expressed this in terms of camels laden with precious metals and perfumes, a picture of the greatest imaginable value brought on the largest "trucks, trains, cargo planes, and ships" known to them at that time. We can be joyful with them within our imaginations without at this point trying to make any New Testament application of this text. The New Testament application can come in our use of the Matthew 2:1-12 account.

Psalm 72:1-7, 10-14

This is obviously a Royal Psalm intended for use at the coronation of a new king or at some commemoration in honor of a king. We notice the high expectations of the songwriter and of the people with respect to their king. They were especially concerned about justice for all and about righteousness in all relationships within the realm. Most of all, they were concerned about justice for the poor.

Within our own experience the theme of justice for the poor becomes extremely significant when national, state, and local governments directly or indirectly withdraw sustenance from those who have the greatest need among us. As members of communities of faith, we have the responsibility to hold our government units accountable through our direct actions and participation in government, advocacy, voting, etc. In addition, we can and should do everything that we can to employ those who are poor, provide skills training opportunities, and to provide immediate assistance in terms of food, rent, mortgage payments, and utility payments. The Day of Epiphany can become a time when we recover some of this kind of service, a service that the Judaisms of the time of Jesus' public ministry, the early Church, and traditionally people within the Islamic tradition have provided. Our efforts locally and through regional and national church bodies have sometimes been very significant. Certainly much more can and should be done.

The mention in Psalm 72:10 of kings from Sheba and Seba in Arabia bearing gifts of great value and falling down in front of the Israelite king — something that was very rare within Israel's history — is apparently the reason for the selection of this psalm in connection with Matthew 2:1-12 on this occasion within our lectionary. The writers of the Matthean tradition probably used both Isaiah 60:1-6 and Psalm 72 when, inspired by the Spirit of God, they prepared the Matthew 2:1-12 account.

Ephesians 3:1-12

This text was most likely chosen for use on the Day of Epiphany because of the mention in Ephesians 3:6 and 8 of participation by Gentiles, along with those who were of Jewish background, in the one Church with its one faith and one Lord. These are very important Epiphany themes.

Matthew 2:1-12

This story is so well known that we may hardly notice how it was constructed. The inspired writers made good use of their Old Testament resources and in the process produced some quite remarkable subtle polemic against the Persian Zoroastrian Magi religion that was still a significant factor in the East at the time of the development of this text. According to the subtle polemic in this text, Zoroastrians who are truly wise will bring their most precious gifts and fall down to worship the baby Jesus. The story is told so simply and beautifully that, accustomed to it as we have been from our childhood, we hardly stop to think about it. With some mature reflection we might ask whether the Herod of history would be so careless that he would not send spies to follow the Magi to the home of any newly born "king of the Jews" who would be a threat to his own plans to be followed in power by one or more of his favorite sons. Also, with mature reflection we might be interested in how differently the Matthean and Lukan redactors developed their infancy narratives. The Matthean writers moved the action from Bethlehem to Egypt, back to Bethlehem, and then north to Nazareth. Luke started in Nazareth, moved the action to Bethlehem, and then returned to Nazareth. If we try to understand the story genre used in both of these infancy accounts, we shall not be unduly troubled by these very different geographical scenarios. Each writer used research, inspiration, and creativity. Their purpose was primarily theological and only secondarily historical. Should our purpose not be the same today, since we believe that we are inspired and led by the same God who inspired and led them?

BAPTISM OF THE LORD
(FIRST SUNDAY AFTER THE EPIPHANY)

With these texts we return to the Gospel According to Mark. In the Baptism of Jesus account in Mark 1:4-11 we have the core of what has often been called the "Adoptionist Christology" of this First Gospel. We read here that Jesus came along with multitudes of people from the rural areas of Judea and from the city of Jerusalem and was baptized by John with John's baptism of repentance for the forgiveness of sins. At this point, Jesus was a human being like the others who came.

According to this text, as Jesus was being baptized, Jesus saw the heavens opened and the Spirit of God coming down as a dove upon him, and heard a voice from heaven saying, "You are my Son, my Beloved Son. In you I am pleased!" With these words, the text portrays God as "adopting" Jesus as God's Son, and Jesus is no longer merely a human being. Because of the embarrassment that Jesus' having been baptized by John in a baptism of repentance for the forgiveness of sins caused followers of Jesus after the time of the writing of the Gospel According to Mark, there can be little doubt about the historicity of Jesus' having been baptized by John. It is not surprising, therefore, that the biblical and post-biblical accounts that depict Jesus being baptized by John include a great variety of theological interpretations, some of which are apparent already in the Mark 1:9-11 story.

The "voice from heaven" implies a very special divine revelation, a divine-human encounter in which Jesus was "anointed" as God's Son with royal power. The descent of the Spirit of God in a manner comparable to the descent of a dove enhances the divine-human encounter. God simply employs a physical means (a dove) to give more objectivity to the descent of the Spirit in this story. As the tradition continued to develop after the composition of this Mark

1:9-11 story, and as the perceptions of the humanity of the Jesus of history receded in order to give way to increasing emphasis on the deity of the Christ of faith, the accounts about Jesus being baptized by John came to be perceived by many — including many within the congregations in which we serve — not as divine-human encounters but as divine-divine encounters, and the creative adoptionistic Christology of the Gospel According to Mark was obscured.

We should praise God for the life of the Jesus of history. We should praise God that the Jesus of history was baptized by John. We should praise God for the biblical and for the post-biblical accounts that provide revealing insights into the theological interpretations given to the event of Jesus being baptized as a human being with a baptism of repentance for the forgiveness of sins. That the Jesus of history was baptized by John is gospel for us. It unites us with the Jesus of history on a human-human level. It places the Jesus of history firmly with us on the human level.

Of course, we are not baptized as Jesus had been with a John the Baptist baptism. Instead, we are baptized with a Christian Baptism in the name of God as Father, in the name of God as Son, and in the name of God as Holy Spirit. That makes our Christian Baptism a divine-human encounter and not a human-human encounter. The Jesus of history was not and could not have been baptized in a "Christian" Baptism, since at that time there was not yet a Christian Baptism. We cannot be baptized as the Jesus of history was baptized in a John the Baptist baptism for the forgiveness of our sins, since there is no longer a John the Baptist baptism. This Mark 1:4-11 account is very important, therefore, to us within our Christian tradition in that it links us to the Jesus of history, and, via our experience of Christian Baptism, we are linked to the Christ of faith in the context of God, who for us is Father, Son, and Holy Spirit.

Let us recapitulate as well as we can the theological process. The Jesus of history was baptized by John. That is a historically verifiable event. During an extensive process of God-inspired theological reflection over this event and its significance, many layers of theological interpretation were given in story form, some of which became sacred Scripture for us. That theological reflection has continued for many centuries and continues today as we consider the significance of all of this for our own lives. Therefore, we perceive the Jesus of history as the Christ of our faith, as our Risen Lord, as our Savior who is one with God perceived as Father and as one with God perceived as Holy Spirit. We ourselves are baptized and we baptize others in Christian Baptism in the name of God as Father, Son, and Holy Spirit.

Certainly it is important and appropriate to have Christian Baptisms on this day in which we reflect upon the Baptism of Our Lord. It is also important and appropriate on this occasion to commemorate our Baptism and the Baptisms of all of the members of the congregations in which we serve. Thus we are tied more closely to Jesus and to Jesus as the Christ, the primary founder of our religion.

As we in our own time and in our own way continue the ongoing process of God-inspired theological reflection upon the event of Jesus' having been baptized by John, the other texts selected for this day provide additional support. Acts 19:1-7 adds the Lukan emphasis on receiving the Holy Spirit, speaking in tongues, and prophesying after being baptized in the name of the Lord Jesus. Acts 19:1-7 also incorporates followers of John the Baptist into the fellowship of followers of Jesus with a Lukan story about a baptism that supersedes John's baptism. In a somewhat similar manner, the so-called "Baptism of the Holy Spirit" with its concomitant gifts is a significant experience for some Christians in our time. The Baptism of the Holy Spirit account in Acts 19:1-7 is a fulfillment by the Lukan writer of the expectation expressed in Mark 1:8 and in its Synoptic parallels that Jesus would provide that kind of baptism for his followers.

The voice from heaven in the baptism of Jesus accounts near the beginning of each of the Synoptic Gospels reminds us of the voice of God ordering and arranging the cosmos in the Genesis 1:1—2:4a creation account. Also, the portrayal of the Spirit of God hovering over the waters in Genesis 1:1-5 is connected to the Spirit of God coming down like a dove in Mark 1:10. Another connection between Mark 1:4-11 and Genesis 1:1-5 is that just as it is written in Genesis 1 that God saw what God had done and it was good, God is presented in Mark 1:11 as being well pleased with Jesus, God's Beloved Son.

In the conclusion of the Psalm 29 hymn to the Lord of the storm, the Lord is said to be enthroned over the flood as king forever. The Lord is then called upon to give strength and power to the people of the Lord. For us as Christians, that strength and that power are perceived as gifts of God received in our Baptism.

SECOND SUNDAY AFTER THE EPIPHANY

In the texts selected for this day, the Epiphany themes of the omniscience of the Lord God and of the Johannine Jesus is proclaimed, along with the guidelines that in response to God we must be open to the revelation of God, especially in terms of our sense of hearing and of sight. This will define for us the message that we should proclaim and the guidelines for life that we should share in our sermon or homily for this occasion.

1 Samuel 3:1-10 (11-20)

The Word of the Lord was said to have been rare during the latter days of the life of Eli. There was no frequent vision. The senses of hearing and of sight were not open to the messages from God. In this text, however, a fresh start is made. The senses of the boy Samuel are alerted when a call and a message come to him from the Lord. This text raises the question also for us whether we today are open to hear and to see new messages from God, as well as the messages that have come to us from God in the past.

Psalm 139:1-6, 13-18

The psalmist marvels at the profound knowledge that God possesses about every thought that the psalmist has ever had or will have. Even when the psalmist was in embryonic form, the Lord God was organizing every detail of the development of the psalmist. Since nothing is hidden from the sight and knowledge that God has, the psalmist must be open to God in every way. Therefore, the psalmist, and we together with the psalmist, must praise God forever.

1 Corinthians 6:12-20

In this text also not only the senses of hearing and of sight but the entire body is emphasized. The body with all of its senses is meant for the Lord. The body is said to be joined to the Lord. The body is a temple of the Holy Spirit within each person. The body was purchased at a very high price. The body is not private property to be used for selfish purposes. We are expected to glorify God in our body. As a temple of the Holy Spirit, the body is the primary place in which revelations of God the Holy Spirit occur. The believer is directed by Paul to do nothing that might hinder the activity of the Holy Spirit of God.

John 1:43-51

Here John the Baptist is depicted as directing the attention of two of his own disciples (one of whom in 1:40 is identified as Andrew, the brother of Simon Peter) to Jesus, who is said to be the "Lamb of God." The disciples follow Jesus and respond affirmatively to his invitation to them to "Come and see." They are portrayed as open, therefore, to God's new revelation in Jesus, providing a model for us also to follow Jesus and to be open to God's new revelation in him.

John 1:43-51 includes a heavy concentration of Christological material. Within these few verses a multitude of Christological titles are applied to Jesus. Jesus is presented as possessing supernatural knowledge, of having seen Nathaniel while Nathaniel had been out of the sight of the other people who were standing with Jesus at that time. Confronted with this supernatural knowledge that Jesus obviously possessed, Nathaniel immediately responds by attributing to Jesus the titles of "the Son of God" and "the king of Israel." Not only does the Johannine Jesus raise no objections to these titles; he also tells Nathaniel that compared to this supernatural knowledge Nathaniel has as yet seen hardly anything at all! Soon he will see far greater things than these. Then the Johannine Jesus tells Nathaniel that he will see the heavens opened (a symbol of God's self-revelation) and will see the angels of God ascending and descending upon the Son of man. Where the psalmist had used poetry in depicting the omniscience of the Lord God, the Johannine writers used narrative.

Certainly, therefore, we should all be perceptive and receptive, especially during this Epiphany season, to God's self-revelation, including new self-revelation to us where we are.

THIRD SUNDAY AFTER THE EPIPHANY

According to each of these four texts, time is short. Human life is brief and transitory. It is a time, therefore, for urgent, decisive action. Four different groups are addressed in four different periods of human history in four different ways by four different bearers of the message. Nevertheless, in each instance a similar message is imparted, namely, that unless people turn to God now, they will miss the good news of the positive action of God and will instead incur only the judgment of God and their own destruction. Is it any different in our own life situations? How shall we express this message next Sunday where we are?

Jonah 3:1-5, 10

There is urgency (judgment and destruction within forty days!) in the message of the Jonah character in this "story about a prophet," even though the Jonah character in this story delivered the message from God so reluctantly. The attitude of the Jonah character was almost totally negative. His delivery of the message was hardly satisfactory. In spite of all of this, the impact was tremendous. The people of Nineveh, from the richest and most powerful to the poorest and least powerful, believed, repented, and fasted. Even the cows in Nineveh fasted! And God did not destroy the city. Despite the immaturity and the inadequacy displayed by Jonah in the story, the grace of God was manifested magnificently, and the "bottom line" of the story was good news for any sinners who repent, just as it is even now.

Psalm 62:5-12

Sharp is the contrast between God (who is my rock and my salvation, my fortress, my deliverance, my honor, my refuge) and humankind (which is only a breath of wind, a delusion, with neither weight nor substance). The psalmist puts trust in God (who is solid, firm, steadfast, and thoroughly dependable) rather than in humankind and in wealth (which are fleeting, transitory, and unstable) and calls upon others to do the same, just as we must call upon ourselves and others to do now.

1 Corinthians 7:29-31

It is obvious that when Paul wrote this material he thought that the end of the world was imminent. How shall we who live more than nineteen centuries later apply what Paul wrote here about urging those who have wives to live as if they do not have them, those who weep as if they do not weep, those who rejoice as if they do not rejoice, and those who buy as if they do not possess anything, because, as it appeared to Paul, the form of this world is passing away?

Within the context of these four texts, it is still appropriate to emphasize, as Paul did, that the time is short, that human life is brief and transitory, and that it is time for urgent, decisive action. However, perhaps, unlike Paul, we should not become so specific in telling people how to live every aspect of their lives and how to conduct their interpersonal relationships in view of the imminent end. Perhaps with the benefit of an additional nineteen centuries of hindsight we might conclude that it would have been better for the Church and for the world if Paul had not tried to be so specific in his parenesis (guidelines for living) at this point.

Mark 1:14-20

There is urgency also in this keynote address of Jesus as portrayed by and for the Markan community in 1:15. "This is the moment!" the Markan Jesus says. "Very soon God is going to take charge of everything directly! Turn to God and believe this good news, that for God to take over the world in a direct way is good news for you, as it will be if you repent and turn to God!" Then there follows immediately in the Markan account the examples of Simon and Andrew, James and John, who left their boats and their fathers and followed the Markan Jesus. The implication is easily seen; this should be the response of everyone who hears or reads this text. Because time is running out, we too should leave everything else and follow Jesus.

From this brief analysis of these four texts, we may conclude that there should be urgency in our message and in the away in which we should present our message next Sunday. Certainly we should urge the people who hear us to turn toward God and toward Christ as Lord and Savior. We should let the Spirit of God direct our lives.

It would be helpful if we would share how we ourselves are trying to turn toward God and toward Christ as our Lord and Savior, and how we try to let the Spirit of God direct our lives. Perhaps we should not try to tell them specifically what they should do in the conduct of their personal relationships as husbands and wives, parents and children, etc. in view of the imminent end. Instead, we should merely try to show what we, and perhaps what others as well, are doing and have done. Then those who hear will be able to see for themselves the implications for their own lives and to draw their own conclusions in their own life situations.

FOURTH SUNDAY AFTER THE EPIPHANY

The issue of absolute authority and of derived authority is the most significant factor that is considered in these texts.

In Deuteronomy 18:15-20 it is said that the absolute authority of God is so awesome that the people of God pleaded that they would not hear the voice of the Lord God again nor see the great fire of God again, lest they die. Therefore, God spoke through the prophet Moses rather than directly to them. God also promised that after the death of Moses God would raise up another prophet who would be like Moses and whose voice the people of God were instructed to hear.

In Psalm 111 the absolute authority of the Lord is recognized as inextricably tied to the everlasting providence of the Lord. The Lord is gracious and merciful, just and trustworthy. A person is wise when that person fears and respects the Lord. It is said to be wise and good to be subject to the absolute authority of the Lord God.

Paul wrote in 1 Corinthians 8:1-13 that "There is no God except the one God." (It is interesting to note that this statement of faith that is based on the Israelite-Jewish statement of faith in Deuteronomy 6:4 is utilized in Arabic as the basis for the Islamic Creed, "There is no allah [god] except Allah [God]." Therefore, the Israelite-Jewish Creed, Paul's Creed in 1 Corinthians 8:4, and the Islamic Creed of Muslims are essentially the same.)

More explicitly, for Paul, according to 1 Corinthians 8:4-6, there is no God except the One God, the Father, from whom all things come and for whom we exist. This absolute authority, wrote Paul, is revealed to us as God the Father of our Lord Jesus Christ. He wrote that many are called "gods" in heaven and upon the earth, but actually there can be and is, of course, only one God, since by logic we perceive that there can be only one absolute authority. Also, Paul wrote, there are many who are called "lords" on the earth, many "bosses," that is, under whose derived authority we function on the earth. But for us, Paul wrote, just as we perceive that there is logically only one God, we perceive that there is logically for us only one Lord, Jesus the Christ. If it were any other way for us, we would be confused in our lines of authority, not certain whom we should serve and obey, especially during those inevitable instances when conflicting orders would be given.

So it is also this way for us today. Institutions, including our own Christian institutions, struggle to define organizational charts so that all can see to whom they are responsible. Families seek to clarify authority structures for the children in the family.

We read in Mark 1:21-28 that Jesus was remembered as a person who taught with authority, even over unclean spirits, which were forced to obey his commands. Because Jesus had been given this authority from the absolute authority of God his Father, Jesus' fame spread everywhere, throughout the entire region of Galilee.

If we are to be faithful to God as God is revealed in these texts, we should start with God, the one absolute authority and work down, so to speak, from God to derived authority and to authority received from derived authority. As responsible leaders in the Church today, we are expected to clarify the authority structures as we understand them. The manner in which we perceive God, the one absolute authority, and the authority derived from God will be expressed in our teaching, in our preaching, and most of all in our lives within our congregations and communities.

We should begin with a clearly worded acknowledgment that God and only God is the absolute authority. We should follow this with the affirmation that the Bible, the Church and its Sacraments, and inspired individuals in interaction with each other within a dynamic process of checks and balances are the principal secondary or derived authorities for us.

Beyond these, there are lower levels of authority, especially as we move into the areas of education, employment, and political and social structures.

Since the time of the early Church, followers of Jesus using Deuteronomy 18:15-20 have enthusiastically identified Jesus as "the prophet like Moses" whom the Lord God would later raise up. As Christians, we have every right, of course, to make this identification. We should always note, however, that we do not stop with the "prophet" designation for Jesus. We take Jesus far beyond that. Also, now that we give greater attention than we have for many centuries to the historical setting of the Jewish Scriptures texts and to the process by which they became and remain sacred Scriptures for Jews and for Christians, we acknowledge that it was Israel seeking clear direction and leadership that spoke within the Deuteronomy 18:15-20 text, Israel as a remnant people wishing to be led back into the "promised land" as once before they had been led by the "prophet" Moses.

FIFTH SUNDAY AFTER THE EPIPHANY

Isaiah 40:21-31

God is acclaimed in this text as not only the Creator of all of the splendor of the universe, but also as the one who watches over and actually mini-manages everything, without ever growing weary or lacking in understanding. Although even young men and women become tired and weak during strenuous activity, all persons, whether young or old, who trust in the Lord God will rise up and soar with wings like the wings of eagles.

Psalm 147:1-11, 20c

God is acclaimed in this psalm with words that have many similarities to the Isaiah 40:21-31 text. These words of praise must be read with much joy and enthusiasm. A perfunctory responsive reading will not suffice. Preparation in advance with lay readers, choirs, and worship committee members is always necessary, but especially when the lections are as joyful as these. The time and effort of preparation will be well spent! The use of lectionary aids such as this by pastors, members of worship committees, lectors, organists, music directors, and choirs can improve the quality of the readings greatly, with reasonable expenditures of time and effort and without embarrassment to any reader.

Mark 1:29-39

Basically, what is attributed to the Lord God in Psalm 147 is attributed to Jesus in Mark 1:29-39. For the members of the Markan community, Jesus heals, casts out demons, and provides hope. Jesus, in turn, is to be praised and served, just as it is said in Isaiah 40 and in Psalm 147 about the Lord God. We will certainly want to share this in our message this coming Sunday within the setting of the congregation at worship, as well as in private counseling situations.

Nevertheless, as the Mark 1:29-39 text indicates, none of us can keep Jesus to ourselves. He withdraws from us to a lonely place. He moves on to other people to serve them also.

1 Corinthians 9:16-23

It was obviously of great importance for the Apostle Paul in his relationships with the followers of Jesus at Corinth not to receive any financial assistance from them during his ministry among them. We know from the letter that he sent to the Philippians later in his life that he did accept assistance from the Philippians for a different reason and in a different situation. Apparently Paul refused assistance from the Corinthians in order that he would have the maximum freedom and flexibility in his difficult ministry among them. He wanted to be able to say what he believed that God was calling him to say and to offer the gospel and himself to many types of persons and in many different ways, without being financially dependent on them.

What are the implications of this for us? What do these texts say to us about our mission? How can we attain the maximum freedom and flexibility in our mission within a changing, merging, and emerging Church?

Not only should we continue to be concerned about our priorities and about our mission. We should also clarify and communicate carefully — as in our reaction to the texts of the previous Sunday — that only God is the absolute authority for us. We are actually called and "hired" by God before we are called and hired by the Church or by a congregation or agency of the Church. We work for God. We work for God among a particular group of people in a particular place at a particular time. When we remember this, we will have the courage and the maximum freedom and flexibility as inspired individuals, with appropriate humility and without arrogance, to be of service in many different ways to many different people, as Paul provided the example for us. We must exercise within the emerging Church of our time the freedom and flexibility that Paul described in 1 Corinthians 9:16-23.

SIXTH SUNDAY AFTER THE EPIPHANY

"Lord God, mercifully receive the prayers of your people. *Help us to see and understand the things we ought to do and give us grace and power to do them* through your Son, Jesus Christ our Lord."

It is in the portions of the Prayer of the Day for this Sunday that are italicized above that we see the unifying factor in the four texts selected for this day. Naaman, the commander of the army of the king of Syria, needed help from the Lord God through Naaman's own servants before he could understand the things that he should do in the cleansing of his body from leprosy in the 2 Kings 5:1-14 Elisha story. The psalmist in Psalm 30, afflicted by a life-threatening illness, needed help that could be given only by the Lord God. The person with leprosy in the Mark 1:40-45 account came to Jesus and was cleansed, but he was not obedient to Jesus' request that he say nothing about his being healed to anyone. He seemed to lack the grace and power to follow through with Jesus' request. Finally, Paul in 1 Corinthians 9:24-27 urged the followers of Jesus in Corinth to see and to understand the things that they should do, and wrote about the self-control needed in order to have the power to do them. The Prayer of the Day is also our prayer on this day as pastors and as people of God at worship. We too need help to see and to understand the things we ought to do, and we too need the grace and power to do them.

2 Kings 5:1-14

This complete story in the entire chapter of 2 Kings 5 is so rich in symbolism and meaning that the limited use of only a portion of it in a lectionary on a particular occasion is a cause for regret. The story about Naaman was especially significant for Israelites while they were in exile in Babylon after 597 and 586 BCE who wondered whether they could worship the Lord God without having "two mule loads of soil from Israel" on which to build an altar (5:17) and whether the Lord God would pardon them if under their condition of servitude they were forced to bow down in a temple dedicated to Marduk, the Deity as perceived in Babylon (5:18).

For us in our time this 2 Kings 5 text is a reminder that we, like Naaman, should do whatever it is necessary that we do and should ask God for the grace and power to do it. We should do this at all times, not only when we are ill and full of disease, but at all times.

Psalm 30

The questions that the psalmist asks of God in verse 9 are fascinating. Faced by a terminal illness, the psalmist argues with the Lord God that it will actually be to the advantage of God to heal the psalmist. If God permits the psalmist to die, the Lord God will receive no benefits from the psalmist. The psalmist will no longer be able to praise God and no longer be able to tell people about the trustworthiness of the Lord. Under similar circumstances, would the line of argumentation that the psalmist uses be appropriate for us today? What prayer possibilities does this open?

Mark 1:40-45

We notice initially that this account is much less developed than is its antecedent in 2 Kings 5. The cleansing from leprosy account in 2 Kings 5 actually depicts a greater miracle than the one attributed to Jesus here in Mark 1. Elisha as a prophet, a "man of God," spoke the word that resulted in the restoration of sound flesh not merely to a leper," but to "Naaman, the commander of the army of the king of Syria." Syria had been the dreaded enemy of Israel at the time depicted in this story, and Elisha spoke the word that led to the cleansing not directly to Naaman but through a messenger. If Elisha performed such great miracles merely through the spoken word as a representative of God, surely Jesus as the Son of God must have performed as great or greater miracles. Such must have been the thinking of many among the early followers of Jesus. As pastors, what are the things that we should see and understand that we ought to do and need the grace and power of God to do? In what areas have we failed to see and to understand what we ought to do, and, not having asked for the grace and power to do them, lost them by default?

1 Corinthians 9:24-27

The verb *hypopiazo* has been almost consistently poorly translated in 9:27. Paul was using the analogy of a boxer here in a fierce struggle with an opponent in an athletic contest in 9:26b. It is not likely that Paul switched from the analogy of striking the body of his opponent in 9:26b to the idea of striking his own body and subduing it in 9:27. The body that he depicted as "my body" in 9:27 was the body of his opponent in the athletic contest analogy, the body that he said was "my body" to subdue. To "pommel" his own body and to subdue it once a boxing match has begun would not gain for him the crown of victory that he sought. That would have been entirely "missing the mark" that Paul wrote in 9:26b that he did not do.

Consider, therefore, the following translation for 9:24-27, because the literal meaning of the verb *hypopiazo* is as a prize-fighting term "I strike under the eye," and because of the way in which Paul used analogies in the other portions of his letters.

> [24]Do you not know that those who run in a stadium all run, but that only one receives the trophy for first place in each individual race? This is how I want you to run your lives so that you will receive the trophy. [25]Every competitive athlete trains strenuously, showing self-control in all ways. They train in order to receive a

victory crown that soon withers, but we to receive one that does not wither. [26]For this I run, not without my goal in sight. For this I box, not beating the air and missing my mark. [27]I hit the body of my opponent right under the eye and subdue it, so that having proclaimed the gospel to others, I might not fail to receive the crown of victory myself. (as translated in Norman A. Beck, *The New Testament: A New Translation and Redaction* (Lima, Ohio: Fairway Press, 2001)

The mark that Paul was referring to in 9:26b was almost certainly the place under the eye of his opponent, the place that he wanted to "hit" in order to win the match and with it the "crown of victory," eternal life with Christ.

Our salvation does not, of course, depend upon our translation of this verb, but our understanding of Paul's theology is enhanced when we translate *hypopiazo* more literally and do not produce the ludicrous situation of Paul giving himself a knock-out punch in order to try to defeat his opponent and gain the crown of victory. Paul's analogy, when translated as it is translated above, provides an illustration that is readily understandable today and helps us to see and to understand the things that we ought to do. It helps to give us the grace and power to do them.

SEVENTH SUNDAY AFTER THE EPIPHANY

In each of these four texts there is an affirmation from God of a sinner or community of sinners and in each text there is an affirmation of God by people. The basic elements of worship are present, therefore, in these texts.

Isaiah 43:18-25

Even though the People of God had not honored God with their burnt offerings and sacrifices, it is said that God would affirm them by providing for them a way in the wilderness for their return to Jerusalem. As we see below, the Apostle Paul made a similar statement of faith in 2 Corinthians 1:18-22 that in spite of their sins God will declare righteous the chosen people of God. There is no particular reason given for this gracious act of God. This "new thing" is simply announced and celebrated. The affirmation from God is evidence of the inscrutable nature of God as noted by Paul in Romans 11:33-36.

The affirmation of God and of God's grace is implied rather than expressed in the Isaiah 43:18-25 text. The affirmation is implied in the proclamation of the good news about the willingness of God to forgive and to forget the sins of the people.

Psalm 41

Within the context of this psalm, the Hebrew adjective *dal* at the end of Psalm 41:1a (in Hebrew, 41:2a) should be translated as "weak" or as "suffering" rather than as "poor," even though the word *dal* elsewhere is used to describe persons who are poor.

Unlike the person in the Mark 2:1-12 account who had been suffering from a serious affliction and says absolutely nothing, the psalmist in Psalm 41 speaks profusely. Most of the psalmist's lament, as in the Job drama, pertains to the attitude taken by enemies of the afflicted person. The psalmist asks for physical recovery so that the psalmist will be able to do to the adversaries what they have done to the psalmist. The psalmist is vindicated, or at least anticipates vindication.

The affirmation of God comes in the doxology at the conclusion of the psalm, which is also the conclusion of Book 1 of the Psalter. The affirmation is appropriate for the day.

Mark 2:1-12

In this text the affirmation of God of the forgiveness of sins and the healing of the paralyzed man is of course mediated through Jesus. Our emphasis as we use this text should be upon the affirmation from God mediated through Jesus rather than on the controversy dialogue inserted in verses 6-10 that makes of this text the first of a series of controversy stories that culminate in Mark 3:6. We are aware from our own experiences how debilitating deep feelings of guilt can be. The text depicts a miracle. The paralyzed man has been affirmed, forgiven, and healed. The proper response is given in 2:12. The man who had been paralyzed rises and walks, and the people who witnessed this miracle of healing glorify God. The circle is complete.

2 Corinthians 1:18-22

This text, which brings the affirmation theme to its climax, asserts that the affirmations from God in history are focused in Jesus Christ, the Son of God. As Paul expressed it in 1:20, "For as many as are the promises of God, in him (the Son of God) they are all kept with the 'Yes!' he supplies." The affirmation is further expressed in the Spirit of God present in the hearts of the followers of Jesus as a continual affirmation from God.

The "Amen" ("Yes, indeed! It is certainly so in our experience!") expresses our affirmation of God in response to the affirmation from God expressed in the life and teachings of Jesus. We are called to live our lives as expressions of this affirmation from God and as affirmations of God.

Perhaps the most significant theme that runs through these four texts is the theme of God's action in providing something new for the People of God. It may be new or renewed life that God as a loving, gracious Father or Husband supplies. It may be new wine to revive and invigorate (certainly not to intoxicate) God's people. It may be a new covenant cut into the lives of God's chosen ones by the ongoing Spirit of God. That which is new is to be recognized as authentic alongside the older written revelation. The new gift of the Spirit of God is exciting to the People of God because they do not yet know what good things it may involve. The new gift may even be considered to be better than the old, for it gives life now in the present situation.

Hosea 2:14-20

Although the People of God were said to have been unfaithful to the Lord God by submitting to the Baals ("Lords") of the land in which they settled and lived and to the "Gods" of the people who had conquered them, the Lord is said to be willing, even eager, to win them back, to attract them again to the Lord and to be like a husband to them again. The Lord God will cause the people to forget the names of their former Baals. The Lord God will provide for the safety of the people by making a covenant even with the wild animals that might otherwise harm them as they come through desolate areas on their way back to Jerusalem. The bow and the arrow, the spear, and all of the other weapons of war that had harmed them in the past will be removed. The people will be joined with the Lord God in a new and better relationship than they had ever experienced in the past.

Psalm 103:1-13, 22

This psalm, which includes in verses 8 and 9 a paraphrase of the great description of characteristics of the Lord God written also in Exodus 34:6-7, Numbers 14:18, Nehemiah 9:17, 31, Jeremiah 32:18, and Jonah 4:2, begins with a reminder to the self to bless the Lord totally and unequivocally. It is a reminder to the self that the Lord God rescues, forgives, and renews life. The Lord is said to be aware of our human limitations. The Lord is portrayed as having pity on us just as a father has pity and compassion for his children. The Lord God is just, but will not punish us as much as we deserve. The Lord gives new life to those who are oppressed. We too can find comfort and hope in this today.

Mark 2:13-22

This text continues the bridegroom analogy that is present in the Hosea 2:14-20 text considered above, but with changes. The Lord God of the Hosea text is now the Lord Jesus, the "bridegroom" of the new developing Christian community of faith. The members of the new community claim that their bridegroom is still with them; therefore, for them to fast during the wedding feast would not be appropriate. They should be celebrating their new relationship with their Lord. They are enjoying "new wine" in "new wineskins." They are to be "new wine" to gladden the spirits of many people. They are still "working" and "fermenting." How can we use these analogies in our life situations?

2 Corinthians 3:1-6

In this chapter and in Romans 7:6 the Apostle Paul definitely claimed something that was "new." He claimed that the new revelation from the Spirit of God regarding salvation in Christ gives life where the older revelation given through Moses and preserved on tablets of stone is actually destructive to life. It may be difficult for us to recognize how radical such statements must have sounded within the Jewish communities of the mid-first century in Galilee and Judea and in the Jewish Diaspora. These statements of Paul that are included within our New Testament are offensive to Jews still today.

Paul could have stressed the importance of the ongoing Spirit of God speaking through himself and through other inspired individuals of his time without this blanket condemnation of the Jewish Scriptures. What he wrote here would be comparable to what one of us might write stating that the words of the Bible are destructive to life, that as a written code it kills, but that what the Spirit of God says through us gives life. How would our ecclesiastical communities respond to us if we were to write like that? What would those who are in authority over us in the Church do?

Instead of Paul's blanket condemnation of written biblical tradition, we today should affirm the ongoing Spirit of God late in this our Epiphany season. As inspired people, we should claim the inspiration of the Spirit of God in our time. There is a new Word of God when we speak in accordance with the Holy Spirit of God. We are the prophets of God in our day and age and in our place. We should claim the Spirit of God when we read and proclaim the biblical texts. The living (spoken) Word of God is efficacious, living and active, sharper than any double-edged sword, as the writer of Hebrews 4:12 indicated. The oral stage of the proclamation is the most vital. It is more cutting, more applicable, than is the written text that eventually may preserve a portion of it. But we would not want to condemn the written word that preserves a portion of the spoken revelation. To do so would be to cut us off from our heritage. The written Word has authority. It is our heritage. It is a means of grace for us.

There is no reason for us to doubt that Paul meant what he wrote in these two places. It is somewhat ironic that Paul's opinion on this subject has come to us in written form in our written religious tradition. At any rate, although followers of Jesus (and of Paul) preserved Paul's opinion on this subject and incorporated it into their expanded biblical canon, they did not reject the written Word, the Jewish Scriptures, but include them as our Old Testament. And we can be grateful for that.

NINTH SUNDAY AFTER THE EPIPHANY

The Ninth Sunday after the Epiphany is rarely celebrated as such among us. The texts selected for this Sunday are used only when Easter is very late in the Church Year and in Churches in which the Last Sunday after the Epiphany is not celebrated as Transfiguration Sunday.

Deuteronomy 5:12-15

Within the guidelines provided in Deuteronomy 5 for the "Ten Commandments," it is written that Israel must "Remember the Sabbath day, in order to keep it holy." By "keeping it holy," it is meant that the seventh day should be set aside and dedicated as a day of rest for everyone in Israel, including all employees and beasts of burden. It is interesting to note that nothing is written in this text about prayer, meditation, and community worship on this day. Neither is there anything written here about activities associated with emergency situations, or about helping people on this day, other than giving everyone an opportunity to rest. It may be implied that certain activities will be necessary on the Sabbath day. For example, babies must be fed, people must eat and drink to preserve their health and lives, soldiers must protect their nation and its people, etc. In our time, rabbis and cantors work to lead worship services in synagogues on the Sabbath and pastors and others work to lead in worship services in churches on Sundays, the Christian "Sabbath" for all except Seventh Day Adventist Christians.

Mark 2:23—3:6

Observance of the Sabbath and activities of Jesus and of his followers on the Sabbath are featured in these two narratives that conclude the series of conflict stories about Jesus and the Pharisees that run from Mark 2:1 through 3:6. It is important to note the structure of these texts, especially of Mark 2:23-

28. The saying of Jesus that the Sabbath was established for the sake of people and that people were not brought into existence for the sake of the Sabbath is consistent with other sayings that without a doubt were expressed by the Jesus of history many times and in many situations. The extensive introduction to the saying of Jesus (2:23-26) appears to be a product of the writer of the Gospel of Jesus Christ According to Mark and of the developing Christian tradition. We can easily fail to see that the Pharisees in this introduction are literary Pharisees set in place by the developing Christian tradition. (Real Pharisees, Jewish Pharisees, would not have been out in the grain fields on the Sabbath to complain about what Jesus' followers were doing.)

The conclusion in verse 28 that the "Son of man" is Lord also over the Sabbath, like other "Son of man" sayings are Christological affirmations developed within the Christian tradition as a result of reflections over the Daniel traditions, and probably do not go back to the Jesus of history.

The best Pharisees and Jews throughout Jewish history would insist, as Jesus insisted in Mark 3:1-6, as well as in Mark 2:27, that people are always more important than institutions and practices, even than the most significant religious practices. After all, the texts in Exodus 20:8-11 and in Deuteronomy 5:12-15 emphasize that the Sabbath Day was designed to help people and beasts of burden by giving them time for the rest that they needed in order to continue to live.

This Mark 2:23—3:6 text will be considered again in Series B on the Sunday between May 29 and June 4, if that Sunday occurs after Trinity Sunday.

Psalm 81:1-10

The connections of this text with the emphasis on what should and should not be done on the Sabbath in the two texts considered above are that God delivered Israel from the burdens imposed by the Egyptians and that the people are called upon to sing praises to the Lord God who delivered them. Therefore, the Lord God has given them rest from their burdens.

2 Corinthians 4:5-12

The Apostle Paul wrote here that although he and other followers of Jesus are afflicted and abused by their Roman oppressors and their surrogates, the ultimate power is held by God and demonstrated in the life of the Risen Christ. Only God is ultimately the giver of rest.

LAST SUNDAY AFTER THE EPIPHANY
(TRANSFIGURATION SUNDAY)

2 Kings 2:1-12

This account is evidence that there was a tendency in the direction of the deification of Elijah within some Israelite traditions, just as there may have been with regard to Moses (Deuteronomy 34:1-12) and earlier within some Semitic traditions with respect to Enoch (Genesis 5:22-24). The accounts of the ascension of Jesus within the Luke-Acts corpus provide the most extensive biblical evidence of the more complete theological development of this nature among early Christians with regard to Jesus.

As we look at 2 Kings 2:1-12, we see that according to this account after a certain point in time Elijah was seen no more, but he was perceived to be alive with God. This was the basis, of course, for the expectation that developed among some of the Israelites — an expectation that is still evident within the Passover liturgy for Jews — that Elijah would return to the earth in a visible form some day. This expectation was used by early followers of Jesus with respect to the person and function of John the Baptist and it was certainly used in the development of the account of the Transfiguration of Jesus that is the dominating text among the four that are selected for our use on this day.

In 2 Kings 2:1-12 the whirlwind and the chariot of fire were the means of transportation in lifting Elijah from the earth and its gravitational force. In the Luke-Acts account Jesus was taken up within a cloud. A cloud was also the setting for the voice from the cloud in the Markan Transfiguration account.

Psalm 50:1-6

Reference to God as speaking and summoning the earth, reference to a devouring fire, and most of all reference to the words, "Gather to me my faithful ones!" link this portion of Psalm 50 to the 2 Kings 2:1-12 text.

2 Corinthians 4:3-6

For Paul, the face of Christ was apparently seen more vividly in the good news of the crucified Jesus being raised by God from the dead as Lord and Savior than in the face of the Jesus of history whom Paul had not seen. That is to say that for Paul the Risen Christ was in a sense transfigured perpetually. Paul saw the glory of God in the face of the Christ. This was for Paul the light that shines unceasingly out of the darkness of death. The face of the Christ was seen, however, only by those who would believe. We who live more than nineteen centuries later are basically in the same position as Paul was. For us also Jesus is in a sense perpetually transfigured.

Mark 9:2-9

This Transfiguration story, along with its parallels in Matthew and in Luke, is considered by the great majority of Christians to be a record of an event that occurred just as it is recorded here. It is likely, however, that much more is involved in these texts than simply a record of an event. If these are simply records of an important, spectacular event that occurred during the public ministry of Jesus, we may wonder why there is no mention of such an astonishing occurrence within the Fourth Gospel. According to popular understanding, the Fourth Gospel was written by John, and John is said to have been present with Jesus on the mountain at the time of this event. How could the writer of the Fourth Gospel have forgotten this profound experience of seeing and hearing men who had lived and died hundreds of years earlier and who remained prominent in Jewish thought?

Although the Fourth Gospel has no mention of this event, Mark, Matthew, and Luke, who are nowhere said to have been present on the mountain, all include this story.

With our understanding of biblical symbolism, we can see that in these Synoptic Gospel Transfiguration stories Moses and Elijah function as symbols for the Torah and for the Prophetic Traditions respectively. The Torah and the Prophets together constituted the sacred Scriptures for most Jews and for the earliest Christians during the time in which the Synoptic Gospels were written. Symbolically, these Transfiguration stories may have been intended to proclaim that Jesus is in the "same league" with Moses and Elijah. By means of these stories Jesus and the words of Jesus are validated as on the same level of authority as the sacred Scriptures as the Scriptures were known at that time. (The so-called Writings had not yet been canonized.) From the standpoint of those who first heard or read the Transfiguration account in Mark, Jesus' words and Jesus as a person were validated within these accounts by God God's self by means of the very impressive voice from the cloud saying, "This is my Beloved Son! Listen to him!" In the story after the cloud moved away, the three awe-stricken disciples are said to have seen no one there except Jesus. Moses and Elijah were gone.

Symbolically, therefore, the Torah and the Prophetic traditions were also no longer to be seen nor heard. At this point the message intended almost certainly was to indicate vividly that Jesus and the words of Jesus have replaced the Torah and the Prophets as sacred authorities for followers of Jesus. The Transfiguration account in Mark 9:2-9, therefore, served to validate the entire Gospel of Jesus Christ (Mark) much as the "Burning Bush" account in Exodus served as a validation of the entire book of Exodus or even of the entire Torah. When the Matthean and Lukan redactors included the Markan Transfiguration account in their expanded Gospels, the Transfiguration accounts served the same purpose in those documents as validation stories for those documents.

The writers of the Fourth Gospel chose to validate their account also but not by using the Markan Transfiguration account. Instead, they validated the Fourth Gospel by their use of the great "I Am" statements that they have the Johannine Jesus express in key places in their document.

Thus we have the Four Gospels validated as "words of Jesus" and actually as "Word of God" that God God's self directly and indirectly is said to have commanded us to hear as we transition from the Epiphany season to Ash Wednesday and to the Lenten season.

ASH WEDNESDAY (A, B, C)

As we ponder the meaning of the season of Lent and the significance we would like for it to have this year for us and for the people with whom we live, we begin with these Ash Wednesday texts.

We see that in Joel 2:1-2, 12-17 and in Matthew 6:1-6, 16-21 the emphasis is on appropriate behavior. In Joel 2:1-2, 12-17 the Lord God commands the people to fast, weep, mourn, repent, and return to the Lord. In Matthew 6:1-6, 16-21 the guidelines are to help those who are in need, pray, fast, and to store up your treasures in heaven where they will never be lost. It is obvious that for those who selected these texts for use on Ash Wednesday the behavior commanded in these texts from Joel and from Matthew were very important, especially for the season of Lent. They then selected a portion of one of the best-known penitential psalms in the Psalter (Psalm 51) to indicate appropriate prayer to accompany appropriate behavior. Finally, the grace of God was brought into this series of texts with the inclusion of the Apostle Paul's passive imperative verb *katallagete* ("be reconciled" to God) in 2 Corinthians 5:20 and in Paul's entreaty in 2 Corinthians 6:1 not to receive the grace of God in vain. The 2 Corinthians reading provides for us, therefore, a very important addition to the appropriate behavior emphasis of the Joel and Matthew texts. The inclusion of the 2 Corinthians 5:20b—6:10 reading suggests that we emphasize the grace of God along with appropriate behavior during Lent each year and perhaps once each three years make it the primary focus.

During the height of the Civil Rights Movement forty years ago, many of us found in Isaiah 58 a message that resonated very well with us. It was that unless we are actively involved in social justice, in addressing the conditions in which people suffer economic and political oppression, as well as in being engaged in immediate and continued direct assistance to the oppressed, our fasting is no way acceptable to the Lord God. As a result, Isaiah 58:1-12 is now an alternative reading to Joel 2:1-2, 12-17 on Ash Wednesday. This inclusion of Isaiah 58:1-12 brings a very important dimension to our observance of Lent.

2 Corinthians 5:20b—6:10

Let us look more closely, first of all, at Paul's passive imperative verb *katallagete* in 2 Corinthians 5:20. From a theological perspective, the passive imperative is one of the most significant grammatical constructions in Indo-European language. Paul exhorts the followers of Jesus in Corinth and, because his exhortation here is sacred Scripture for us, also exhorts us to be reconciled to God by the grace of God. We believe that God makes this reconciliation possible by means of the life, death, and resurrection of Jesus the Christ, through the great atonement proclaimed by Paul and elaborated upon by other Christian theologians later.

What, then, is our role in this reconciling action? According to the grammatical construction, we are passive. God in Christ is the active one. We are to be passive, to have this done to us. "Be reconciled to God!" we are told. We can, of course, choose to reject this reconciliation, but Paul urges his readers and hearers to permit it to be done, to be forgiven, to become a new creation in Christ, as described in the 2 Corinthians 5:20a portion that precedes this text. All are strongly urged to accept this grace of God from God and to live in this grace. In 2 Corinthians 6:3-13 and continuing in 7:2-4 Paul claims that he and his co-proclaimers are trying to put no obstacles in anyone's path. He wants no obstacles of any kind to keep this message of passive reception of grace from anyone who might want to hear it.

Our work, therefore, on Ash Wednesday and throughout the Lenten season, in accordance with this 2 Corinthians

5:20b—6:10 text, is to prevent any and all obstacles from hindering God's action of reconciling us and others to God through Jesus as the Christ.

Let us look now at the other texts appointed for us for this day in the light of Paul's admonition to us that we should "Be reconciled to God by the grace of God through Jesus Christ our Lord." Let us, as Martin Luther insisted, interpret Scripture by the use of Scripture. In this way, we shall be letting the "gospel" — which in the texts chosen for this day is in the "epistle" — shed light on the other texts selected.

Psalm 51:1-17

The portion of Psalm 51 selected here puts emphasis on the penitential prayer. The obstacles to be removed in this instance are the psalmist's sins (and our sins). These sins are great, but the appeal is that God's mercy is greater than our sins. From our Christian standpoint, the forgiveness of our sins is accomplished by God through Jesus' death and resurrection. We recognize, however, that the Israelites and Jewish people prior to, during, and after the pre-Christian era called upon the mercy of God with no reference to Jesus, and we can and should assume that God has been able to forgive them. To assume anything less would be to try to limit God.

In the portion of Psalm 51 that follows verses 1-13, the psalmist shows an awareness that God does not need burnt offerings and other sacrifices in order to be able to forgive sins. God is interested in our broken and contrite heart. When our hearts are contrite, then the offerings and sacrifices will have value.

Has this changed since the time the psalmist wrote or sang this psalm? Which is the more inclusive concept, atonement or forgiveness? Do we today always require atonement of each other (of our children for example) before we will forgive them? Within our cultural milieu is it possible that an overemphasis on atonement theology places an unnecessary limitation upon God and upon our perception of God?

Atonement theology is useful and valuable within our understanding of God's grace, but perhaps it should be seen as only one of the ways in which we may perceive God's action in Christ and in history. Atonement theology was a way in which some of the followers of Jesus after the crucifixion of Jesus saw some very important good that God had brought about through that tragic event. Atonement theology is one of the ways in which we continue as Christians to see the crucifixion of Jesus, but it is only one of the ways in which we understand the crucifixion of Jesus. Considered together with the resurrection of Jesus, we see the action of God as a vindication of Jesus and of his life. God did not prevent the Romans from crucifying Jesus, but we believe that God vindicated Jesus and made the Romans powerless via the resurrection of Jesus from the dead. For more about this, see Hans Kueng, *On Being a Christian* (Garden City, New York: Doubleday, 1976), pp. 419-436.

Joel 2:1-2, 12-17

This text elaborates on the ideas of Psalm 51 beautifully and even more vividly. Again in relation to this text, let us consider the issues and questions raised above about atonement and forgiveness. Atonement is very important in "classical" Christian theology. There is no subject, however, in which Jews and Muslims are more significantly different from Christians than on the subject of atonement. Jews and Muslims understand and teach that no person, even God, can atone for the sins of someone else. For Jews and for Muslims, each person is totally responsible and accountable for that person's own sins.

Forgiveness, on the other hand, is very important for Jews and for Muslims, as well as for Christians. We agree within these three religions that we should always seek forgiveness from people whom we have harmed and then also from God, asking God to spare God's people, as this Joel 2 text indicates.

For more about the understanding among Jews and among Muslims that no one can atone for the sins of someone else, see Hassan Hathout, *Reading the Muslim Mind* (Plainfield: American Trust, 1995), pp. 33-35, and my *Blessed to be a Blessing to Each Other: Jews, Muslims, and Christians as Children of Abraham in the Middle East* (Lima, Ohio: Fairway Press, Revised edition, 2010), pp. 51-54.

Matthew 6:1-6, 16-21

A glance at the Synoptic parallels shows that except for Matthew 6:19-21 the components of this periscope are peculiar to Matthew. We can say, therefore, that the materials in Matthew 6:1-6 and 16-18 are best understood as teachings of the leaders of the Matthean community in Jesus' name. The positive aspects of these teachings are certainly applicable for us today as Christians. We should help those who are in need, we should pray to God, and we should fast, but we should do none of these in order to be praised. The negative anti-Jewish aspects that condemn the Jews and their leaders in these verses are not applicable for us today.

Isaiah 58:1-12

As indicated above, the inclusion of Isaiah 58:1-12 as a text to be read and reflected upon on Ash Wednesday and throughout the Lenten season brings a very important dimension to our observance of Lent. It reminds us that if we want to do something that is truly important during Lent or at any other time, we should help people who are in need, especially those who are oppressed economicly, politically, socially, and in any other way. That is what the inspired speaker and writer in this Isaiah tradition text said and apparently did. That is what the Jesus of history said and that is what the Jesus of history did. There can be no doubt about that.

Lent is the season of the Church Year in which we focus in our study and reflection upon the Jesus of history. There are a multitude of texts in the Four Gospels that are evidence of words and actions of the Jesus of history in support of those who were oppressed during that time. There is very little evidence in support of Jesus himself fasting, other than at the beginning of his public service in the Synoptic Gospels, and nothing about his giving up for a few weeks a bad habit that was obviously harmful to himself or to others. If we want to be like Jesus during Lent, or better yet throughout the year and during our entire lives, let us do whatever we can to change systems that rob the oppressed and give excessive bounty to the rich within our own nation and throughout the world.

FIRST SUNDAY IN LENT

These four texts are linked by the themes of covenant and of baptism, as well as of trust and of obedience. All are appropriate for the Lenten season. They provide many possibilities for Lenten keynote messages.

Psalm 25:1-10

The psalmist makes no attempt to present before the Lord a facade of sinlessness. Instead, the psalmist stakes everything on trust in the Lord. The psalmist reminds the Lord that the Lord is widely known and characterized by mercy and steadfast love. Therefore, the psalmist asks the Lord to concentrate on the goodness of the Lord and to teach that goodness and that way of life to those who, like the psalmist, are humble sinners who are eager to live according to the terms of the covenant that the Lord God has established with God's people. Although this psalm may be nearly 3,000 years old, it is not outdated. It provides an excellent model for us, and for the people among whom we serve, for Lent and for all seasons.

Genesis 9:8-17

Among the various covenants described within our biblical accounts, this covenant of God with Noah, with the descendants of Noah, and with every living creature is the most inclusive and perhaps the most gracious on the part of God, the mighty power in the covenant. In this covenant God makes no demands; God makes only promises. It is affirmed in the text that every rainbow that every living creature will ever see will be a reminder to God and to every living creature of God's everlasting mercy and grace.

1 Peter 3:18-22

The Lenten theme of redemption in Christ is extended in this text to those who, at the time of Noah, did not obey God. Through the waters of the great flood in the Noah story God destroyed all who were disobedient; in the waters of baptism now God saves those who are obedient. The covenant of baptism links the believer to Jesus the Christ, who is raised from the dead and ruling in the heavenly regions. By means of the baptismal covenant with Christ, the believer is endowed with the righteousness of Christ and linked to God the Father. First Peter 3:18-22 is a principal reason that 1 Peter, along with Paul's letter to the Romans and the Gospel According to John, were the favorite New Testament documents for Martin Luther.

Mark 1:9-15

If Jesus was obedient to God in coming to John the Baptist to participate in a baptism for the forgiveness of sins, how much more should not those who wish to follow Jesus as the Christ come to the Church, the Body of Christ, for baptism in Christ's name? In the Gospel According to Mark the baptism of Jesus by John the Baptist marks the beginning of a very special covenant relationship of God with Jesus, a covenant between Father and Son, a covenant in which Jesus is declared to be very pleasing to God. In this text Jesus is depicted as obedient to God even when Jesus is tempted by "Satan" in the wilderness. In this text Jesus proclaims the kingdom of God's grace and rejects the kingdom of Roman power. He overcomes the temptation of "Satan," the temptation to try to help Jesus' fellow oppressed Jewish people by cooperating fully with the alluring, satanic power of the Roman state. Jesus is depicted in this text as not believing that by his cooperating fully with the oppressive Romans the Roman oppression will be reduced. With his life and with his words Jesus will speak out against the satanic power of the Roman state, the state that will near the end of the Gospel According to Mark and at the end for us of the season of Lent this year crucify Jesus. Nevertheless, the Roman state will not, even with all of its power and glory, be able to prevent God from raising Jesus from the dead on the third day, Easter morning for us. That is the Easter message that we will anticipate in a few short weeks when the season of Lent has run its course.

SECOND SUNDAY IN LENT

Genesis 17:1-7, 15-16

This text is a story about the covenant between the Lord God and Abram and his descendants. The story provides an etiology of the origin of the custom of the circumcision of all Israelite males as a sign of this covenant. The story also describes the name changes from Abram to Abraham and from Sarai to Sarah as commanded by the Lord. Since the Lord is proclaimed in this text as God Almighty, Abraham and his descendants are commanded to walk (live) under constant scrutiny of the Lord God and be blameless. The childless marriage of Abraham and Sarah will be blessed by God by the birth of a son, Isaac, even though Abraham, who is 100 years old and Sarah 90, laughs (v. 17) at the possibility of a child for himself and for Sarah. As an important factor in the Christian story of salvation (*Heilsgeschichte*), this account is appropriate for use in Christian worship services during the Lenten season.

Psalm 22:23-31

After crying out to God in despair while suffering from a life-threatening illness and describing his physical distress, the psalmist promises to offer a heartfelt testimony of gratitude to God in the presence of other Israelites. The psalmist proclaims that in the future all people in every nation will bow down in humble adoration of the Lord God, who has total power and authority over them.

Romans 4:13-25

The Genesis 17:1-7, 15-16 text chosen for this day puts no emphasis on the faith of Abraham. In fact, it states that when Abraham heard the Lord say that Sarah and he would be blessed with a son in their advanced age, Abraham laughed in disbelief. Instead of this text, the Apostle Paul used

Genesis 15:6, in which it is written that Abraham believed the Lord, to support Paul's argument in Romans 4:13-25 that the promise to Abraham and to Abraham's descendants had been established by their faith and that the Lord would keep the promise the Lord made.

Alert members of our worshiping Christian congregations will wonder why those who compiled our lectionary did not use Genesis 15:1-6 rather than Genesis 17:1-7, 15-16 in conjunction with this text in Romans 4:13-25. Paul here in Romans 4:18 argued that Abraham believed with a hope that went far beyond all reason to hope and did not weaken in his faith even when he considered his own body and the prolonged infertility of Abraham and Sarah. This is in sharp contrast to the Genesis 17:17 note that Abraham laughed at the idea that God would bless Sarah and Abraham with a son when they were so old.

Mark 8:31-38

Mark 8:31 includes the first of three predictions by Jesus (to be followed in Mark 9:30-32 and 10:33-34) of his rejection, of his being seized in the Garden of Gethsemane, being crucified by the Romans, and after three days being raised to life by God. As used here on the Second Sunday in Lent, it serves as a projection toward Good Friday and Easter in our Church Year calendar. It also raises questions among thoughtful people today how Peter and the other disciples of Jesus could have responded so vehemently in protest to Jesus' prediction of his death and ignored completely Jesus' prediction of his resurrection that will occur three days after his death.

This account in Mark 8:31-38 provides for us much evidence of the inspired creativity of the Markan writer and of the earlier tradition. It is a particularly fascinating text to study, because three life situation levels can be discerned within the history of the tradition of this text up to the level of the Markan account.

The first life situation level is the level of the activities of the Jesus of history with some of his closest followers. We can see two rather loosely connected sayings of Jesus (Mark 8:36-37 and 8:38) at this Jesus of history level, as well as a hint in 8:31 that the Jesus of history had talked with his followers about the likelihood that he would be killed by the Roman occupation authorities as a Jewish messianic figure. There is further evidence in 8:32-33 that, when the Jesus of history talked about the likelihood that he would be killed by the Roman authorities as a Jewish messianic figure, Peter (and perhaps others among Jesus' followers who were present) objected strenuously to his talk about an imminent violent death. In spite of this, Jesus had refused to be deterred. He had resolutely continued his bold and courageous advocacy of the cause of God even when he was confronted by the fears of his disciples and their understandable attempts to dissuade him. During this first life situation, there would have been no prediction of and no expectation of the resurrection of Jesus three days after his death.

Behind this Mark 8:31-38 text, therefore, there may have been at least three separate situations within the activities of the Jesus of history. Let us try to reconstruct them as well as we can.

On one or more occasions, the Jesus of history probably said something about the likelihood that he would be killed by the Romans. As a highly intelligent and perceptive human being, he would have foreseen the likelihood that the military and political leader of the Roman occupation troops would order his arrest and crucifixion because Jesus was a Jewish messianic figure, passionately concerned about his fellow oppressed Jews and not afraid of the Roman authorities. Because he was helping his fellow oppressed Jews actively and openly, and because significant numbers of men and women from among his own people were often gathered around him, Jesus was perceived correctly by the Roman authorities to be a Jewish messianic figure and, therefore, a potential threat to the security of the Roman forces.

Although it is not likely that the Jesus of history ever encouraged his followers to use military actions and resistance against the Roman occupation authorities, the Romans could not be sure about that. Even though he himself would not encourage military resistance, which was not his purpose and which would have been foolhardy even if it had been, some of his excitable young followers might have attempted such action. Both the Roman occupation forces and the "Herodians" (Jewish religious and political leaders who cooperated fully with the Romans and opposed any attempts by Jewish Zealot types to foment a revolt or revolution that would almost certainly be crushed by the Romans with heavy loss of Jewish life, property, and position) were nervous, therefore, about the Jesus of history and about the excitable young men who were often gathered around him.

Eventually, of course, the Roman occupation leader, Pontius Pilate, did order the arrest, torture, and crucifixion of Jesus in Jerusalem. Pilate correctly considered Jesus to be a Jewish messianic figure, one among many others at that time. We note the inscription on the cross, "Jesus of Nazareth, King of the Jews." This inscription would demonstrate plainly and publicly to the Jewish populace what the Roman occupation authorities did to Jewish messianic figures. The "King of the Jews" inscription had probably been used many times (whenever the Romans crucified a Jewish leader of prominence) both before and after it was used as a designation of the reason that the Romans were crucifying Jesus. This was done by the Romans in order to keep the Jewish population subdued and to keep the number of Roman troops needed to control the Jewish population as small as possible.

On many occasions the Jesus of history probably talked about integrity and courage (and demonstrated great integrity and courage) in a way that was remembered, repeated, and recorded in the words of Mark 8:36-37, "What gain will there be for a person — even if the person should gain control of the whole world — if the integrity of that person is lost? For what could a person possibly give in exchange for that person's integrity?"

Also, it is likely that the Jesus of history talked about the Son of man and about other terms and ideas commonly spoken about within Jewish apocalyptic circles at that time. The words of Mark 8:38, "Whoever is ashamed of me and of my words within this adulterous and sinful generation — the Son of man will be ashamed of that person when the Son of man comes in the glory of his Father with the holy angels," probably are a reflection (with some additional development) over what the Jesus of history had said about these things. The Son of man is spoken about in the third person grammatically here, and "in the glory of his Father" may also be a part of this additional development of the text.

The second life situation level is the level of the reminiscences of followers of Jesus after he had been crucified. The words of 8:34b, "If anyone wishes to follow after me, let that person deny that person's self and let that person take up that person's own cross and follow me," were probably developed during this period of reminiscence when the cross symbol was becoming meaningful to followers of Jesus. At this level the words of the Jesus of history about this "adulterous and sinful generation" would be changing from internal criticism of Jews by a Jew (the Jesus of history) to external criticism of Jews by those who were not Jews (the Christ of faith and the early Christians). At this level of reminiscences of followers of Jesus after he had been crucified, the predictions of the Jesus of history that he would probably be killed by the Roman military forces would often be recalled — privately but not publicly and not in written form.

During this level of reminiscences, followers of Jesus would gradually have added details to the passion predictions *ex eventu* as they came to believe that Jesus was now raised from the dead and with God. Here (or at the Markan level) the important step of adding the resurrection prediction was probably taken in what was to become Mark 8:31. This step was taken because it was thought that Jesus as God's Son must have known that God would raise him from the dead; since along with his divine power he would also have omniscience. During this period of time the statement in Mark 8:36 that whoever loses life or integrity for Jesus' sake would have been developed as incentive and motivation for followers of Jesus. Also at this level (and at the Markan level during the Jewish revolt of 66-72 CE) followers of Jesus who were transmitting the tradition would have been careful not to say anything publicly or in written form about the Romans as those who would kill Jesus, so that their own lives would not be further endangered. Jewish authorities could be blamed, since they did not have political and military power over followers of Jesus, especially after 67 CE.

After Pilate had been discredited and removed from his office by the Romans, it became safe for followers of Jesus to speak publicly and to write about Pilate's involvement in the crucifixion of Jesus. If Pilate had been retained in office and advanced in position by the Romans, it is probable that followers of Jesus would not have been able to speak publicly or to write about Pilate's involvement in condemning Jesus to death. As it was, followers of Jesus were careful to present Pilate and the Romans only as rather passive participants rather than as the active agents that they were in ordering the arrest of Jesus, torturing him during the night, and crucifying him the next morning. It was perfectly safe, however, to blame the Jews by making them the active, aggressive instigators of the death sentence of Jesus. A few Jews, of course, the Herodians, may have been willing participants, but not the overwhelming majority of the Jews. We must be aware of this as Christian leaders today, and we must share our awareness of this with the people in our congregations.

The third life situation level, the level of the Markan composition of the document "the Gospel of Jesus Christ" that became canonical, brought together by the use of redactional connectors a variety of oral and written traditions into what we now have as Mark 8:31-38. At this level, additional detail was added, especially elements such as the words "and for the sake of the gospel" in 8:35.

Beyond this third level the Matthean redactors added details such as "to go away to Jerusalem" in Matthew 16:21 (Mark 8:31) and "May God mercifully spare you this! This must never happen to you!" in Matthew 16:22 (Mark 8:32). The Lukan writer-redactor went a different way by eliminating the rebuke by Peter (Luke 9:21-22).

There is an active debate currently about whether our proclamation should be limited to the canonical level of the tradition, or whether we should sometimes base our proclamation or use in our proclamation on other levels that are now accessible to us through use of exegetical methodologies. Personally, I think that we should be able to use all levels in our proclamation. Actually, whenever we place our emphasis on a particular portion of a text, we are choosing a particular level in the development of a text. If we use both Matthew and Mark, or Luke and Mark, or Deuteronomy and Exodus, or 1-2 Chronicles and 1-2 Kings, etc., we are actually using materials from more than one level of development of the traditions within the biblical account. Was not the tradition inspired at every level of its development? Particularly, I suggest that we should use the earliest discernible level of the development of texts from the Four Gospels. To limit our use to the canonical level would be reductionistic and would separate us unnecessarily from the Jesus of history. Of course, canon criticism and the canonical level are vitally important. So is text criticism that reveals changes in the text after the canon was established.

Mark 9:2-9

For this, please see the notes in the Transfiguration section on page 96.

THIRD SUNDAY IN LENT

John 2:13-22

Within Series B of this lectionary, the Gospel account for the Third Sunday in Lent (John 2:13-22) is, in a sense, a sequel to last Sunday's Mark 8:31-38 passion-resurrection prediction. This John 2:13-22 passion-resurrection prediction of the Johannine Jesus is couched in typical Johannine terms that are much more obscure and symbolic than are those within the Synoptic traditions. Not only is the cleansing of the temple placed near the beginning of Jesus' ministry rather than at the end where it is in the Synoptics, but also the Johannine writers placed this passion-resurrection prediction near the beginning of their account of Jesus' public ministry rather than well into the account as was done in Mark, Matthew, and Luke.

Further comparison of the cleansing of the temple accounts indicates that the Johannine tradition made the temple cleansing action of Jesus much more violent than in the Synoptics by having the Johannine Jesus form a whip of thorn bushes and use it to drive from the temple court those who had been selling animals there for use in the temple sacrifices and changing Roman coins into Jewish "tokens" that would be acceptable as temple offerings. Such comparison of texts also reveals that the Johannine tradition used its temple cleansing account as the basis for its passion-resurrection prediction in this John 2:13-22 text. (Note how the play on words in John 2:13-22 is dependent upon the cleansing of the temple account in John 2:13-17.) As with so many other texts, we are impressed by the creativity of the inspired writers of these traditions. We can say that this John 2:13-22 text is basically a product of the inspired Johannine community.

Among the indications that this John 2:13-22 text is a product of the inspired Johannine community are the following. First, there are the words of the Johannine Jesus in 2:19, "Destroy this temple, and (or If you destroy this temple,) within three days I will raise it up," and second, there is the use of the words "the Jews" in 2:13, 18, and 20. Let us look more closely at these two factors.

The words of John 2:19 are characteristic of a Divine Sovereign who cannot be limited or removed by death. Even though his temple-body might be destroyed by evil people, he has the power of self-resurrection at whatever time he designates. A human being, on the other hand, cannot accomplish self-resurrection. (Even Egyptian pharaohs who had mammoth pyramids constructed in which their bodies were to be placed could not accomplish self-resurrection.) We see that the words of the Johannine Jesus, here and elsewhere within the Fourth Gospel, are expressions of what the people of the Johannine community believed about Jesus as they perceived him. Their perception bordered on what was later to be called Docetism (that Jesus only seemed to have been human), although they guarded against that somewhat with their "and the Word became flesh" in the Johannine Prologue.

The distance between the Jesus of history and this account as we have it here is also portrayed in the use in this text of the expression "the Jews." By the time and in the place of the full development of this text, the members of the Johannine community were far removed theologically from Jews who remained Jews. They had in effect "forgotten," or perhaps we should say "chosen to forget" that the Jesus of history had lived and died as a Jew. Because of the way in which they used the expression "the Jews" in this and in many other Johannine texts, most Christians have also "forgotten" or "chosen to forget," or at least have not realized that Jesus himself was a Jew. As a result, destructive and hateful anti-Semitism became accepted and inherent within the Christian Church and in many Christian people.

Before we take up the practical question of what we shall proclaim next Sunday using this text as our primary biblical basis, let us consider for a moment a few thoughts about the resurrection predictions in John 2:13-22 to supplement our reflections over the passion-resurrection predictions in Mark 8:31-38 last week.

We can see and understand how resurrection predictions would be attributed to Jesus after followers of Jesus began to believe that Jesus who had been crucified by the Romans was alive again, raised from the dead by God or even self-resurrected, was in the Spirit of God truly present with them, and was uniquely one with God the Father. Resurrection predictions such as these are a natural development *ex eventu*. They are classic examples of *vaticinia ex eventu* (predictions made after the event has occurred).

Once it was perceived that Jesus was the unique Son of God, soon to be considered to be "God the Son," it is in no way surprising that followers of Jesus would have believed and taught that Jesus was and is omniscient. Therefore, it was reasoned or at least assumed that Jesus must have known prior to his death precisely when and how he would be killed and when and how he would rise from the dead.

Resurrection *vaticinia ex eventu* were therefore an entirely normal development. After it was proclaimed and taught, however, that Jesus had known and had revealed to his disciples that within three days after his death he would be raised from the dead, it became necessary to emphasize that his followers could not understand and did not remember Jesus' resurrection predictions until after Jesus' death and resurrection had occurred. For if his male disciples had believed and remembered Jesus' resurrection predictions, presumably they would have waited confidently for three days to pass, gathering early in the morning on the third day at the tomb of Jesus to welcome him back from the dead, never doubting that they would soon see him alive again, instead of doubting the word of the women who had experienced and then announced his resurrection to male followers of Jesus.

It is important for us to try to discern Jesus' own perception of the suffering that he would soon endure in Gethsemane, during the horrible torture by the Roman soldiers of the crucifixion squad during the night, and on the cross. The earlier Gospels, Mark and Matthew, retained an emphasis on Jesus' agony and suffering by utilizing the first verse of Psalm 22, "My God! My God! Why have you forsaken me?" as the only words of Jesus on the cross. On the other hand, the later Gospels, Luke and especially John, portray Jesus as essentially in control of the situation even while he was dying on the cross and as never in despair.

Now let us face the practical question of what we should proclaim based on this text this coming Sunday. We can portray how clever Jesus was, how adamant "the Jews" were, and how slow the disciples were to recognize and to process what Jesus had said. We can marvel at the daring and strength of Jesus as he drove men and animals from the temple court. Or, as a result of a more intense study of this text within the broader context of the Fourth Gospel and of the Synoptics, we can proclaim that this text reveals some of the things that the people of the Johannine community believed about Jesus and wrote about some of the Jews who were contemporary with the Johannine community during the time of the development of the Fourth Gospel. We can demonstrate how the people of the Fourth Gospel community formulated this passion-resurrection prediction as an additional inducement to faith in the Johannine Jesus, the Lamb of God who takes away the sin of the world. It will be helpful to get back as much as possible into the situation of the people who developed and first used this text. It will be helpful to express our faith as they expressed their faith, but without condemning the Jews. Certainly, we want our proclamation this coming Sunday to be both faith-inducing and edifying.

1 Corinthians 1:18-25

It is probable that this text was chosen to be used with John 2:13-22 because, like John 2:13-22, it is an indication that many Jews during the decades after the death of Jesus were asking those who were followers of Jesus for some indication that the human condition and especially their human condition was improved as a result of the death of Jesus and the efforts of Jesus' followers. From the standpoint of the Jews, there was an expectation that when the Messiah would come, a new age of peace, security, joy, and happiness for all people would occur. They were asking for indications of this sort, not for miracles as such, but for radically changed political, social, and spiritual conditions. If the political, social, and spiritual conditions not only of the Jews but of all people had improved dramatically as a result of Jesus' life and death, most Jews probably would have accepted Jesus as having been the Messiah.

Most Jews, however, saw little evidence that the human condition had improved dramatically as a result of the life and death of Jesus. Instead, as a result of the attempt by nationalistically minded Jews to attain their autonomy in Galilee and in Judea that had been crushed by the Romans with terrible suffering by the Jews, the condition of Jews had decreased horribly. Pressure from followers of Jesus who were placing the blame for Jesus' suffering and death on the Jews and were at the same time trying to persuade Jews to become followers of Jesus certainly did not improve the human condition of the Jews. By our becoming aware of this, we as Christians can have a better understanding of why antagonism against the Jews by Christians, why anti-Jewish polemic in the New Testament documents and in the Church, and why anti-Semitism by Christians throughout most of the

120

history of the Church have always been so counterproductive for Christians, especially when some of them have continued to try to "convert" Jews to Christianity. It would be helpful if we could explain some of this in our message this coming Sunday.

Paul wrote that the Jews ask for signs and that the Greeks seek wisdom, as apparently many of them did during the first century of the common era. Was not their search valid? Should not our proclamation also be intellectually respectable? Paul's point here, however, apparently was that his message centered on the crucifixion and on the resurrection of Jesus. So should our message as well. Are we not called in our situation to proclaim that message in ways that are appropriate and helpful where we are, just as Paul was called to do in his situation?

Psalm 19

The reason this text was selected for the Third Sunday in Lent in Series B is probably the connection between Psalm 19:7b, "The testimony of the Lord is sure. It makes even the simple person wise," and Paul's insistence in 1 Corinthians 1:18-25 that the message of Christ crucified brings the power and the wisdom of God to everyone who will accept this message. Psalm 19:7-14, of course, provides for us an important insight into how Jews traditionally have regarded the Torah. These verses are similar in this respect to the greatly expanded Psalm 119:1-176.

Exodus 20:1-17

Since the Torah has been acclaimed in Psalm 19:7-14, the "heart" of the Torah in the Decalogue in this Exodus 20:1-17 priestly account is then added as the Old Testament reading. In this connection, see the article, "Commandments in Context: The Function of Torah in Early Israel," by Paul D. Hanson in the *Lutheran Theological Seminary Bulletin*,

Gettysburg, Pennsylvania (Summer, 1981), pp. 14-24. Copies are available for a nominal charge for postage and handling from the Business Office, The Bulletin, Lutheran Theological Seminary, Gettysburg, Pennsylvania 17325.

FOURTH SUNDAY IN LENT

The series of passion-resurrection predictions during these Series B Lenten texts continues here with a third text (John 3:14-21), and it is extended further with a fourth text (John 12:20-33) for the Fifth Sunday in Lent. All three of these Johannine Jesus passion-resurrection predictions (John 2:13-22 on Lent 3, John 3:14-21 on Lent 4, and John 12:20-33 on Lent 5) are expressed in similar Johannine style, obscure and symbolic, in contrast to the straightforward Mark 8:31-32a with which this series of passion-resurrection predictions began in the Gospel account for Lent 2.

John 3:14-21

In typical Fourth Gospel style this passage begins with a setting (in this instance a meeting involving Jesus and Nicodemus) for which is provided an extended dialogue and here eventually changing into a monologue. Nicodemus fades out of the picture somewhere around the place where our 3:14-21 text begins. Within 3:14-21 it is actually the Johannine writers and community who collectively are speaking about Jesus as "the Son of man" being lifted up, as "God's only-begotten Son," and as "the Light of the world." It is virtually impossible to discern where the Johannine Jesus stops speaking here and the Johannine writers and community begin. Red-letter editions of the New Testament generally code all of John 3:14-21 as words of Jesus. Actually, throughout the entire Fourth Gospel it is the Johannine writers and community who are speaking. True to the gospel genre, these writers and this community of believers say what they believe about God, about Jesus, and about themselves and others in words of Jesus within a ministry of Jesus vehicle.

What these writers and community have provided for us can become for us to share a three-part message about

Jesus as 1) the Son of man being lifted up, 2) God's only-begotten Son, and 3) the Light of the world. The passion-resurrection prediction about the Son of man being lifted up to provide life for all who believe in him just as Moses was said to have lifted up the serpent in the wilderness to preserve life for all who look at it is largely a *vaticinium ex eventu*, an interpretation of the significance of the death of Jesus after that death had occurred and an expression of belief that God had raised Jesus from the dead. Is that not what we also do (especially during the Lenten and Easter seasons), i.e., we provide interpretations of the death of Jesus and of the significance of that death for all people, and we proclaim that God raised Jesus from the dead and will raise us also with Jesus into a glorious life? John 3:15-18a (especially John 3:16, which is so important to us) is "gospel" in positive, non-judgmental terminology. John 3:18b-21, however, brings in condemnation of all who do not follow this Johannine "one way." Which of these shall we emphasize next Sunday? What are we called to proclaim, good news, or condemnation, or both?

Numbers 21:4-9

It is somewhat surprising that this account was incorporated by the Israelites into the Torah, since the serpent was a Canaanite symbol. Perhaps the most satisfactory commentary on this text is provided in Wisdom of Solomon 16:6-12 in the Old Testament Apocrypha, in which the bronze serpent is described as a symbol of salvation, and in which it is said that those who looked at the serpent were saved from the effects of the poisonous snake bites not by the power of the bronze snake but because they were obedient to the word of the Lord given through Moses.

Theologically, the account in Numbers 21:4-9 says that the people had sinned by speaking against God and against Moses. God punished them. The people repented and asked

Moses to intercede for them. Moses interceded in behalf of the people. God forgave them and provided a tangible way in which they could now be obedient to God and receive healing benefits from God.

The details of the account were undoubtedly based on experiences with poisonous snakes within the Sinai Peninsula and in the southern Negev region and upon the popular belief that the creature that caused pain and death should also be the creature through which deliverance from pain and death could be accomplished. This is a principle that is similar in some ways to what occurs in medical immunizations.

Ephesians 2:1-10

In this summary of Paul's message elsewhere, the writer here presents those who will read and hear as already figuratively raised up with Christ by God and caused to sit with Christ Jesus in the heavenly places. What shall we say about this? Was this bordering on Gnostic Christian perceptions? What the writer apparently wanted to emphasize was the certainty of the salvation that God provides through Christ. In our own ways we too should express this conviction.

Psalm 107:1-3, 17-22

This psalm of thanksgiving to God for the salvation in this life of deliverance from the devastating effects of serious illnesses is an appropriate complement of the other texts selected for this occasion. Together with the Numbers 21:4-9 text, it places its emphasis on salvation within this life here and now, providing for us a balance against the other-worldly emphases in the John 3:14-21 and Ephesians 2:1-10 texts.

FIFTH SUNDAY IN LENT

John 12:20-33

In this interesting text that concludes this series of passion-resurrection predictions there are two different symbols used by the Johannine writers and community in describing Jesus' death and the life that is by faith a result of that death.

The first of these two symbols (in 12:23-25) uses an analogy from life experiences in an agricultural society. Unless a kernel of wheat or of any other grain dies (rots, decays, germinates) after it is placed into the ground, it remains a single kernel. But when it dies (germinates), the sprout that grows from it has the potential to produce many other kernels. The death of the kernel (representing the death of the Jesus of history) is therefore predicted — again *ex eventu* — as well as declared to be essential if the Jesus of history is going to be used by God to produce life in many other persons. This analogy is particularly interesting, because the "sprout" that resulted in the growth of the early Church did not appear until after the death of the Jesus of history.

The second symbol (in 12:26, 32-33) that was introduced in the John 3:14-21 text that we used last Sunday is more obscure. If Jesus is lifted up from the earth, it is said that he will draw all people to himself. Although this analogy is said in the text to have indicated the nature of Jesus' death (on a cross "between heaven and earth"), all people are not to be crucified with him. Instead, as the "Lamb of God," by means of his death he will have the power to take away the sins of all people. The way in which 12:26 is expressed suggests that reference is being made not only to the crucifixion, but also to the return of Jesus to the Father. Anyone who wishes to serve the Johannine Jesus is directed to follow him to the cross and on his return journey to the Father. It is through the passion-resurrection return of the Johannine Jesus that the

Johannine Jesus (here self-designated as the Son of man) is glorified. This text is, therefore, a theological interpretation of the significance of Jesus' death and physical absence from his followers in the Johannine community.

In comparison to the accounts in Mark and in Matthew, there is relatively little emphasis in the Fourth Gospel on Jesus' agonizing over his death and of his suffering during his crucifixion. Instances such as John 12:27 and 13:21 are brief and fleeting. The Johannine Jesus is in almost complete control of every situation, even when he is dying on the cross. That is the way, therefore, in which we shall depict the Johannine Jesus if we are going to follow closely the pattern of the Fourth Gospel texts. (This reminds us of a major disadvantage of our current lectionary in which during Series B, the year of Mark, we repeatedly are jumping back and forth between Markan and Johannine texts, making a consistent, coherent pattern of presentation difficult.)

Hebrews 5:5-10

Although this text speaks about Jesus appealing to God and being heard by God just as the Johannine Jesus is depicted as having appealed to God and having been heard by God in John 12:20-33, if we look more closely we see that this Hebrews 5:5-10 text does not fit well with John 12:20-33. Certainly in John 12:20-33 the Johannine Jesus does not bring to God prayers and supplications with loud cries and tears. Such a description hardly fits even the Markan and Matthean accounts of Jesus in Gethsemane and on the cross, much less the Johannine presentations. Our emphasis in our use of this Hebrews text along with John 12:20-33, therefore, should be on Hebrews 5:9 in its proclamation of Jesus as the source of eternal salvation for those who are obedient to him.

Jeremiah 31:31-34

There is little direct connection between this well-known "New Covenant" text and John 12:20-33. We can establish a link, of course, by proclaiming that God forgives the sins of individuals through the death of Jesus as the "Lamb of God" in the Johannine sense. It has been traditional within Christianity to see the Church and the New Testament as the "New Covenant" prophesied in Jeremiah 31. Perhaps if we look at this text in its own context rather than from our Christian perspective, we will be able to see a promise and a hope that is still futuristic, still to be realized fully for us as Christians just as it is still fully to be realized for Jews, for Muslims, for Hindus, and for others.

Psalm 51:1-12

This psalm portion is similar to Jeremiah 31:31-34 in its plea for God "to create a clean heart and a new spirit within me." In a general sense, that is our prayer during Lent and at all times. Is this not what we are asking in all of these texts, that God would take control of our lives more directly, both now and in the future? This is the emphasis that unites these texts.

Psalm 119:9-16

In this segment of Psalm 119, as in a variety of ways in each segment of this extensive acrostic psalm, the psalmist asks that God take control of the life of the psalmist by guiding the psalmist in the joy of living in accordance with the commandments that God has provided in the Torah. If the psalmist will meditate on God's commandments, the way that the psalmist will live will be pure and blessed forever.

SIXTH SUNDAY IN LENT
(PASSION SUNDAY or PALM SUNDAY)
LITURGY OF THE PALMS

There is a long tradition on the Sixth Sunday in Lent for many people within Christianity of reading one of the texts each year that portray Jesus riding on an animal into the city of Jerusalem. This "Palm Sunday" tradition can be maintained by reading and by dramatizing Mark 11:1-11 or John 12:12-16 during the Series B year as the Processional Gospel at the beginning of the worship service. The experience will be even more profound if the readings and dramatizations of one of these "Triumphal Entry" of Jesus into Jerusalem texts is preceded by a dramatic reading or dramatization of Psalm 118:1-2, 19-29, either with the entire worshiping congregation processing into the church building or with choir members and other liturgists with strong voices beginning outside the entrance to the building and processing in to join the worshiping congregation already seated.

We should take every opportunity to dramatize these texts. They are action texts. Our dramatizations during worship should not be limited to Christmas and Easter. The more services utilizing dramatic action that we have during the Church Year the better and more vibrant our praise and worship of God will be. This also involves more of our people, especially youth, makes our worship services more memorable, and increases attendance at our worship services.

After the processional using the Psalm 118 and Mark 11 or John 12 texts, the reading of texts from the Liturgy of the Passion and a brief interpretative message that applies the texts to our own life situation should follow.

LITURGY OF THE PASSION

Isaiah 50:4-9a

Most people who participate in Christian worship services and hear this text on the Sunday prior to Good Friday associate the claims of daily direct inspiration of this portion of the third Servant Song of the Isaiah tradition with Jesus, as though Isaiah 50:4-9a was written about Jesus or as prophecies pointing to Jesus. We as Christians can certainly interpret the Older Testament in whatever ways that we choose, and it is helpful for us to visualize Jesus as we read or hear this Isaiah text. It would be appropriate, nevertheless, for us as leaders in Christian worship services to share in some way with our congregations a recognition that the Suffering Servant Songs have a context of their own as a composite expression of the Israelite and Jewish prophetic tradition at its best. For Jews, the Prophetic tradition itself and those who are inspired and courageous leaders among the Israelite and Jewish people have the experiences that we as Christians associate with Jesus. We can gain a greater appreciation for the perspective of Jewish people regarding what we as Christians label as the Suffering Servant Songs (Isaiah 42:1-4; 49:1-6; 50:4-11; and 52:13—53:12) if we read the entire Isaiah document, or at least Isaiah 40-66.

Psalm 31:9-16

Our use of this individual lament within a Christian Order of Service clearly indicates that for us also, as for the psalmist, complete deliverance is still to come; it will happen in the future. For us the complete deliverance will be experienced in the Easter appearances of Jesus the Risen Christ, and in our own Easter appearances. Nevertheless, together with the psalmist, we too cry to the Lord God for deliverance here and now.

Philippians 2:5-11

This magnificent poetic expression of faith in Jesus as the Christ has been considered by many, perhaps by most, commentators to have been quoted by Paul from a previously existing source. If, however, Paul was using a beautiful expression of faith of someone else in which much of what is written in Isaiah 45:23 about faith in the Lord God "to whom every knee shall bend and every tongue shall acclaim" is ascribed to Jesus as the Christ, Paul did not introduce it as a quotation. The content of this expression of faith is not unlike what Paul had written elsewhere, in Romans 5:19 for example, and the way in which Philippians 2:5-11 continues without a "wrinkle" what Paul wrote in Philippians 2:1-4 suggests to me that this beautiful expression of faith is Paul's own composition.

Most commentators also have thought that the words in 2:6 in which it is written that Jesus as the Christ was *en morphe Theou* is a statement that expressed a belief in the divine pre-existence of Jesus. These words are then considered to be similar in thought to the high Christology of John 1:1-3 and Colossians 1:15. When seen, however, in the context of Paul's entire letter to the Philippians and of his other letters, Paul was writing in 2:6 that Jesus was a person created by God to be, as indicated in Genesis 1:26-27, "in the form and image of God," just as Adam, the first man and all of humankind, including everyone of us, was and has been. What was so strikingly different about Jesus, according to Paul in Philippians 2:7-8, was that Jesus, unlike Adam and all of the rest of us in humankind, did not consider divinity as something "to be grasped," but lived as a servant of God, in his words and deeds a courageous advocate of God and of God's oppressed people. As a result of the way in which Jesus had lived, willing even to be tortured and crucified by the Romans, God highly exalted Jesus as the Risen Christ, giving to him as the Risen Christ a name that is greater than any other name, etc.

Unlike most other commentators, therefore, I personally consider what we have as Philippians 2:5-11 to have been written by Paul himself and to be consistent with Paul's Christology elsewhere, which is not pre-existence Christology, but a Christology in which Jesus was made to be the Christ, the Divine Son of God, by God, in and through Jesus' death and resurrection.

Paul, therefore, provides for us on this Sunday of the Passion a beautiful panorama of the entire Christ event, a most fitting preparation for our reading and hearing of the passion of Jesus texts that were developed after Paul himself had been executed by the Romans, and for the Easter texts that will follow for us one Sunday later.

Mark 14:1—15:47

In vivid detail, and from a theological perspective, the Markan writer and the redactors and other writers of the Gospel traditions who followed him, provided passion of Jesus as the Christ accounts. As we read them, it is very important that we read and hear them in the context of the life situation of those who composed them. We should be aware that although portions of the passion accounts are based on historically verifiable information, providing historical information was not their writers' primary purpose. From the perspective of an historian, it can be said with certainty that Jesus was seized in the Garden of Gethsemane by a contingent of Caiaphas' bodyguards, who were obeying orders given by Caiaphas, who reported to Caiaphas later that same night that their mission had been accomplished. Under orders from Caiaphas, his "goons" then delivered Jesus over to the night duty segment of Pontius Pilate's crucifixion squad, who tortured Jesus during the remainder of the night, along with the two other young men who had been designated for crucifixion the next morning. The men who tortured their three victims were relieved in the morning by the day shift of the crucifixion squad, who also under previously issued orders from Pilate, dragged Jesus and the other two young Jews through the streets of Jerusalem and crucified them. From the perspective of an historian, the "trials" of Jesus are historically verifiable. They occurred during the merciless beatings by the soldiers during the night.

Decades ago, when I was a child and a student at home with my parents, our family attended Lenten services in our congregation every Wednesday evening throughout the Lenten season. From Ash Wednesday until the Wednesday during "Holy Week," we heard a composite harmonized King James Version of the passion accounts, with sermons based on the lengthy segment read that evening.

Now, with our three-year lectionary and since the early 1990s the Revised Common Lectionary, we are urged to read the entire passion account, and during this year of Series B, this means Mark 14:1—15:47, or perhaps only Mark 15:1-39 (40-47). When I was a child, I heard the portions of the passion accounts in which the Jews are presented as putting heavy pressure on "poor Pontius Pilate," practically forcing him to give the order for the crucifixion of Jesus, and I had no questions whatsoever about the historicity of those portions. Later, however, I began to have some questions about what actually may have happened on the night prior to the crucifixion of Jesus. I began to wonder why Jesus' own people would have been so hateful and almost rabid about wanting Jesus to be killed in such a horribly painful way. I could not understand this, especially since Jesus was such a kind and considerate person, healing and encouraging so many of his fellow Jews.

It was not, however, until I participated in several Lutheran-Jewish consultations in Minnesota and Wisconsin in 1975 and 1976 that I had the opportunity to hear directly from Jewish scholars how they felt about those hateful texts that accused Jews of deicide. As a result, I began a serious study of the passion accounts and other portions of the New Testament in which Jews are condemned as cruel, hateful, and hypocritical. This resulted in the research and writing of my book, *Mature Christianity: The Recognition and Repudiation of the Anti-Jewish Polemic of the New Testament* (Selinsgrove, Pennsylvania: Susquehanna University Press, 1985), which, after additional work, I published as *Mature Christianity in the 21st Century: The Recognition and Repudiation of the Anti-Jewish Polemic of the New Testament* (New York: Crossword, 1994). My next step in this process was to prepare a new translation of the New Testament that is sensitive to both the anti-Jewish and the sexist materials in these documents. The result was *The New Testament: A New Translation and Redaction* (Lima, Ohio: Fairway Press, 2001). In this translation, in addition to being sensitive in my translation of the religiously racist and sexist texts, I placed the segments that are the most viciously anti-Jewish and the most degrading to women in small-print form, in order to make it easier for the reader to respond as each reader wishes.

I have shared all of this in order to suggest that instead of the shorter reading of Mark 14:1—15:47 using only Mark 15:1-39 (40-47) that is suggested as an option in the Revised Common Lectionary, pastors and other worship leaders might wish to read Mark 14:1-54, 66-72 and Mark 15:16-47, passing over Mark 14:55-65 and Mark 15:1-15, the most anti-Jewish portions on this occasion. In addition, by using my translation listed above for this reading, there will be further sensitivity to the faith and commitment of millions of Jews and of women.

If you are interested in more details about my own struggles with these issues, please see my articles, "Appropriate Christian Responses to the 'Teaching of Contempt' for Jews in the New Testament," in *Defining New Christian/Jewish Dialogue*, ed. by Irvin J. Borowsky, New York: Crossroad, 2004), pp. 15-25, and "Replacing Barriers with Bridges," in *Faith Transformed: Christian Encounters with Jews and Judaism*, ed. by John C. Merkle (Collegewille, Minnesota: The Liturgical Press, 2003), pp. 71-89. For an analysis of our need for greater sensitivity to the issue of anti-Jewish materials within the New Testament documents as we revise our lectionaries, see "Removing Anti-Jewish Polemic from our Christian Lectionaries: A Proposal," http://jcrelations. net/en/?item=737 (also in Spanish).

HOLY WEEK
MONDAY OF HOLY WEEK
(A, B, C)

John 12:1-11

Monday of Holy Week is introduced with this account that is only in the Fourth Gospel, about an anointing of the feet of Jesus by Mary, the sister of Martha and of Lazarus, whom Jesus, according to John 11:1-44, had resurrected from the dead. The account makes a major contribution to the plot of the Fourth Gospel, with Jesus speaking in support of what Mary was doing and in opposition to Judas Iscariot, who was complaining about the pouring of the expensive perfume on the feet of Jesus when the perfume could have been sold and the proceeds given to the poor. The statement of the Johannine Jesus that "you are always going to have poor people with you whom you can help, but you are not always going to have me" presents the greatest challenge for us even today. It raises fundamental questions about how the financial resources of a congregation should be allocated.

Hebrews 9:11-15

The writer of the Epistle to the Hebrews presents Jesus in a way that is very different from the ways in which Jesus is depicted elsewhere in our New Testament documents. Within each of the Four Gospels Jesus is opposed by the priests who manage the Temple under contracts purchased from the Romans; he is certainly not presented as the honored priest entering into the Holiest Place in the Temple to offer his own blood to God. This very different way in which Jesus was portrayed by the writer of this document was a major reason that the Epistle to the Hebrews was one of the last documents to be accepted into the New Testament canon.

Isaiah 42:1-9

By using this "Servant of the Lord" text, as it is designated by Christians, on the Monday of Holy Week, we are identifying the Servant of the Isaiah traditions with Jesus as we as Christians perceive him. That identification, of course, does not give ownership of the Servant concept to us as Christians. The Servant of the Lord still primarily belongs to the Jews, not to us as Christians. The statements in this text about God putting the Spirit of God upon the Servant in order that the Servant may establish justice on the earth in a sense unites Christians with Jews, since, when we are at our best, we as Christians, together with Jews, long for justice and work together to "repair" the world and to be righteous and just in all that we and Jews do.

Psalm 36:5-11

Here also, when we as Christians use this psalm, or any of the psalms, or any portion of the Old Testament for that matter, ideally we use these materials together with Jews, as devotional guides along with Jews, even during our so-called Holy Week. Although our experiences and our understandings of the intended meanings of the texts in the Old Testament are different from those of Jews, we must remember that these were Israelite and Jewish documents before we began to use them and that they remain basically Jewish documents today.

TUESDAY IN HOLY WEEK
(A, B, C)

John 12:20-36

All except the final verses 34-36 of this text are used also on the Fifth Sunday in Lent and were commented upon on in the Fifth Sunday in Lent, Series B, section earlier. There we considered the two symbols that are used in this text to signify the death of the Johannine Jesus. His death is compared to the "death" of a kernel of grain, a change and germination that is necessary in order that new life will result. His death is also depicted in this text as a situation in which the Johannine Jesus is lifted up between the earth and the sky on a Roman cross.

On this occasion, let us look more closely at verse 25, a Johannine explication of the "death" and germination of a kernel of grain as a symbol of Jesus' death on the cross. Most translations of verse 25 into English indicate that the Johannine Jesus here said that the person who loves the person's own life loses it, but that the person who hates the person's life here in this world will retain it eternally, expressing the form of the Greek verb *miseo* here with the word hates. In most instances of the use of forms of the Greek verb *miseo* in our literature, the English word hate is appropriate. Here and in Luke 14:26, however, there are better and more nuanced ways in which this Greek form should be expressed in the English language. It is not a good translation here in John 12:25 to say that a person should hate the person's own life here. In the context of this verb in John 12:25, I suggest that the verse should be translated as I express it in my *The New Testament: A New Translation and Redaction* (Lima, Ohio: Fairway Press, 2001) as follows: "The person who selfishly wants to retain that person's life is going to lose it, and the person who selflessly gives that person's life to others in this world will actually retain it into life eternally."

In the three verses (John 12:34-36) that are used here but not on the Fifth Sunday in Lent the Johannine depiction of Jesus as "the light" is used. The idea that the Johannine Jesus will not be physically present within the Johannine community much longer, as expressed more extensively in the "farewell discourses" in John 14-16, is included.

1 Corinthians 1:18-31

In this text the Apostle Paul proclaims Christ crucified as the one whom God, through the resurrection of Jesus as the Christ, made the primary manifestation of the power of God and of the wisdom of God. The word of the cross (Christ crucified) makes us wise, makes us righteous, makes us holy, and redeems us from the power of sin. This is what God does, not what we do. Therefore, we should not boast about what we have done. We should boast about what God in the death and resurrection of Jesus as the Christ does.

Isaiah 49:1-7

In verse 3 of this second of what we as Christians call the Servant Songs of the Isaiah tradition the Servant is identified as "Israel." This identification was probably added to the text at some point after the initial composition and use of this text. It is difficult to see, however, how the Servant could be Israel when it is written in verse 5 that the Servant is commissioned by God to bring Jacob back to God, to gather Israel back to God and in verse 6 to bring back to life the tribes of Jacob, to restore those who will be preserved in Israel. Our Christian identification of the Servant with Jesus as the Christ does not work perfectly either, unless we make the followers of Jesus as the Christ to be the "New Israel." When we do this, we should call ourselves at most "a new People of God," rather than "the New Israel." When we call ourselves "the New Israel," we are being arrogantly supersessionistic.

Within the context of the Isaiah traditions, the Servant, and, farther along in the traditions as we have them, the Suffering Servant, should probably best be understood as a composition of poetic expressions by a variety of inspired Israelites of the ideal prophet, the ideal inspired person in that tradition. In that sense, the Servant or Suffering Servant concept can be used both by Jews and by us as Christians today, with neither group preempting the concept.

Psalm 71:1-14

The psalmist, during the "senior years" of the psalmist's life, calls upon God to rescue the psalmist from those who are cruel and oppressive, from those who are showing no respect. The psalmist affirms that the psalmist has depended upon the Lord God ever since the Lord gave life to the psalmist when the psalmist was born.

WEDNESDAY OF HOLY WEEK
(A, B, C)

John 13:21-32

Not only is the Johannine Jesus in this text depicted as having the foreknowledge of which of the twelve disciples will "betray" him, the Johannine Jesus is portrayed as in a sense mandating that betrayal by saying to Judas Iscariot, "That which you are going to do, do it soon." Various interpretations have been given to this saying within Church history. One is that Judas was predestined by God to betray Jesus so that God's plan of salvation would be accomplished. Personally, I have never felt comfortable theologically with that interpretation. I think that a much better interpretation within the context of the Fourth Gospel is that here as throughout the Fourth Gospel, but not in the Synoptics, Jesus is portrayed as being in charge, in command of the entire situation, as the Lamb of God who takes away the sins of the world from the beginning of the Fourth Gospel until he dies on the cross with the words in John 19:30, "All that I have come to do has been done!" The Johannine Jesus directs the orchestra, he is the producer and the director of the play, he is the coach who calls the plays on the field.

Hebrews 12:1-3

The writer of the Epistle to the Hebrews has a Christology that uses words that differ considerably from the words used by the Johannine writers. Nevertheless, the Christology is similar in many respects to that in John. For the writer of the Epistle to the Hebrews, as in the Fourth Gospel but not in Mark and Matthew, Jesus is completely in charge of God's salvation drama. In the Epistle to the Hebrews, Jesus himself goes into the most holy place in the Temple and offers his own blood as a sacrifice to God for sin, not for his own sin but for the sins of other people. Here in Hebrews 12:1-3

Jesus is presented as the founder, the pioneer, the one who makes our Christian faith perfect, the one who is now seated at the right hand of the throne of God.

Isaiah 50:4-9a

The ideal prophet to the writers of the Isaiah tradition is given directions each morning by the Lord God. Therefore, the ideal prophet is able to stand up with confidence against those who are evil and to help those who are in need. For those of us who are Christians, Jesus the Risen Christ is like that and even more than that. This does not mean, however, that our interpretation of Isaiah 50:4-9a is the only valid interpretation. Our interpretation was certainly not the original and was not the earliest interpretation, and Jewish interpretations will always remain valid and helpful to us, as well as valid and helpful to Jews.

Psalm 70

For anyone who is suffering distress, whether because of adversaries or because of illness, the cry to God for help at the earliest possible moment expressed by the writer in this psalm is certainly understandable. Since this cry for help contrasts with the situation of the Johannine Jesus more than it complements it, Psalm 70 would be more appropriate in a Christian lectionary when the Gospel reading is from Mark or Matthew rather than from John. Within our message on this Wednesday of Holy Week, we can apply Psalm 70 to us but hardly to the Johannine Jesus.

HOLY THURSDAY
(A, B, C)

John 13:1-17, 31b-35

For most of us who have been accustomed since our childhood to observe this day as Maundy Thursday and to associate this night with Jesus' words of the institution of the Eucharist on the night when Jesus would within a few hours be seized in the Garden of Gethsemane, it seems somewhat strange that we read Jesus' words of the institution of the Eucharist in the 1 Corinthians 11:23-26 text from the Apostle Paul rather than from one of the Synoptic Gospels. Of course, in the Revised Common Lectionary the Words of Institution (Mark 14:22-25; Matthew 26:26-29; and Luke 22:14-20) are read each year, but only in the context of the lengthy Liturgies of the Passion, one of them each year. Unless we are rigidly bound to follow the Revised Common Lectionary with no deviation, we can, of course, supplement the reading from John 13:1-17, 31b-35 of Jesus washing the feet of his disciples on Holy Thursday each year with a reading of the Words of Institution from one of the Synoptic Gospel texts each year. We would then, however, have a nearly duplicated reading of the Words of Institution from Paul in 1 Corinthians 11:23-26 within the same service.

The Johannine reading that has the Johannine Jesus washing the feet of each of his disciples, even of the feet of Judas Iscariot, may appear at first and has often been considered to be an illustration of Jesus' humility. A more detailed study of this text in John 13, however, indicates that what the Johannine Jesus is represented as doing here is not an act of humility, but of control. Simon Peter was not given the option of refusing the washing. Neither was Judas Iscariot or any of the other disciples. Jesus also, not Peter, had the choice of how much of Peter's body Jesus would wash. In addition in this text, the Johannine Jesus does not merely urge his disciples to love each other; the Johannine Jesus commands them to do this. As leaders in worship in the Church we are not, of course, the Johannine Jesus. We should, however, use appropriate care when we talk about humility and when we attempt to be humble, so that our actions will be genuine and not be expressions of a false humility.

1 Corinthians 11:23-26

It is essential that we look closely at the context in which Paul presents the Words of Institution of the Eucharist here. We can easily overlook the fact that Paul's primary concern in 1 Corinthians 11:17—14:40 is not the Words of Institution. Instead, Paul's primary concern is to command the followers of Jesus in Corinth to change the ways in which they were eating food when they were gathered together. The ones who were affluent had not been sharing their food with the ones who were poor. Apparently, even when they used the Eucharistic words, they were not participating together, but separately. Some of them were very disrespectful of others in the community of believers. Because they were not resolving these difficulties and problems, Paul sternly chided them for their behavior. He was not scolding them for their lack of intellectual understanding of the mystery of the Eucharist. He was chiding them for their segregated behavior, for not eating and drinking in the Eucharist together, for not having love for and respect for one another.

It is tragic and disrespectful to Jesus and to Paul that even into the twenty-first century the "sharing of pulpit and altar fellowship" is still so limited within the Church, even within the same denomination, as it is in my own Lutheran Christian denomination. If Paul, not to mention Jesus, were physically present and evaluating us today, Paul, as Paul indicated in 1 Corinthians 11:17—14:40, would chide us sternly, not because we have not achieved a single identical understanding of the mystery of the Eucharist, but because of our segregated behavior, because so many of us refuse to receive the Eucharist together with others or to permit others to receive the Eucharist with us. Many of us who are Lutheran Christians refuse to permit even other Lutheran Christians to join with us at our altars and in our pulpits, because we have decided they these other Lutheran Christians are not "Lutheran" enough, that they do not segregate themselves sufficiently from other Christians who are not Lutheran Christians. What would the Apostle Paul, whom especially we who are Lutheran Christians claim to honor so highly, say about us and our failure to honor the Church as the "Body of Christ," comprised as Paul put it in 1 Corinthians 12 of many diverse parts (ears, eyes, feet, etc.)?

We need much more serious study of Scripture in the Church, especially of Scripture in the context of other Scripture. We need to study and to use the Words of the Institution of the Eucharist in 1 Corinthians 11:23-26 in the context of 1 Corinthians 11:17—14:40, not isolated from their context as we do in the Holy Thursday selections in the Revised Common Lectionary. It would be preferable on Holy Thursday to be using the Words of Institution in the context of their place in Mark 14, Matthew 26, and Luke 22 in successive years, not every year as they are in a secondary position in 1 Corinthians.

Exodus 12:1-4 (5-10) 11-14

This text in the Priestly tradition in which the Israelite Passover observance is commanded and which is read when the Seder meal is celebrated in Jewish homes today provides a segment, but only a small segment, of the background for the Christian Eucharist. The sacrificial slaughter of an entire yearling sheep or goat to be eaten during the course of one night by a family or two neighboring families has evolved for Jewish families today into the use of only a single bone of a lamb as a symbol of the entire lamb in a Jewish Seder. There is a lamb bone on the table, but meat from a lamb is not necessarily a part of the menu for the Seder meal today.

There is very little direct connection between the Israelite Passover observance as commanded in Exodus 12 and the bread and wine by means of which we as Christians receive the "Body" and the "Blood" of Christ in the Eucharist. There is symbolism, however, in the belief that we have as Christians that because of the death and resurrection of Jesus as the Christ in which we as Christians participate in the Eucharistic action, God "passes over" our sins and we, like the ancient pre-Israelite slaves in Egypt, are spared. It is important that we make this connection on Holy Thursday.

Psalm 116:1-2, 12-19

There are a few connections between these portions of Psalm 116 and the other texts selected for this day in our lectionary. Somewhat like the Israelite slaves in Egypt, the psalmist testifies that the Lord has set the psalmist free from that which had enslaved the psalmist, in this case a very serious illness. We as Christians can link the reference by the psalmist to "the cup of salvation" that the psalmist will raise up and will call upon the name of the Lord to the cup within the Eucharist, especially on this Holy Thursday.

GOOD FRIDAY
(A, B, C)

Psalm 22

As followers of Jesus reminisced about the suffering that Jesus had experienced while he was being tortured and crucified by the Romans and about the significance that they saw in Jesus' suffering for their own lives, no texts within the Hebrew religious traditions were more helpful to them in describing the crucifixion of Jesus than were the Psalm 22 and the Isaiah 52:13—53:12 readings that have been selected in this lectionary for Good Friday each year.

Followers of Jesus used the vivid details of these texts as they told and retold their descriptions of Jesus' crucifixion in order to fill in the gaps within their own knowledge and recollections of that horrible event. Most of the portions of these two texts that could not be used in their recounting of the events during the crucifixion of Jesus because they did not "fit" Jesus' situation were simply not used. Psalm 22, as a detailed individual psalm of lament, and Isaiah 52:13—53:12 both served well to depict what his followers concluded must have been Jesus' inner struggles as he was dying and to depict how Jesus had suffered, even though neither of these two portions of the Hebrew religious traditions were originally intended to describe the thoughts of Jesus or of anyone else who was dying on a Roman cross centuries later.

Our Christian hymns written to express Jesus' thoughts as he was dying develop these details even further than the New Testament texts develop them, and as we sing these hymns the words that we sing are implanted into our memory. It is important that we read the entire Psalm 22 within its own life situation before we use the Psalm in telling the story of Jesus' passion and death.

Isaiah 52:13—53:12

Most of that which has been written about Psalm 22 above applies also to this climax of what we as Christians call the Suffering Servant Songs of the Isaiah traditions. We can, of course, merely continue to see these texts as amazingly accurate prophecies that describe in vivid detail Jesus' suffering hundreds of years before he was crucified. We can also say that it was necessary for Jesus to suffer and to die in a specific way in order that he might fulfill these Scriptures. It will be in much greater accord with what actually happened, however, and more helpful to the people whom we serve if we suggest within our proclamation that followers of Jesus probably used details from Psalm 22 and from the Isaiah 52:13—53:12 texts as they told and retold what they understood about the death of Jesus during the decades after his crucifixion. Is this not essentially what we ourselves do when we prepare and share sermons and homilies to express our faith and to encourage other people in the development of their faith in God? We too use what we can and what works best within the religious documents that are available to us.

John 18:1—19:42

If these entire two chapters are read, the time that will be used within the service for this reading will mean that if there is a sermon or a homily these proclamations will be very brief and will probably provide very little reflection over most of the details in the reading. If, because of the length of the reading, there will be no sermon or homily of reflection at all, the impression will be given that everything written in the two chapters is simply a compilation of historical facts.

There are three segments in this extensive reading in which the narrative depicts the Jews as extremely cruel and sadistic in their insistence that Pilate order the crucifixion of Jesus. It would be admirable if we would shorten the reading somewhat by not including these three segments (John 18:28b-32, 38b-40, and 19:4-16a) in our reading. These are the three segments that are the least edifying, the least historically verifiable, and the least appropriate for Christian proclamation. It would be even more desirable to begin our reading with John 19:16b and read until the conclusion of the suggested reading with John 19:42. This is the portion of the two chapters that actually depict actions on Friday that were witnessed by followers of Jesus rather than on Thursday evening in which no followers of Jesus were present, but only assumed occurred.

It is not surprising that when we compare the passion accounts in all Four Gospels, we see that in the Fourth Gospel Jesus speaks quite extensively, unlike the other three in which Jesus says only a few words. This is consistent with what we have seen throughout the Fourth Gospel in which the Johannine Jesus is basically in charge of the entire situation, even until he dies on the cross with the words, "It is finished," i.e., "I have completed everything that I have come to do."

Also, as we compare the passion accounts in all four of the Gospels, we see that although in the Synoptic accounts there are said to have been various women present at the scene of the crucifixion of Jesus, no mention is made of the mother of Jesus being there. Also, in the accounts in Mark and in Matthew it is stated that all of Jesus' male disciples had fled, including Peter who had at least gone along to enter the courtyard of Caiaphas to attempt to see what the bodyguards of Caiaphas would do to Jesus. Apparently the Fourth Gospel presents a different scene in order that its hero, "The Disciple whom Jesus Loved," would be shown as continuing Jesus' responsibilities by taking the mother of Jesus into his own home, or, if the "Beloved Disciple" is a symbol or representative of the Johannine community, into its home. This Johannine story about the mother of Jesus and the "Beloved Disciple" being present during the crucifixion of Jesus is not primarily a contradiction to the Markan and Matthean accounts. It merely presents a different scene for a different purpose.

Hebrews 10:16-25

As an encouragement for those who read or hear this text to enter into the most holy presence of God, made possible because of the blood shed by Jesus on the day that for us has become a Good Friday, this text is appropriate for our use on Good Friday every year. In the words of the writer of the Epistle to the Hebrews, let us rejoice in our new and life-giving access to God through the "curtain" that Jesus as the Christ has opened for us.

Hebrews 4:14-16; 5:7-9

The prayers and the supplications of Jesus mentioned in Hebrews 5:7 help to bring this document somewhat closer to the depictions of Jesus in the Four Gospels. The designation of Jesus as "a ruler-priest after the order of Melchizedek" in 5:9 takes it farther away from them. We experience an echo of this "great high priest" language applied to Jesus the Christ in the Great Thanksgiving portion of our Holy Communion liturgy. There are those among us, however, who are still somewhat less than comfortable with this "great high priest" terminology in our Communion liturgy, even after many years of usage.

Finally, these texts selected for our use on Good Friday provide the setting for a general appeal for sensitivity during our Good Friday experiences. Our Jewish friends tell us that even now in this country they are at times still somewhat uneasy on this day that we as Christians designate as Good Friday. They remember the instances that their parents and grandparents have told them about verbal and physical abuse suffered by their people in Europe when after "Good Friday" worship services Christians poured out from their church buildings to attack Jews. Some of them remember the abuse that they themselves experienced within this country from Christian children who ridiculed and chased them as "Christ-killers." There are many Christian people who do not realize that it was a Jew who was crucified by the Romans on that first "Good Friday," and that it was a Jew who became our Lord and Savior within the process of Christian theological development. Rembrandt realized this when he asked a Jew to pose for him while Rembrandt painted his portrait of Jesus, but most other Christian artists have not and neither have most Christian preachers. Perhaps on Good Friday this year, and every year, we might remember this and in some way share the fact that Jesus lived and died as a Jew. If we do this, we might even be able to invite Jews whom we know to join with us in some way on Good Friday in our remembrance of the crucifixion of Jesus the Jew by the oppressive Roman occupation forces in Jerusalem.

HOLY SATURDAY
(A, B, C)

Matthew 27:57-66

There are two disparate materials in this selection. The first, verses 57-61, is an expression of kindness and love shown to the body of Jesus by Joseph, a relatively rich man from Arimathea. The second, verses 62-66, depicts the chief priests and the Pharisees as gaining permission from Pilate to have guards stationed at the tomb of Jesus to make certain that Jesus' body will remain there. The materials in verses 57-61 are edifying and appropriate for consideration on this Saturday, when we are experiencing with the early disciples of Jesus the sadness of facing the reality of Jesus' death. There is nothing that is edifying or appropriate for our use in the second account. It and its sequel in Matthew 28:4, 11-15 are malicious polemic against the Pharisees, developed and included only by the Matthean reactors. Matthew 27:62-66 and 28:4, 11-15 provide for us in narrative form information about the animosity that developed between some of the Matthean redactors and Pharisees with whom some of the Matthean redactors were having many experiences of frustration over not being able to "convert" Pharisees to the theological position of the Matthean redactors. They provide neither historical information, nor theological information that we can use as we, together with the early disciples of Jesus, experience the sadness of facing the reality of Jesus' death, a sadness that we should feel on Holy Saturday.

Therefore, it is regrettable that Matthew 27:62-66 and 28:4, 11-15 are included in our New Testament documents. It is even more regrettable that they are included in our lectionary. Since they are included in the lectionary, I suggest that we have four viable responses. We can read these verses and use nothing from them in our sermon or homily. We can read them and express in our sermon or homily that we regret that they are in the text and that they are in the lectionary. We can read and use only the edifying and appropriate Matthew 27:57-61 portion. We can attempt to have the hateful verses no longer included in our lectionary.

John 19:38-42

For the reasons discussed above, the use of this text is much more appropriate than would be our use of Matthew 27:57-66. Here we have the Fourth Gospel's version of the burial of Jesus, a version that includes Nicodemus, a figure who is included only in the Fourth Gospel within the New Testament, along with Joseph of Arimathea from the Synoptic Gospels participating in the kind and loving action of providing an honorable burial of the body of Jesus. Here Nicodemus, described in John 3:1 as a prominent Pharisee and in John 7:5-52 as urging his fellow Pharisees not to judge Jesus unfavorably without listening to Jesus, is presented as bringing a large quantity of spices to place around the body of Jesus. This is the best account within the Four Gospels to read and to use in our worship services on Holy Saturday.

1 Peter 4:1-8

The message of this text, which includes references both to the suffering of Jesus as a human being and the proclamation of the resurrection of Jesus as the Christ, is in every way appropriate for our use on Holy Saturday, the day between the death of Jesus and the proclamation of his reappearing as the Risen Christ. It is also helpful that this text includes both proclamation of the good news of the resurrection of Jesus and parenesis (guidelines for living) that are to be expected of followers of Jesus, since our sermons and homilies should on most occasions include both of these elements and not one without the other.

Psalm 31:1-4, 15-16

The thoughts expressed in these portions of Psalm 31 can be applied to the situation of Jesus on Holy Saturday, as well as to us. The psalmist expresses resolute faith in the Lord God, asks to be rescued from the "hidden net," and commits the psalmist's spirit into the hands of God.

Job 14:1-14

This text also is appropriate for this Holy Saturday day of death. It is said, poetically, that the human life and that the human condition is short and fragile, like a flower, like a shadow, like a river the water of which evaporates on the dry sand, unclean. When a tree is cut, there will usually be a new, vibrant, green tree sprouting from its stump. If a man dies, however, it is entirely uncertain, from the perspective of reason, whether the man will ever live again. It may be implied that God has the power to change the human condition, but that hope is not expressed here.

Lamentations 3:1-9, 19-24

In terminology similar to that in Job, the writer of this portion of Lamentations expresses the distress into which God has placed the writer. Although there is no escape from the afflictions that God has brought upon the writer, because the writer believes in the faithfulness of God and in the mercies of God that are new every morning, there is hope. So also it was for Jesus, even as he died on the cross and was dead on Holy Saturday, and so also it is for us.

OLD TESTAMENT READINGS AND PSALMS (A, B, C)

Genesis 1:1—2:4a

This classic Priestly creation account is cosmic in scope. As in other Priestly materials in the Torah, the number ten is used, perhaps to teach children with the Priestly teacher keeping the gathered children involved by counting off each part on each of the teacher's and the children's ten fingers. Here ten times we read and hear (in Genesis 1:3, 6, 9, 11, 14, 20, 24, 26, 28, 29) "And God (Elohim) said." At some point in the development of the text, these ten statements were apparently shaped into a seven-day framework of six days of work by God, followed by one day in which it is written that God finished God's work and rested from all of the labor that God had done. We see, therefore, that a primary purpose of the account became that of establishing the concept that God, already in God's wondrous creative activity, instituted the Sabbath. If God rested on the seventh day and made that day holy, so also should the Israelites, as is implied in Genesis 2:2-3. This Priestly creation account was then placed at the beginning of the Torah in front of the Genesis 2:4b-25 folktale account in which the primary purpose, as we have it, is to show that God instituted monogamous marriage.

Finally, it should be noted that this creation account is not designed to give detailed scientific or historical information. Instead, it is designed to be a detailed expression of faith. We should recognize this and improve our translations into modern languages by beginning the account and most of the other sentences in it with the words "We believe that," as in "We believe that in the beginning God created (called into existence) everything (the skies/heavens and the earth)."

These are all statements of faith, not of scientifically or historically verifiable facts. As statements of faith, they are far more important and substantial than are any so-called facts that can be disproved by new and additional evidence. When we are cognizant of this, we avoid much of the destructive conflict between science and religion that has been detrimental to Christianity during recent centuries.

Psalm 136:1-9, 23-26

Our Easter Vigil in which we recount highlights in our story of salvation (in our *Heilsgeschichte*) continues with this beautiful expression of thanksgiving to the Lord God. Verses 4-9 especially recapitulate portions of the Genesis 1:1—2:4a creation account. Every one of the 26 verses in this psalm includes the worshiping congregation's refrain "for God's steadfast love endures for ever."

Genesis 7:1-5, 11-18; 8:6-18; 9:8-13

The most reassuring segment of this Noah's flood story is the rainbow symbol and the promise that God will never again use a flood that will cover the entire earth.

Psalm 46

The awesome power of God is acclaimed in this well-known psalm. It is a power designed to bring peace upon all of the earth.

Genesis 22:1-18

In this frightful story of the binding of Isaac, God is presented as rewarding the obedience of Abraham. An animal is substituted as the offering. The reader is assured that God will provide, and Abraham and his descendants will be blessed. From our Christian perspective, God offered no substitute later but freely offered Jesus as the Christ, the Son of God, as a sacrifice for our sins.

Psalm 16

The psalmist has faith that God will revive the health of the psalmist and grant to the psalmist an extended period of physical life and pleasure.

Exodus 14:10-31; 15:20-21

In the Revised Common Lectionary it is stated that "A minimum of three Old Testament readings should be chosen" for this Easter Vigil and that "The reading from Exodus 14 should always be used." Why do you think that this directive about Exodus 14 was given? It is a salvation story, but the action that saved the Israelites is presented as resulting in the death of large numbers of men in the Pharaoh's army, some or even many of whom may have been morally good young men with parents, wives, and children waiting for them to return. The Exodus 15:20-21 Song of Miriam, likewise exults in the death of the Egyptian soldiers.

Exodus 15:1b-13, 17-18

This alternative, which includes the more extensive Song of Moses and of the people of Israel, also expresses rejoicing that God has destroyed the Egyptian soldiers in the waters of the sea. There is the salvation element, of course, in the expectation that the Lord God will establish the Israelite people in their own nation, with a political and religious capital in Jerusalem.

Isaiah 55:1-11

This poetic expression of salvation in restoration Jerusalem is certainly positive and edifying, providing guidance regarding how to live in accordance with the words and thoughts of God. As such, it is in every way appropriate for use in our Christian Easter Vigil.

Isaiah 12:2-6

This too is appropriate for our use here. It is a song of salvation, of faith in God, of praise to God, and of encouragement to live in the peace that God will provide.

Baruch 3:9-15, 32—4:4

As the exile of the former inhabitants of Jerusalem continues, the inspired writer urges Israel to learn wisdom, that is, to walk in the way of God by obeying the commandments and guidelines that God has provided in the Torah.

Proverbs 8:1-8, 19-21; 9:4b-6

Wisdom speaks, calling upon men to seek her, offering to them fruit that is better than the finest gold and silver, the gifts of righteousness and justice, and a place at her table where they may eat of her bread and drink of her wine.

Psalm 19

All of creation proclaims the glory of God. Nevertheless, the Torah that God has given is even more wondrous, more to be desired than the finest gold, sweeter than the most pure honey.

Ezekiel 36:24-28

God will gather the remnants of Israel from among the nations, sprinkle pure water upon them, give them a new heart, and put the spirit of God within them.

Psalm 42 and 43

In both of these psalms the psalmist is oppressed, asking God for help and vindication. Then, when God responds, the psalmist will again be able to return to Jerusalem to worship the Lord God there.

Ezekiel 37:1-14

When the dry bones in the valley strewn with desolation hear the word of the Lord God, breath will come back into them and they will live again. God will open their graves and raise the entire house of Israel from the dead. Therefore, this text is entirely appropriate for use in our Easter Vigil, especially when we recognize its original situation in life in ancient Israel.

Psalm 143

During the darkness of night the psalmist prays to hear in the morning of the steadfast love that the Lord God has bestowed. The psalmist does not claim to be perfect and righteous. Only God is said to be perfect and righteous.

Zephaniah 3:14-20

This is a joyous expression of faith that the Lord God will return to Jerusalem, whose inhabitants will then no longer fear evil and disaster. Its people will be brought home, and the Lord God will restore their fortunes.

Psalm 98

The People of Israel are commanded to sing to the Lord God a new song, for the Lord has been victorious over all evil. All of nature is commanded to join with Israel in this song, the sea roaring, the floods clapping their hands, and the hills singing for joy.

NEW TESTAMENT READING (A, B, C)

Romans 6:3-11

As proclaimed in this text by the Apostle Paul, by means of our Baptism in the name of Jesus Christ we are united with Christ so completely that our sins actually died with Jesus when Jesus was killed by the Romans. Therefore, when God raises Jesus from death to life, with Jesus Christ we now live in a new relationship with God that is a new life of grace. This means that Easter morning is immeasurably important to us as Christians, by far the most important time in the Church Year.

Psalm 114

The psalmist considers the Lord God who brought the ancient Israelites out of slavery through the sea and across the Jordan to be so powerful that the entire earth trembles in the presence of the Lord. For us as Christians, this is comparable to the power we ascribe to God in bringing Jesus, who had been crucified and buried, out from the earth that can no longer contain him, for Jesus is now the Risen Christ.

Gospel:
Mark 16:1-8

With the reading of Mark 16:1-8 and our reflection over this text, our Easter Vigil is complete. Our period of waiting is over. We welcome with grateful appreciation to God the power and the glory of the Risen Christ. The season of Lent is ended! We again and anew sing the Alleluia! Praise the Lord!

RESURRECTION OF THE LORD
EASTER DAY

First Reading

Acts 10:34-43

As the Lukan playwright presents it, Peter announces to Cornelius in this text that Jesus as the Risen Christ has been appointed by God to be the judge of both those who are living and of those who have died and that everyone who believes in Jesus as the Risen Christ receives forgiveness of sins through Christ's name. Peter and all of us are to be eyewitnesses of this and to share the message as eyewitnesses.

Isaiah 25:6-9

The reading of this very significant expression of Jewish hope has become traditional for us as Christians on Easter Day. We realize, of course, that the expression of hope in Isaiah 25:6-9 is still largely futuristic for Jews, for us as Christians also, for Muslims, and for others. They wait. We wait. Must we have animosity toward each other as we wait? Is our animosity pleasing to God? What can we do together as we wait? Dare we include questions such as these within our Easter message this year? Perhaps we can no longer afford not to include them.

Psalm 118:1-2, 14-24

This beautiful, extensive "individual hymn of praise" used by the Israelites as the last in the collection of Hallel psalms (Psalms 113-118) in the Psalter has its decisive futuristic element in 118:17, "I am not going to die — because I am going to live! And I am going to declare the deeds of the Lord." In its original setting this meant that "I am going to live longer in this present life as I know this life here and now" because the Lord God has rescued me from death and has given to me a new lease on life. Later, for Jews within apocalyptic circles and for Christians, this "I am going to live!" became "I am going to live eternally!" The future growing out of the present became the future after life and death here.

Second Reading

1 Corinthians 15:1-11

The Easter message is stated clearly and unequivocally within each of the four New Testament texts selected here for the second reading and the Gospel on Easter Day. The Apostle Paul in 1 Corinthians 15:4 wrote that Jesus as the Christ "was raised from the dead on the third day in accordance with the scriptures." The Lukan playwright in Acts 10:40 has Peter proclaim to Cornelius that "God raised Jesus from the dead on the third day as the Christ, and gave the Risen Christ the ability to become visible to whomever the Risen Christ wished." The writer of the Gospel According to Mark in Mark 16:6, speaking through the words of the *neaniskos* (young man) in the empty tomb says, "Do not be astounded. I know that you are looking for Jesus, the man from Nazareth who was crucified. He has been raised from the dead! He is not here. See the place where they placed him." The writers of the Gospel According to John in John 20:18 have Mary Magdalene joyously announce to the male disciples, "I have seen the Lord!"

This Easter message is expressed joyfully and enthusiastically within our Easter hymns and throughout our Easter liturgies. Certainly it is to be expressed joyfully and with enthusiasm in the reading of all of these texts and in our proclamation of the Easter message. Anything less would be totally inappropriate on this most important day of our Church Year.

It is often noted that Paul in 1 Corinthians 15:1-11, writing prior to the formation of the Four Gospels, placed his emphasis on appearances of Jesus as the Risen Christ rather than on the empty tomb, the Easter setting in each of the Four Gospels. If we use 1 Corinthians 15:1-11 and John 20:1-18 on Easter Day, our emphasis also should be on appearances of Jesus as the Risen Christ, including the appearance to Mary Magdalene. The difference is that Paul cited a variety of appearances of the Risen Christ, primarily to males and to the more than 500 that would presumably have included women, while in John 20:1-18 the dramatic appearance is to a woman, Mary Magdalene. What shall we do with this?

Acts 10:34-43
For this, please see above.

Gospel

John 20:1-18
Among the Easter accounts within the Four Gospels, this is the most fully developed and complex. The text begins and ends with Mary Magdalene. Told by Mary Magdalene that the stone had been rolled aside from the entrance to the tomb and that the body of the Lord had been taken from the tomb, Peter and "the disciple whom Jesus loved" are said to have run to the tomb. That the other disciple ran faster than Peter and arrived first at the tomb is usually considered to be an indication that Peter was relatively old and could not keep up the pace of the younger "disciple whom Jesus loved." Within the context of the Fourth Gospel, however, in which "the disciple whom Jesus loved" is repeatedly portrayed as "one up" on Peter, there is the possibility, perhaps even the likelihood, that "the disciple whom Jesus loved" is more than a single individual, that this "disciple" is a symbol,

a self-designation of the Johannine community, while it considered Peter to be a representative symbol of the much larger extended Markan community.

The Johannine community was then perhaps in its document claiming to have been "reclining close to Jesus" at the meal on the night on which Jesus was betrayed (John 13:23-25). The Johannine community then was claiming to have been present at the foot of the cross to be given and to accept the responsibility from the Johannine Jesus to take the mother of Jesus into its care, thereby doing what the Johannine Jesus previously had done (John 19:26-27). The Johannine community then was perhaps claiming in its document to have outrun Peter and the Markan community to the empty tomb and was the first to "believe," as it claimed in this John 20:3-8 text. The Johannine community then is the one about whom the Johannine Jesus says to Peter in John 21:20-23, "If I want 'him' (or 'it') to remain until I come, what concern is that to you?" The Johannine community then, not merely a single individual, is the witness concerning all of the things that are written in the Fourth Gospel. The Johannine community then is said to have been the one who has written the Fourth Gospel (John 20:24).

There is a certain arrogance in the claim in the Fourth Gospel that there was one disciple "whom Jesus loved." Did not Jesus love all of his disciples? There is still a certain level of arrogance if the community was symbolically claiming that it rather than Peter and the larger Markan community was especially loved by Jesus, but the arrogance is more understandable and acceptable if it was the community members who felt that they were special and that they were especially loved by Jesus, than if one person is said to have been the one "person whom Jesus loved." A community of faith may feel that its members are especially loved and blessed and happily express that within the community and even discreetly beyond the community without saying explicitly, "We are better than you are!" Perhaps this is what happened and what we have in the Fourth Gospel, the validating document of the Johannine community, the document in which it expressed its faith and its claims.

It is of great interest also to note the progression from Mark to Matthew to Luke to John in who is presented as announcing for God the Easter message to followers of Jesus. In Mark 16:5-7 the message is announced by the *neaniskos* (a young man) here clothed in white. We note that the word *neaniskos* is used in Mark 14:51-52 to describe the young man in the Garden of Gethsemane who, after the twelve disciples of Jesus had fled, remained until some of the bodyguards sent by Caiaphas to seize Jesus reached for him, when he tore loose, leaving his garment and running away "naked."

Now in Mark 16:5-7 it is a *neaniskos* clothed in white who announces for God that Jesus has been raised from the dead. We cannot be certain, but if this first Gospel was written by John Mark, it is possible that John Mark was that *neaniskos*, who was in Gethsemane along with the twelve somewhat older young followers of Jesus, the young teenager who lived with his mother in Jerusalem and in whose home the women who had come with Jesus to Galilee may have been guests, providing meals for Jesus and his male disciples who had come with him from Galilee, while Jesus and the other males camped each night in Gethsemane. In the Gospel According to Mark, much of the material (chs. 11-16) is about Jesus in Jerusalem, so much so that some commentators have described Mark as a passion account with an extensive introduction. This may have been because the young man John Mark had seen and been with Jesus only during the final week of Jesus' life. Rather than for John Mark as the writer of this Gospel to make the critically important proclamation, "Jesus has been raised from the dead!" he may have put himself into his Gospel as a minor character in 14:51-52 but as a major character in 16:5-7 who made this announcement. (For a literary portrayal of this and of many other incidents in the life of Jesus portrayed as a man, see my movie script, "Jesus, the Man," available at the Texas Lutheran University Bookstore www.tlu.edu.)

Instead of the *neaniskos* clothed in white in Mark 16:5-7, the Matthean redactors in Matthew 28:2-7 portray an angel of the Lord clothed in white as making this all-important announcement. The Lukan redactor expanded Mark's *neaniskos* clothed in white in Luke 24:4-7 into two men who were in clothing as bright as lightning! The Fourth Gospel redactors went one step farther by having two angels in bright apparel (John 20:12-13) appearing to Mary Magdalene. Had there been a Fifth or Sixth Gospel, we might expect that the announcement would have been made by a whole chorus of angels, much as the Lukan writer has a chorus of angels announce the birth of Jesus to the shepherds in the field in Luke 2:13-15. We continue this progression in our Easter worship services as we and our congregations' choirs and our congregations joyously sing the Easter hymns and proclaim the Easter message.

Mark 16:1-8

The secondary source that has been most helpful to me in my appreciation of the resurrection of Jesus accounts in the Synoptic Gospels is a short book written by the British Baptist scholar Norman Perrin just before his death at the University of Chicago in 1976 as a result of both cancer and heart disease. In his *The Resurrection According to Matthew, Mark, and Luke* (Philadelphia: Fortress, 1977) Perrin explained how the passion and resurrection of Jesus account in the Gospel According to Mark depicts the failure of Jesus' male disciples to believe and trust in him, and how these disciples fade away after Jesus is seized in Gethsemane. Even the women followers of Jesus, who, although unlike the men, are with Jesus in Mark's Gospel watching from a distance as Jesus dies on the cross, watching also as Joseph of Arimathea places the body of Jesus in Joseph's tomb, and preparing to anoint the body of Jesus early in the morning after the Sabbath, when told by the *neaniskos* that Jesus has been raised from the dead, fail Jesus because they say nothing to anyone about what the *neaniskos* has said to them, because they are afraid.

Perrin described the resurrection of Jesus account in Mark 16:1-8 as a "primordial myth," an almost primitive, primeval expression of the theme and experience of "suffering/death/ the overcoming of death," evidences of which Perrin wrote "are found everywhere in human culture" (p. 34).

The readers and hearers of the passion and resurrection account in Mark that ends, or rather that is left unended with the words "for they were afraid," do not have the assurances of appearances of Jesus as the Risen Christ that are provided by the Apostle Paul in 1 Corinthians 15 and by the redactor-writers who produced Matthew 28, Luke 24, John 20-21, and the various "endings" attached after Mark 16:1-8 in later centuries. The readers and hearers of the passion and resurrection accounts in Mark are given no expressions of proof of Jesus' resurrection, or of their own! So also it is for us as we read and hear Mark's "primordial" story. They, and we as well, who live after the "ascension" of Jesus, do not physically see Jesus the Risen Christ. The first readers and hearers of Mark's story, and we as well, read, hear, and believe. They, and we as well, have no physical proof. Together, we live by faith, a primordial, primitive, primeval faith. That is why Perrin resonated so well with Mark's account. What about you? What do you think about this? If you use Mark's story, what will you proclaim and how will you proclaim it?

EASTER EVENING
(A, B, C)

Isaiah 25:6-9
For this, see First Reading for Easter Day on page 161.

Psalm 114
For this, see Easter Vigil on page 160 (Series A, B, and C).

1 Corinthians 5:6b-8
In this section of 1 Corinthians Paul was chiding the Corinthians for being tolerant of immoral behavior among them and exhorting them to remove the old "yeast" of sin that was multiplying and spreading among them. He urged the followers of Jesus in Corinth to celebrate the Passover with the Passover bread of pure motive and truth. Can we see Eucharistic connotations here?

Luke 24:13-49
There are obviously Eucharistic connotations in this Road to Emmaus and appearance of Jesus to a large group of his followers account. Not only does Jesus break the bread and give it to the two men at Emmaus; Jesus actually is depicted as eating a piece of broiled fish to show a group of his followers that he was indeed physically resurrected from the dead. Easter evening is unquestionably the ideal time for us to read and to consider this text. This text is as "concrete and foundational" as the Mark 16:1-8 text is primordial. Here Jesus is presented as, in terms of the prepositions used by Martin Luther, "in us, with us, and under us" as we receive the body and blood of the Risen Christ in the Eucharistic action.

SECOND SUNDAY OF EASTER

Psalm 133

Since the only texts selected from the Old Testament for the Sundays after Easter in Series A, B, and C of this lectionary are the readings from the Psalms, with selections from the Lukan literary drama Acts of Apostles used for the First Reading instead of texts from the Old Testament, the selections from the Psalms should be given special attention during the coming six weeks.

Who could disagree with the beautiful statement of the blessings that are the result of people living together peacefully, as expressed in the first verse and throughout Psalm 133? Who would not enjoy the analogies utilized in this wisdom psalm? The statement in verse 1 has universal application, especially appropriate for us as Christians during the Easter season and throughout the year. The analogies that follow verse 1 are thoroughly Israelite-Jewish, but useful also for us.

Acts 4:32-35

At first glance, this text follows Psalm 133 very well, providing an excellent example of how productive and harmonious it is when members of a religious community live together in peace and harmony, sharing their resources for the benefit of all. Attempts at communal living and sharing are common within past and current religious communities, including Christian communities. Various Christian monastic communities have functioned well for long periods of time. Others, such as John Calvin's Geneva and a number of communities in the USA during the nineteenth century, were viable only for a generation or two. What the Lukan playwright depicts as problems beyond this text in Acts 5:1-11, however, is fairly typical of the attempts at communal sharing within religious communities.

What degree and level of sharing do you consider to be most advantageous within the congregation in which you serve? Would it be desirable to have a higher level of sharing within your congregation, perhaps for a relatively brief period of time, for example during the Easter season each year? Would a very high level of communal sharing be more likely to be successful in a small, new "mission" congregation supported by other congregations than in a large, well-established congregation? In your opinion, how much communal sharing is ideal within a Christian community of faith?

John 20:19-31

Like the Luke 24:13-49 text and unlike the Mark 16:1-8 texts considered above, this John 20:19-31 text is a proof of Jesus' physical resurrection account. It is somewhat different from Luke 24:13-49, however, in that here in John the Risen Christ is depicted as passing through doors without opening them, as a "spirit," while at the same time having the same body as before his death, even having scars from wounds inflicted upon him prior to his death. Here he has the same body, but it is a body that no longer has the mortal limits of time and of space.

Here Jesus as the Risen Christ greets his disciples with a message of peace. Here he shows to his disciples his wounded hands and side. He breathes on them and tells them to receive the Holy Spirit. He gives to them power to forgive and to retain sins. He tells them to believe.

Within our worship services this coming Sunday, we shall want to share within the congregations in which we serve everything that Jesus is said to have shared with the disciples in this text. Many of our claims within the Church are based on accounts such as John 20:19-31. We believe because those who have delivered to us these traditions have believed. We are called to deliver these traditions to others.

It is regrettable that those who wrote the Gospel According to John included the words *dia ton phobon tōn Ioudaiōn* (which is usually translated into English as "because of the fear of the Jews") in 20:19. The Johannine community had apparently experienced "fear of the Jews" in its recent past (probably during the decade of 81-90 CE) because of its contention with Jews who remained Jews. It is likely that negative experiences of frustration over the inability of members of the Johannine community to attract Jews to believe what the members of the Johannine community believed about Jesus had caused pejorative statements about the Jews in general to abound as the members of the Johannine community told their own story.

Grammatically, the genitive case in the Greek expression *tōn Ioudaiōn* can be translated into English either as a subjective genitive "the Jews' fear," that is, because of the fear that the followers of Jesus as Jews had of the Roman occupational authorities who had tortured and crucified Jesus, or as an objective genitive "the fear of the Jews," in which the Jews are the object or reason for the fear that the disciples of Jesus had. If John 20:19-31 were a documentary of the activities of the disciples of Jesus the third night after Jesus had been crucified by the Romans, these disciples of Jesus could indeed be portrayed as being afraid as Jewish followers of Jesus that the Roman authorities who had killed Jesus as a threat to Roman security in Jerusalem might come to seize, torture, and crucify them also.

The Four Gospels are not objective documentaries, however. Instead they are largely theological accounts, expressions of faith. Within the context of the Fourth Gospel, in which in most instances "the Jews" are presented as opponents of the Johannine Jesus and of his followers within the Johannine community, we must translate into English within the context of the Fourth Gospel and of the perspective of the Johannine community during the last decades of the first century.

Nevertheless, we can and should translate the words *dia ton phobon tōn Ioudaiōn* with sensitivity. We can include some nuances when we translate these words into English during this twenty-first century. Accordingly, in my *The New Testament: A New Translation and Redaction* (Lima, Ohio: Fairway Press, 2001), I have translated John 20:19 as follows: "During the evening of that day, the first day after the sabbath, while the doors where the disciples were staying were locked because they were afraid of what Annas and Caiaphas might do to them, Jesus appeared and stood among them and said, 'Peace be with you.' "

Incidentally, the expression *dia ton phobon tōn Ioudaiōn* is the only overtly anti-Jewish expression within chapters 20-21 of the Fourth Gospel. Most of the anti-Jewish polemic in the Fourth Gospel is centered in chapters 5-12.

1 John 1:1—2:2

This reading from the beginning portion of 1 John complements the John 20:19-31 Gospel selection for this day beautifully. It is made-to-order as a companion reading for the account of the disciples of Jesus seeing the Risen Christ with their own eyes and of Thomas being asked to touch the hands and the side of the body of Jesus where the nails had pierced his hands and the sword had gashed into his side. It also expresses very well the concept of atonement accomplished by the Christ, who is described as the expiation for our sins.

THIRD SUNDAY OF EASTER

Having had the most convincing proof of Jesus' physical resurrection story from the Fourth Gospel traditions as our Gospel reading this past Sunday, we turn now for next Sunday to the most convincing proof of Jesus' physical resurrection story in the Gospel According to Luke (Luke 24:36b-48).

We are grateful for proof of Jesus' physical resurrection stories, even though by faith even without them and with only Mark 16:1-8, we could believe that God raised Jesus physically from the dead. We are grateful for them because they indicate belief that after God has also raised us from the dead we too will be able to eat food, to touch and be touched, etc. We express our belief through the use of these texts that we too shall not be limited to a "spirit" existence. More than any other factor, this belief that after God has raised us from the dead we shall be able to relate to God and to one another physically has made Christianity the religion that has the largest number of members in the world today. It is not our ethical system or the exemplary manner in which we have lived that has led to the immense popularity of Christianity. Instead, it has been this teaching and belief in a meaningful physical being after death and resurrection that has been the most attractive feature within Christianity. (The Greek concept of the immortality of the "soul," for example, did not result in the ongoing development of a major "world" religion, although some of this concept was incorporated into Christianity. The Sikh concept of the faithful member being "absorbed" into God has not made the Sikh religion widely attractive either.)

We are called to proclaim this physical resurrection belief clearly and joyfully. We should proclaim it with the firm conviction that God is active and will continue to be active in our history through Jesus Christ our Lord, without in any way attempting to restrict God to our own limited understanding and experience. This is the challenge that we face throughout the year, and especially during the Easter season and on this Third Sunday of Easter in Series B.

Luke 24:36b-48

This is a typically Lukan account in style, vocabulary, and literary genre. Just as in other accounts that are peculiar to Luke-Acts, this story provides answers in vivid literary drama to questions that "Theophilus" or any other Christian who "loves God" might ask during the last two decades of the first century of the common era. It provides the same answers for us also today.

There are two distinct portions in this text. Luke 24:36b-43 is a "proof of Jesus' physical resurrection" story. It answers questions that must have been asked frequently among the followers of Jesus decades after his death, questions such as "Was it a spirit of Jesus or the spirit of Jesus that the disciples saw?" "Could this appearance have been merely the result of the imaginations of those first disciples?" "Is their testimony of having seen Jesus alive again perhaps only the wishful thinking of those who missed him and his presence so much after his death?" The answer given to all of these questions in this Luke 24:36b-43 account is the confident affirmation that Jesus was indeed and in every way physically present when he appeared to his disciples numerous times after his resurrection. He had the marks of his crucifixion on his body. The scars remained. Even more convincingly, he actually ate a piece of fish, this story says. A disembodied spirit does not eat fish!

The second part of this text (Luke 24:44-48) is a Lukan "fulfillment of scripture" account in which the disciples of Jesus are given specific directions and told that they are to anticipate a gift of power from God. It anticipates the Acts of Apostles sequel to Luke's Gospel. We notice because of Hans Conzelmann's *The Theology of St. Luke* that the Lukan

"Stay in Jerusalem" command is significantly different from Mark's and Matthew's "Go to Galilee." In view of the menu items (bread and fish) served in the feeding of the multitudes accounts and in this story about Jesus eating fish, it is surprising that fish sandwich meals have not been more significant within Christian communities.

1 John 3:1-7

The most obvious connection between this text and the Luke 24:36b-48 Gospel selection is "We do know that when the Son appears we shall be similar to the Son, because we shall see the Son just as the Son is" in 1 John 3:2b. Because the relationship between the Son and the Father is so intimate, there is ambiguity in texts such as 1 John 3:2b about whether the masculine pronoun is intended to have the Father, the Son, or God as its antecedent. It is also difficult to determine whether "he" (the Son) or "what we shall be" from the previous sentence should be considered to be the subject of "is revealed" in 1 John 3:2b. Church usage throughout the centuries, including the juxtaposition of Luke 24:36b-48 and 1 John 3:1-7 in this lectionary, suggest that the Son, or the Son and the Father as God, should be considered to be the subject of "appears" or "is revealed" here.

Acts 3:12-19

For those of us who have been sensitized by the Holocaust and the long history of the horribly damaging effects upon Jews, as well as of the dehumanization of Christians, caused by Christian anti-Semitism, it is deplorable that we have texts with verses such as Acts 3:13b-15 and 3:17-19 in this lectionary, to be read in Christian corporate worship settings.

A decision was made by Roman Catholic liturgical experts during and after Vatican II to use texts from Acts of Apostles rather than from the Older Testament as the "Old

Testament" First Readings during the Sundays in the Easter season after the Day of Easter in each of the three years of the lectionary cycle. This was done because presumably there were very few texts in the Old Testament that could be construed, even with the most skillful fine footwork of casuistry, to be "predictions" fulfilled in the resurrection of Jesus. These liturgical experts and their ecclesial superiors and administrators unfortunately, in spite of their very commendable development and approval of the document Nostra Aetate, in which the Roman Catholic Church rejected the history of Christian anti-Semitism, included blatantly anti-Jewish verses such as Acts 3:13b-15, and 3:17-19 in their lectionary. The other Christian denominations and groups and their leaders who have used the lectionary developed by the Roman Catholics after Vatican II, including those who modified it somewhat to produce the Revised Common Lectionary, have also been deplorably insensitive to the use of blatantly anti-Jewish verses such as Acts 3:13b-15 and 3:17-19 in Christian corporate worship.

There is plenty of edifying material in our Bibles to use in three-year, four-year, or even ten-year lectionaries that is not blatantly defamatory to Jews. I had no difficulty whatsoever in finding far more than adequate edifying material that is not condemnatory of Jews when I prepared the Four-Year Lectionary that I published as an Appendix in my *The New Testament: A New Translation and Redaction* (Lima, Ohio: Fairway Press, 2001). It is unconscionable for us to continue to read verses such as Acts 3:13b-15 and 3:17-19 in our Christian corporate worship.

Acts 3:12-19 is not even appropriate as a pericope in terms of form and structure. It starts within the middle of an account that begins in Acts 3:1 about Peter, John, and a man who had been lame from the time of his birth and it breaks off in the middle of a sentence that continues into 3:20. A pericope should have a beginning, body, and conclusion.

Acts 3:12-19 begins in the middle of a pericope and ends within that pericope. To use it as we have it is somewhat like coming into a movie thirty minutes late and leaving thirty minutes before its ending.

Since the Acts 3 account is lengthy and actually with its continuation in Acts 4:1-4 has thirty verses, if our First Reading for the Third Sunday of Easter in Series B must be from Acts, the text chosen and used should start with the beginning of the Acts 3:1—4:4 account and include only the edifying and appropriate Acts 3:1-13a, 16. This adjustment from Acts 3:12-17 to Acts 3:1-13a, 16 should be made by lectionary revisers within all of the denominations and groups that are using this lectionary. Our adjustment to Acts 3:1-13a, 16 this coming Sunday and in succeeding years will contribute to this process.

Psalm 4

This psalm of entreaty and of trust can easily be interpreted from our Christian perspective, in the context of our belief that God raised Jesus from the dead. Our belief in the resurrection of Jesus puts joy into our hearts! It enables us to lie down and to sleep, to live securely. Within our lectionary this psalm also previews the texts for the Sunday that follows this one, the Great Shepherd of the Sheep Sunday, with its Psalm 23 and John 10:11-18 texts.

FOURTH SUNDAY OF EASTER

John 10:11-18

Among the John 10 texts selected in this pericope series for the Fourth Sunday of Easter (the Great Shepherd of the Sheep Sunday), we have this year in Series B the central text. It is the only one of the three (John 10:1-10 in Series A, John 10:11-18 in Series B, and John 10:22-30 in Series C) that focuses clearly on the Johannine Jesus as the Great Shepherd of the Sheep. It is therefore the premier text among these three.

Although it is certainly the Johannine Jesus rather than the Jesus of history who speaks here, in the deepest sense we are confronted by the Jesus of history in this text, since there is much evidence within our tradition that the Jesus of history functioned as a great shepherd of the sheep among his fellow oppressed Jews who because of his courageous advocacy for God and for people — particularly for people who were in need of much help and protection — was tortured and crucified by the Romans. Jesus could have avoided that torture and crucifixion if he had discontinued his work or possibly if he could have explained carefully to Roman authorities that he was in no way encouraging his fellow oppressed Jews to try to use force or violence to improve their condition.

Once Jesus had been delivered over to the Roman crucifixion squad by the group of bodyguards (goons) who were employed by Caiaphas, there was no opportunity for Jesus to explain anything to the Roman authorities. Jesus' followers also could not rescue him at that point, at least not short of a planned, concerted suicidal massive frontal attack on the Roman garrison, and there is no reason for us to think that the Jesus of history would have desired such an attack and the heavy loss of life that would have occurred in such an attempt to rescue him. He would have continued his work after such a rescue, and a second arrest would have been inevitable.

Actually, what Jesus was doing by proclaiming that soon the Lord God would in some way come and that after that only the Lord God would be ruling over the oppressed Jews in Galilee and in Judea was giving hope for freedom that did pose a threat to the Roman security forces in Jerusalem. What Jesus was doing before he was seized, tortured, and crucified was "liberating" in every way. Whenever the oppressed have hope of being set free, their oppressors are unavoidably threatened. It cannot be otherwise. In that sense, the Jesus of history did put down his life for the sheep, did go to the cross, or, as we say in our time, did "go to the wall" for them, and for us. It seems that the best people in every age "go to the wall" for us!

Of course, in a different sense it is not the Jesus of history during his work prior to his crucifixion who speaks in this John 10:11-18 text. Instead, it is the Sovereign Lord of the Johannine community who voluntarily put down his life for his sheep (the members of the Johannine community) and has the power to take it up again who speaks in this text. Actually, it is leaders in the Johannine community, inspired by God, who speak in this text and throughout the Fourth Gospel. For the Johannine community and its leaders, Jesus as the Risen Christ was the Sovereign Lord with divine power.

The Fourth Gospel is an expression of what the members of the Johannine community believed about Jesus raised from the dead as the Sovereign Lord, but, true to the "gospel" genre, this expression is in a "ministry of Jesus" framework. The events of the Gospel According to John chapters 1-19 are presented as pre-Easter events, but actually in terms of what the community and its leaders believed about Jesus as the Sovereign Lord the entire Fourth Gospel is post-Easter.

The Fourth Gospel reveals more about what happened to the people who became the Johannine community after the crucifixion of the Jesus of history than it reveals about what happened to the Jesus of history before he was crucified by the Romans. For the members of the Johannine community, Jesus as the Risen Christ was the Great Shepherd of the Sheep, the Light of the World, the True Bread from Heaven, the Way, the Truth, and the Life, etc., even though it is not likely that the Jesus of history ever made such claims for himself. The Jesus of the Synoptic Gospels never talks that way. John 10:16 in this text and John 17:20-23 in the "High Priestly Prayer" are indications of the desire of the members of the Johannine community to draw the "other sheep" from the Synoptic communities into the Johannine fold where there would be "one flock with one shepherd."

1 John 3:16-24

The writer of 1 John made believing in God's Son Jesus the Christ and loving one another within the Johannine community of faith a commandment of God. It is consistent with much of the thought of the Fourth Gospel to consider faith and love to be commandments. Perhaps as a result of the experiences of the leaders of the Johannine community with the people of the Johannine community, it appeared to them to be necessary to command faith and love rather than merely to exemplify faith and love in their own lives as appropriate responses to our gracious God. Shall we exemplify faith and love or shall we command faith and love where we are as leaders in the Church and in our congregations today?

Acts 4:5-12

In this text the Lukan writer brilliantly portrays the belief that God has raised Jesus from the dead. It is entirely proper for us along with the Lukan writer to emphasize that we are saved from sin and from eternal suffering in the name of Jesus as the Christ. We can emphasize this belief today without making the exclusivist "one way" claim that God acts only in Christ or only in us. There is, of course, only "one way" for us, and that is God's way!

We should always proclaim that God provides salvation for us in Christ. That is "good news" for all of the people of the world. There is no necessity for us to proclaim that there is salvation only in Christ, for that is "bad news" for most of the people of the world. The exclusivist "one way" claim made here by the Lukan playwright and by the leaders of the Johannine community in John 14:6 comes across to many people, including many Christians, as irrational, arrogant, and imperialistic. It causes many people not to want to be associated with people who make that claim. Therefore, it hampers rather than enhances the effectiveness of the gospel of Jesus Christ. It is a minority claim within the New Testament documents, made in only two verses, John 14:6 and Acts 4:12, which become the favorite Bible verses of some Christians, often of Christians who want to assert their control and their understanding of Christianity over all other Christians and over all other people who live in this world. Let us respond to them in Christian love with the suggestion that, yes, there is indeed only one way, God's way, and let us seek that way together with them and with all of the other people of the world.

Psalm 23

It is most interesting to compare the psalmist's perception of "the Lord" as "my shepherd" with the Johannine community's perception of Jesus raised from the dead as its "Great Shepherd of the Sheep." The Risen Christ in the New Testament texts for this Fourth Sunday of Easter is essentially what "the Lord" is for the psalmist in Psalm 23.

FIFTH SUNDAY OF EASTER

John 15:1-8

Within the "Farewell Discourses" of the Fourth Gospel, John 15:1-8 is quite harsh and demanding. According to this text selected for our use next Sunday, every branch that is not bearing fruit is summarily taken away to be thrown into the fire and burned (and anyone who has ever burned a compacted mass of grapevines knows how flammable dry grapevines are and how quickly and intensely they burn and are consumed). The obvious implication is that anyone who does not remain within the Johannine community will be destroyed by an intense fire.

The words of this John 15:1-8 text, therefore, indicate that at the time when these words were written and incorporated into the Fourth Gospel tradition the Johannine community had many of the distinguishing characteristics of a religious cult. For various reasons, not all of which can be discerned today, the leaders of the Johannine community had isolated the community and themselves even from closely related other groups of followers of Jesus. They were claiming that they alone were composed of fully productive "pruned" branches of the "true vine," i.e., of the Johannine Jesus.

Other branches, such as those of the members of the extended Markan communities that had produced the Gospels According to Mark, Matthew, and Luke, were not, in the opinion of the leaders of the Johannine community, yet "pruned" and fully productive. The leaders of the community-fellowship of the Johannine Jesus considered themselves to be already "pruned" because of the words that the Johannine Jesus had spoken to them and because of their fidelity to Jesus as they perceived Jesus during the time when many who had been among them had departed and were therefore "pruned" from their community. Through the words of this John 15:1-8 text they were admonishing each other to remain

182

within their community and its fellowship, the community and fellowship of the Johannine Jesus. They state that only if their members remain in the community and fellowship of the Johannine Jesus would the Johannine Jesus remain in community and fellowship with them. If they remain, they will be given whatever they ask. Their fruit and productivity is tied very closely to their being accepted as disciples of the Johannine Jesus. Unless they are producing fruit, they are not disciples. It is apparent that "church discipline" and more than "church discipline" is involved here. There is also an exclusiveness in which the leaders of the community claim in the name of Jesus the authority to "prune away" all who do not conform to the beliefs and practices of these leaders.

We may ask, "Why is this text so harsh and demanding in comparison to John 14:1-31 that immediately precedes it?" "Has a shadow come over the Jesus of history on his last fateful night of freedom and of life, causing him to set aside the comforting and pastoral words that he had just employed in John 14:1-31?" That is possible, of course. In view, however, of what appears to be a conclusion of the farewell discourse in John 14:31c with the words, "Get up. Let us go away from here," and other considerations within the Fourth Gospel there are indications that the document went through several editions and incorporated the work of several writers during the course of its development. It is likely, therefore, that John 15:1-8 is material from a stage in the formation of the Johannine tradition that is different from that of John 14:1-31.

The branches cut away from the true vine that is the Johannine Jesus and community almost certainly refer to the many disciples who in John 6:66 are said to have left the Johannine Jesus and no longer were walking in the group with him. The branches cut away from the true vine are described as follows by the writer of 1 John 2:19. "Those people who left our community went away from us. Actually, they were never truly members of our community. For had they truly been members of our community, they would have remained with us. They went away, in order that it might be revealed that they had never truly been members of our community."

We know from sociology of religion studies that participants in a religious cult become in many respects harsh and defensive in their interactions with those who have left their group and increasingly demanding and controlling of their own members. It is important for us to realize this about the community that through inspiration by God produced this Fourth Gospel. It helps us to have a more adequate understanding of this John 15:1-8 text, of the entire Fourth Gospel, and of the congregations in which we serve.

In our proclamation of the gospel this coming Sunday we should emphasize the positive aspects of John 15:1-8 and the grapevine analogy as an illustration of our relationship with God through Jesus our Lord. We are dependent upon God. We are accountable to God. Apart from God we wither and die. We are expected to be productive, to produce good grapes.

There are many ways in which we can be productive. We know that our situation is not identical to the situation of the members of the Johannine community who wrote John 15:1-8. We should be open and receptive to whatever new things God may be saying to us today, together with what God is saying to us through this John 15:1-8 text.

1 John 4:7-21

This text continues the emphasis of John 15:1-8 on the necessity of being fruitful. It urges the members of the community to show their love for each other by what they do for each other; not merely to show their love by speaking words of love. First John 4:7-21 is an early commentary on John 15:1-8 and on similar texts in the Gospel According to John. We might consider it to be a brief sermon or homily on

John 15:1-8. Therefore, it provides a helpful model for us as we prepare our sermon or homily for next Sunday.

Acts 8:26-40

In this vivid scene in the Acts of Apostles literary drama about Philip and the Ethiopian court official, the Lukan playwright utilized a portion of the Suffering Servant Song (Isaiah 53:7-8), applied it to Jesus, and dramatized the spread of the new Christian movement to African lands, as well as along the Mediterranean coast of Judea.

Psalm 22:25-31

By using this final portion of Psalm 22 along with the Acts 8:26-40 account, we associate the psalmist's suffering with the suffering of Jesus. In this way, we are able to make the psalmist's song of praise our song of praise within our present context in a very meaningful way. We are challenged to apply these Acts 8:26-40 and Psalm 22:25-31 elements of our biblical tradition to our own new situation is such a way that, by our being inspired by God as the Lukan playwright and the psalmist were inspired by God, new tradition is formed within and for the people of God. We welcome and embrace that challenge!

SIXTH SUNDAY OF EASTER

John 15:9-17

Few texts within the Fourth Gospel reveal more about the way in which the Johannine community and its leaders perceived themselves than does this pericope. The text is principally about the relationships of the members of the Johannine community to each other and to their Johannine Jesus.

According to this text, the members of the Johannine community in this portion of their "Farewell Discourse" of Jesus reflected about the significance of the life and of the death of Jesus and expressed their belief that Jesus had put down his life for them (John 15:13). Elsewhere in the Fourth Gospel, such as in John 3:16-17, there are indications that some within the community, or perhaps the community at an earlier stage in its development, had perceived that God had sent Jesus because of God's love for "the world" (a concept that is much broader than that of the community itself). Here, however, in John 15:9-17, Jesus' death is said to have been for the members of the Johannine community, for Jesus' much loved "friends." The members of the Johannine community were obviously very proud of this designation of themselves as *hoi philoi* ("the friends") of Jesus. The leaders and members of the Johannine community, inspired by God, were affirming that Jesus had put down his life for them! For the members of the Johannine community, this was their basic statement of faith.

At one time they had considered themselves to have been "servants" of Jesus, but now they considered themselves to be Jesus' much loved "friends." They were his much loved friends, "the Disciple whom Jesus loved," because Jesus had revealed to them (so they claimed) everything that Jesus had heard from his Father (John 15:15). According to these accounts within the Fourth Gospel, Jesus may have revealed some things to people in other groups, but to the members of the Fourth Gospel community Jesus had revealed everything that Jesus had heard from the Father. In this sense, the leaders and members of the Johannine community were similar to the Gnostic and Gnosticizing Christians in their claims that they had been chosen to have within themselves knowledge of everything about God.

Nevertheless, the claims of the Johannine community as we have them in the Fourth Gospel were not as absolute as were the claims of the Gnostic Christians. The claims of the members of the Fourth Gospel community and their relationship with Jesus were still somewhat conditional. They stated that they would be Jesus' much loved friends if they would continue to do the things that Jesus was commanding them to do (John 15:14). What they believed Jesus was commanding them to do most of all, according to John 15:9-10, 12-13, 17, was to continue to love each other. The admonition to love each other became so important (and apparently so necessary!) within the Johannine community that it even became a "new commandment" of the Johannine Jesus to the community in John 13:34-35, as well as here in this John 15:9-17 text. This "new commandment" to love each other was reiterated many times elsewhere in the Fourth Gospel and in 1 John and in 2 John.

From a superficial reading of the Fourth Gospel and of 1 John and 2 John, we get the impression that the people by whom and for whom these documents were written were members of a most loving and congenial community of faith. A closer look, however, indicates that they were, in effect, "protesting too much" about their love for each other. Love for one another was apparently greatly needed within this community, so needed that they were in the process of making love for each other a requirement and of perceiving love for one another legalistically. If they would love each other, then the Johannine Jesus would be happy with them and their joy would be completed, perfected, fulfilled (John 15:11). Then they would go and bear fruit that would remain. Then whatever they would ask the Father in the name of the Johannine Jesus would be given to them (John 15:16).

1 John 5:1-6

According to this text, Jesus is the Christ because he came not only with the water of baptism but also with the blood of the cross. The person who believes that Jesus is the Christ shall demonstrate that the person is a child of God by keeping God's commandments. Because the person who has been and is "born of God" has overcome the temptations of the world, it is not a burden for that person to keep the commandments of God.

Although the view of the writer of this 1 John 5:1-6 text regarding our ability to keep the commandments of God differs greatly from the view of the Apostle Paul as expressed in chapters 1-5 of Paul's letter to the Romans, the Church included both documents within its developing New Testament canon and has lived under the authority of these documents for many centuries. The inclusion of these differing views illustrates the ongoing, creative tension that exists in Christian theology and practice and in the theology and practice of other theistic religions between the importance of adequate faith and right living. Adequate faith and right living are important within a theistic religion. We should not raise one of these factors above the other, nor should we exclude one in favor of the other. Both factors are firmly imbedded within the New Testament documents and, of course, within the Old Testament documents as well. We see them also throughout the Qur'an of Islam. Both should be emphasized in their ongoing, creative tension in our proclamation and in our parenesis.

Acts 10:44-48

This text was particularly important during the latter years of the first century of the common era and later as a validation of the inclusion of non-Jewish background followers of Jesus as full participants in the new religion along with those who were of Jewish background. Today this text is significant as a biblical basis, together with other texts in Acts of Apostles, for the claims of some Christians that they have received special gifts from the Holy Spirit of God. All of us have the right to claim special gifts from the Holy Spirit of God and the responsibility to note that these gifts are intended for the entire Church and not only for a few gifted individuals and groups.

Psalm 98

The struggles and anxieties apparent within the three New Testament texts chosen for our use next Sunday seem to melt away in the words of this psalm, "Let us sing to the Lord a new song!" In this psalm, rather than in the three texts from the Newer Testament, the "gospel" is expressed most joyfully. In this psalm the texts for this day reach their highest point of love, joy, and acclamation of God. Therefore, we may wish to alter the sequence of the readings so that this psalm is read last among the texts used on this occasion.

ASCENSION OF THE LORD (A, B, C)

The Ascension of the Lord texts in Luke-Acts (Luke 24:44-53 and Acts 1:1-11) accomplish four major objectives. First, they provide an explanation of where the Risen Christ is now. Second, they provide an explanation of why the Risen Christ was seen by many followers of Jesus during the first few weeks after his crucifixion and resurrection but is being seen in the same way no longer. Third, they provide assurance that the Risen Christ is still with us spiritually and that the Risen Christ will return. Finally, they establish more clearly the responsibilities of the followers of Jesus to be witnesses of the Risen Christ throughout the world.

These are very important objectives, and we miss our opportunity to follow through with a dramatic culmination of our forty-day Lenten season and of our forty-day Easter season if we do not have a meaningful and memorable worship service on Ascension Day each year.

Psalm 47

Our use of this psalm on our Christian Ascension Day is an indication that we consider the Risen Christ to be our Lord and God in a way that is quite similar to the way that the ancient Israelites perceived the Lord God for them. They perceived the Lord God to be the one who had won the victory for them over their enemies and over all evil and as the one who was, as it is stated in the picturesque language of this psalm, "sitting on the holy throne of God" the "Most High King over all of the earth." As Christians, we perceive Jesus the Risen Christ in much the same way as the Lord God was and is perceived and acclaimed by Israelites and by Jews in Psalm 47.

Psalm 93

There are numerous similarities between Psalm 47 and Psalm 93. The Lord is acclaimed in Psalm 93 as the king clothed with power and majesty, whose throne is established eternally. The Lord's rule is holy and just and will be for ever.

Acts 1:1-11

Since the principal literary antecedent of Acts 1:1-11 is the Septuagint text of 2 Kings 2:1-18, it is helpful to review the 2 Kings text in preparation for a Christian Ascension Day worship service. Genesis 5:21-24 and Deuteronomy 34:1-7 should also be read to provide the Enoch and Moses analogies.

We note that the inspired Lukan writer linked the Ascension account closely to the Lukan empty tomb account by having "two men clothed in white robes" interpreting the significance of the ascension of the Risen Christ in Acts 1:10-11 just as the Lukan writer had "two men in dazzling apparel" interpret the significance of the resurrection of Jesus in Luke 24:4-7. Perhaps we could benefit from the use of this Acts 1:1-11 drama best if we would begin the Ascension Day service outside the church building with the reading of this Acts 1:1-11 text. It would not be necessary for anyone to play the role of the Risen Christ, but it would help to dramatize the event to have two of the men of the congregation dressed in white robes appear from around a corner somewhere at the point of Acts 1:10 in the reading while the rest of those gathered for the worship service are standing together "gazing up into the heavens." The two men should appear and say to the group, "Why are you all standing here, looking up into the heavens? This Jesus, who has been taken up from you into heaven, will come again as you have seen him going into the heavens!" The worship service can then continue with the people entering into the sanctuary, singing an Ascension Day hymn, and using an Ascension Day liturgy.

Ephesians 1:15-23

At least once during our three-year cycle in the lectionary that we are using, it would be effective to utilize this Ephesians 1:15-23 reading as the primary text for the Ascension Day message. This text articulates what is desired for the People of God in the Church on Ascension Day. It refers specifically to the thought that the Risen Christ is sitting at the right hand of God in "the heavenly places." It uses the analogy of the ancient throne scene to depict how some people in the early Church late in the first century perceived the Risen Christ. What is said here about the power of the Risen Christ over the Roman emperor and all of the political authorities who are persecuting and threatening the early Christians should be emphasized as we consider this text.

Luke 24:44-53

The Lukan themes of understanding the Scriptures and of claiming that everything about Jesus' life, death, and resurrection written in the Israelite Scriptures has now been fulfilled are prominent in this text. What the Lukan writer did not say in this text about the expected return of Jesus as the Risen Christ is supplied in the Acts 1:1-11 reading. What Luke 24:44-53 does emphasize is the great joy of the followers of Jesus and their constant worship and blessing of God. Let us continue this joy and this worship and blessing of God for the Risen Christ now and always!

SEVENTH SUNDAY OF EASTER

John 17:6-19

For the members of the Johannine community while this text was being developed, Jesus was "no longer in the world." But the members of the Johannine community were "still in the world." Our own situation is somewhat similar to this on the Sunday after the Ascension. We too are "in the world" without having Jesus physically present among us. To us also Jesus' word has been given (and in a more "seasoned" form than it had been given to the members of the Johannine community). We may not be experiencing the hatred of the world as much as the members of the Johannine community apparently were experiencing it, but that may be merely because we are so much more "worldly" than were the members of the Johannine community. It may be because we do not function as a sectarian group as the members of the Johannine community functioned.

Nevertheless, according to John 17:14 the members of the Johannine community realized that they were, even in their situation, not "out of the world," nor did they want to think that Jesus was actually "out of the world" either. Neither do they have their Johannine Jesus ask God that Jesus' followers be taken "out of the world." He asks only that the Father would keep them from "the evil one" (John 17:15).

Incidentally, "of the world" is an inadequate translation of *ek tou kosmou* in John 17:14b, 16. The translation "of the world" is a translation that is not warranted by the context. It is to the credit of the leaders of the Johannine community that they felt that they had been sent "into the world" (John 17:18) and that they were not living "out of the world." We today also need to feel that we are being sent "into the world" rather than that we are not "of the world." We are physically and biblically "of the world," and it is not helpful to encourage us to think that we are not "of the world" by providing for popular use translations that are interpretations not warranted by the context of a text. If those who shaped the Johannine traditions had wanted to say that they were not "of the world" rather than that they were not "out of the world," they could easily have avoided the use of the word *ek* in John 17:14b, 16. An adequate translation into English of the Greek word *ek* in its context in John 17:14-16 would be "I have given them your word, and the rulers of the world have hated them, because they are not derived from the world, just as I am not derived from the world. I am not requesting that you take them out of the world, but that you keep them safe from the evil one. They are not derived from the world, just as I am not derived from the world."

Unless it is perceived that the reference to the loss of the "son of destruction" as being necessary for the Scripture to be fulfilled is a *vaticinium ex eventu* (prediction made after the event has occurred), we give the impression that John 17:12 teaches that Judas was predestined by God for destruction and that Judas had no free will to make his own decisions. When we see that there is a "prediction after the event has occurred" in John 17:12, we shall not declare that God predestined Judas for destruction. It is appropriate to declare that Judas did whatever Judas did because Judas wanted to do that, just as we do what we do — whether good or evil — because we want to do that also. Whatever we say next Sunday, may it be spoken as John 17:12 puts it, in order that the worshiping congregation where we are and the world may have the joy of Jesus fulfilled among them and that, in accordance with John 17:17, 19, the people and the world may be made holy.

1 John 5:9-13

It was the intention of the writers of this text to assure the people who remained within the community of faith in which they were leaders that God had given to them eternal life in the person of Jesus the Risen Christ, the Son of God. In order to give the people of the community greater confidence and to encourage them to remain within the community even though there were some teachings within the community that they found to be difficult to accept, the writers claimed in 1 John 5:12 that "the person who does not have the Son of God does not have life." We today and next Sunday would fail in our responsibility if we would not believe and proclaim that those who believe in the name of Jesus the Risen Christ as the Son of God have life now and eternally. It is not necessary for us to make the negative judgment that those who do not have Jesus as the Risen Christ, the Son of God, do not have life. God is to be the judge of that.

Acts 1:15-17, 21-26

The link that is most apparent between this text and John 17:6-19 is the reference to Judas, whose manner of death as described here differs considerably from the account in Matthew 27, and Papias' second-century account about Judas' death differs from both New Testament presentations. The Lukan playwright apparently chose to develop an account that would present the death of Judas in the most vivid and horrible way possible, writing with regard to Judas in Acts 1:18 words for Peter expressed in my English translation as follows: "As you know, Judas purchased a parcel of land with the coins that he had received for his dastardly act. And having fallen headlong, his body burst apart in the middle and all of his internal organs poured out their contents!" This cannot be harmonized with the Matthean account in which Judas is described as repenting, throwing the coins that he has received into the Temple treasury and then going out and hanging himself (Matthew 27:3-5).

It was not the primary purpose of these accounts to provide historical information about the death of Judas. The primary purpose was to portray Judas' death in a way that would be appropriate in view of what Judas is presented as having done as one of Jesus' own chosen disciples, helping Caiaphas to obey the command of Pilate by guiding the contingent of bodyguards sent by Caiaphas to locate Jesus in the darkness of the Garden of Gethsemane.

What is written in the Four Gospel accounts about the actions of Judas Iscariot and concerning his motives in guiding the contingent sent by Caiaphas is based on assumptions of the disciples of Jesus who were with Jesus in Gethsemane and of later followers of Jesus, not upon explanations given by Judas himself. One of these assumptions is almost entirely theological, the interpretation that God had predestined Judas to betray Jesus in order that God would be able to carry out God's plans for our salvation. Personally, I have never been attracted to that interpretation, because of the inconsistency of that interpretation with the biblical portrayal of human free will and accountability.

Other assumptions are that Judas chose to hand Jesus over to the Romans in order that Jesus would be "forced" to exhibit his divine power and subdue his enemies, or that Jesus knew when Jesus chose Judas as one of the twelve that Judas would betray him, but chose him in spite of this for a variety of possible reasons. I prefer the assumption that Judas was a "loner" who had been duped by the leader of the bodyguards into helping them find a suitable place to camp that night, that he thought that he was helping his new friends and did not intend to do anything that would be harmful to Jesus, and that he was aghast when he saw what was being done to Jesus. That is the assumption that I use in my portrayal of Judas in my "Jesus, the Man" movie script that is available at the Texas Lutheran University Bookstore (www.tlu.edu).

Psalm 1

According to this well-known psalm that was placed at this most prominent position in the Psalter by the editors of this collection, there are two ways in which to live. There is the way of the one who rightly chooses to meditate on and live by the commandments presented in the Torah, "Word of God," and there is the way of the one who wrongly chooses to follow the way of the wicked, the scoffers, the sinners. Those who are wise will choose the right way.

This psalm, therefore, previews the non-festival half of the Church Year in which the importance of our choosing the right way is emphasized on the Sundays after the Day of Pentecost and Trinity Sunday.

DAY OF PENTECOST

On this day we enter into the period of each year in which we celebrate the ongoing activity of God in our lives. The activity of God has a special meaning for us as Christians because of the life of Jesus. The texts appointed for this day, however, are a reminder to us that the activity of God and God's relationships with people did not begin with the life of Jesus. The activity of God and God's relationships with people take on new meaning for us because of Jesus' life, death, and resurrection, and for that we are grateful.

Analysis of the Hebrew Bible (the Old Testament for us as Christians) indicates that within those documents various hypostases (words used to represent God, anthropomorphic expressions used in attempts to describe activities of God) were developed. Among the most important and frequently used of these are the Word of God, the Glory of God, the Wisdom of God, the Presence of God, and the Spirit or Breath of God. These words became valuable vehicles for communicating effectively that God is indeed actively involved in the world even though we cannot actually see or touch God. These hypostases are helpful as we endeavor to talk about God and to God. We realize that as we attempt to talk about God we must use words, descriptive words drawn from our human experiences.

On this Day of Pentecost, our attention is focused on one of these hypostases used within the Hebrew Bible, namely the Spirit or Breath of God. The Spirit of God is the principal unifying factor in these five texts. Within the development of specifically Christian theology, the Spirit of God became one of our three most basic hypostases for God, most useful in our struggling attempts to talk about God and about the activities of God in our lives. As an hypostasis for God, the Spirit of God concept did not originate during the first century of the common era, nor on the day of creation, nor at any point within recorded history. We believe that the Spirit of God is a God-given means by which we are enabled to talk about God.

Within the Day of Pentecost observance in the Christian calendar, the dominating text is obviously the Lukan playwright's Pentecost story that we have in Acts 2:1-21. We could hardly celebrate this day in the Church Year without using it. The Lukan writer's Pentecost story brought the Christian observance of Pentecost into existence. Therefore, let us turn to this text.

Acts 2:1-21

Just as in early Christian tradition recorded in the Synoptic Gospels the Last Supper of Jesus was placed within the context of the Israelite-Jewish Passover observance, here in this sequel to the Third Gospel tradition the Lukan writer placed the inception of Christian prophecy within the context of the Israelite-Jewish celebration of Pentecost.

By the time of the first century of the common era, the Israelite Feast of Weeks (in the Greek language known as Pentecost) had evolved from an agricultural festival in which groups of Israelites came together to enjoy the first fresh fruits and vegetables of the season and to give portions of these first fruits and vegetables to God by sharing them with those who functioned as priests among them to become for them also a commemoration of the giving of the Torah. Apparently the Lukan writer — or a source utilized by the Lukan writer — took the process of development one step further, taking the Jewish celebration of the giving of the Torah and transforming it for followers of Jesus into the occasion on which Christian prophecy began. This account in Acts 2:1-21, consistent with many others in early Christian traditions, took an Israelite-Jewish custom or ceremony and adapted it for Christian use in a supersessionistic process. By means of this account, early Christianity was able to claim not only to have its own "Torah" in the Synoptic Gospel accounts, but also its own "Prophecy" here in the utterances of these early Christian leaders, all of whom were depicted by the Lukan playwright as gathered together in one place. There are some what we might call "rough edges" in this Acts 2:1-21 account (an indication perhaps of the freshness of the construction). There is a disagreement among those who in the text heard the voices of the disciples as to whether the utterances were incoherent babblings such as might be made by intoxicated persons or whether the utterances were excellent translations of a single message into a variety of languages and dialects such as those provided during sessions of the United Nations General Assembly. Nevertheless, the message intended by the account is clear.

In our Day of Pentecost proclamation it is the message, not the details of the account, that is of primary importance. In the best ways possible for us, we shall certainly want to proclaim that God through the Holy Spirit inspires us also today within the priesthood of all believers, comes over us with mighty power, gives to us the ability to prophesy (that is, to speak forth for God), and fulfills the biblical expectation in our time. Certainly we must claim the Spirit of God as we celebrate our Day of Pentecost. It is not sufficient for us to repeat or to paraphrase this Acts 2:1-21 account only as something that happened in a certain way during the first century. We must claim the Spirit of God also for the Church and for us today.

Ezekiel 37:1-14

It is the Spirit of the Lord God that leads Ezekiel in this fascinating account and places him into the valley filled with dry bones. It is the Spirit of the Lord God that commands Ezekiel to speak to the wind (the breath of God) and call it back into the bodies of the Israelites who had been rendered lifeless. Spirit/wind/breath comes from God for the restoration of life. This is also our God-given claim as Christians, Jews, Muslims, and others today.

Psalm 104:24-34, 35b

In this delightful poetic expression of God's initial and continuing creative activity, it is said that, as in Genesis 1:2, when the Spirit of God is sent forth, all creatures, even the sportive Leviathan, are brought into existence and sustained. We are called to share this message about the power of God today, especially as we continue to be reminded of the destructive powers being marshaled not only by large nations in the world, but also by smaller nations and by terrorist groups.

Romans 8:22-27

According to the Apostle Paul in this account, the entire creation has been groaning and in agony like a woman who is suffering with labor pains that never end. Paul wrote that within all of creation, all people have been struggling in agony under the bondage of sin until the time of the death and resurrection of Jesus as the Christ. For Paul, the Spirit of God is now with us at all times to provide the support that we need, because by ourselves, Paul wrote, we do not even know how to pray. The Spirit of God, therefore, intercedes for us with prayers that are so profound that we can neither imagine nor describe them.

John 15:26-27; 16:4b-15

In these texts the Spirit is described as the Paraclete, the Spirit of Truth, who proceeds from the Father and is to be sent by the Johannine Jesus after he leaves the Johannine community. The Paraclete will glorify Jesus, will take from the things that belong to Jesus and declare them to the Johannine community, will condemn the sinful world and convince the members of the Johannine community that the righteousness of God is fully known within the Johannine Jesus. The Paraclete is described as in some sense the surrogate for Jesus who cannot come unless the Johannine Jesus will go. The Paraclete is a guarantee that there will be more of the grace and truth of God to come and that the revelation will continue for the Johannine community.

In our use of this text, particularly on the Day of Pentecost, it is important that we claim participation in the ongoing revelation of God, that we as pastors, leaders in worship, and congregations as a whole affirm that we are expressions of the work of the Paraclete, the Spirit of Truth, in our time and place. The work of the Johannine Jesus, of the Paraclete, of the Spirit of Truth, did not in any way end during the first few decades in the development of Christianity. The work of the Spirit of Truth continues among us where we are, and among others, even among those who are very different from us.

SEASON AFTER PENTECOST
(ORDINARY TIME)
TRINITY SUNDAY
(FIRST SUNDAY AFTER PENTECOST)

The Festival of the Holy Trinity is an occasion on which we are called to speak boldly and as well as is humanly possible about our faith in God and about how we perceive God. The texts selected, the liturgy, and within the liturgy especially the hymns provide resources for our use. Beyond these, there are people, and ultimately there is God.

We speak about God from within the context of this world and of our experiences. In many ways we ourselves are limited to this world, speaking about God whom we believe is not limited to this world. Nevertheless, we are inspired by God to speak within the limits of this world about God whom we believe is not limited to this world.

As Christians, we believe that God is totally transcendent, totally beyond, all powerful, all knowing, perfect in every way. We also believe that God is always here among us as pervasive Spirit, like the air, the wind, always necessary for us, that we might breathe in and breath out, permitting us to do evil as well as good, though guiding us to do only that which is good. Finally, we believe that God is active in our lives, coming to us most of all in the birth, life, death, and resurrection of Jesus, whom we believe to be the Risen Christ, here among us, but also ascended to the Father. We believe in God perceived as God the Father, as God the Son, and as God the Holy Spirit.

Within the texts appointed for this day in Series B, there is no explicit expression of our Christian concept of the Holy Trinity such as we have it in the post-biblical ecumenical creeds and in the writings of post-biblical Christian theologians. We do not have the explicit reference to God as Father, Son, and Holy Spirit such as we have this in

Matthew 28:19 appointed for Trinity Sunday in Series A. It is surprising that the benediction "May the grace of the Lord Jesus Christ and the love of God and the fellowship of the Holy Spirit of God be with all of you" (2 Corinthians 13:14) was not selected for use anywhere in the Revised Common Lectionary. Second Corinthians 13:11-13 is used on Trinity Sunday Series A in the Revised Common Lectionary, but not 2 Corinthians 13:14. Unless we are strictly bound to use the Revised Common Lectionary with no variations, I think that we should include 2 Corinthians 13:14 in Series A on Trinity Sunday each series A Cycle.

Isaiah 6:1-8

In this magnificent "call of Isaiah" text we have the threefold acclamation of the Lord of hosts in Hebrew as kadosh, kadosh, kadosh, in Greek hagios, hagios, hagios, and in English "Holy, Holy, Holy." In Hebrew and for the Israelites and Jews the repetition of this word that means "Most Awesome" or "Totally Set Apart" is a way to indicate emphasis on and great respect for the Lord God as they perceived and continue to perceive God. We as Christians see in this text an indication, even a prophecy for some, of the threefold being of God and proclaim our understanding of this most notably in the words of Reginald Heber, combined with music provided by John B. Dykes, in one of our favorite hymns: "Holy, Holy, Holy, Lord God Almighty," with lines one and four concluding with the words that have been perhaps more influential than the Isaiah 6:1-8 biblical text itself, "... God in three persons, blessed Trinity!"

We should note in our study of these concepts that in the Greek language in which most of the earliest development of our Christian theology was expressed the Trinity concept was depicted by using the Greek word, in the plural form *hypostases*, by which they meant three ways of perceiving God. The Latin writers used the Latin word *personae* to express this, and English translators rendered this word as "persons," as we see it in the favorite Trinity Sunday hymn mentioned in the previous paragraph.

In terms of belief in one God, it is better that we speak about God on Trinity Sunday and throughout the year as "one in three" rather than as "three in one," one God whom we perceive in three principal ways rather than as three whom we perceive as one. In dialogue with people who are Jews and Muslims, this is especially important. We as Christians are monotheists, not tri-theists.

Psalm 29

Within the context of these Holy Trinity Sunday texts, the Lord God is revealed in Psalm 29 as the God of the storm, with powerful and frightful winds, as "the voice of the Lord" sweeping over the land from the Mediterranean Sea to the desert in the east, with the elements of a storm of lightning and thunder, strong winds, and heavy rain. The phenomenon of nature is used very effectively in this ancient hymn to the Lord as the Lord of the storm. It is appropriate also for us.

Romans 8:12-17

The Aramaic "Abba" in this text can be translated as "Daddy!" here rather than retained in a transliteration. In either case, it provides one of the closest links through the liturgical practices of the earliest followers of Jesus between the Jesus of history and the Apostle Paul. Paul's use of the words Father, Christ, and Spirit of God in this text provide additional materials for us in our teaching and in our proclamation on this Festival of Trinity Sunday.

John 3:1-17

The key verses for us for our use next Sunday are John 3:5-8 and John 3:16-17. They also are the portions of John 3:1-17 that most likely were the first portions of John 3:1-

17 developed within the Johannine community, prior to the addition of the anti-Jewish segments that surround them in this text.

We have elements in John 3:5-8, 16-17 with which to speak from our hearts about God as God is revealed to us. Our Christian traditions depict God as the Father of Jesus and consequently as "Our Father." Through our use of John 3:1-17 and Romans 8:12-17 next Sunday, we shall certainly proclaim that the Risen Christ is God for us. We believe that the Holy Spirit of God, the Spirit of God, and the Spirit of Jesus is blowing among us wherever God wishes. We cannot see God, but we can feel God — just as we cannot see the wind but we can hear it and we can feel it — and we can see the effects of what God does. We believe that God certainly is revealed also in other ways, but for us as Christians these three are by far the most important. Throughout all of this, we remember that God is, after all, "One," actually most significantly "Number One," as indicated in the theology of Jews, Christians, Muslims, Hindus, Sikhs, Baha'is, and other theists.

PROPER 4
ORDINARY TIME 9
SECOND SUNDAY AFTER PENTECOST

Sunday between May 29 and June 4 inclusive (if after Trinity Sunday)

Apparently those who participated in choosing the readings for Series B in the Revised Common Lectionary that we are using were more interested in providing sequential pericopes from Mark 2-6 and 2 Corinthians 4-12 for these Sundays during the first portion of the post-Trinity Sundays after Pentecost than they were in choosing texts for this Second Sunday after Pentecost in which a unifying motif can easily be seen. The Sabbath does figure prominently in the Deuteronomy 5:12-15 and in the Mark 2:23-28 readings, but in the former text the Sabbath is commanded, and in the latter other considerations are said to be more important than the Sabbath observance.

There are also rather tenuous connections between "Remember that you were a servant in the land of Egypt" in Deuteronomy 5:15, "We are serving you because of Jesus" in 2 Corinthians 4:5, and "I relieved your shoulder... and your hands of the burdens that you carried as slaves of the Egyptians" in Psalm 81:6. In view of this, perhaps we will serve best if we base the message for next Sunday on Mark 2:23—3:6 and on 2 Corinthians 4:5-12 with only fleeting references to the other texts. Therefore, we shall concentrate here primarily on Mark 2:23—3:6 and on 2 Corinthians 4:5-12.

Mark 2:23—3:6

This pericope is composed of the fourth and fifth controversy dialogues between the Markan Jesus and various Jewish groups in Mark 2:1—3:6. These fourth and fifth controversy dialogues in the first of two Markan series of controversy dialogues (the second beginning at Mark 11:27) are indicative of the lifestyle and of the attitude of the members of the Markan community regarding observance of the Jewish Sabbath.

Analysis of Mark 2:23-28 and of its parallel texts in Matthew 12:1-14 and Luke 6:1-11 suggests that the core saying that most likely was retained from the *ipsissima verba Jesu* is "The Sabbath was established for the sake of people; people were not brought into existence so that they could observe the Sabbath" (Mark 2:27). The new introduction, "And he said to them," that sets this saying apart from the other words attributed to Jesus in Mark 2:25-26, as well as the content of the saying in Mark 2:27 and the fact that this saying is not included in the Matthean and in the Lukan redactions of Mark 2:23-28 are all indications that the Jesus of history actually had said what we have in Mark 2:27, probably on many occasions. It is likely that the story contained in Mark 2:23-26 and given a Christological punch line in Mark 2:28 was developed within the early Christian tradition and gathered into the series of controversy/conflict dialogues that became Mark 2:1—3:6.

The issue of Sabbath observance was important to and frequently discussed by Jews. We have every reason to think that the Jesus of history would have taught that "The Sabbath was established for the sake of people; people were not brought into existence so that they could observe the Sabbath," and it is likely that most if not all of the Pharisees who were contemporary with Jesus would have agreed with him. We know that according to 1 Maccabees 2:39-41 if the enemy attacks on the Sabbath, one must fight back rather than to remain passive and be killed. In Mekilta 109b of the Rabbinic Literature with reference to Exodus 31:14 Rabbi Simeon b. Menasya is quoted as having taught that "the Sabbath is delivered to you, and you are not delivered to the

Sabbath," which is very similar to the Mark 2:27 saying of Jesus. More recent Jewish writers such as Israel Abrahams in *Studies in Pharisaism and the Gospels, 1* (Cambridge: Cambridge University, 1917), page 129, C.G. Montefiore in *The Synoptic Gospels, 1* (London: Macmillan, 1927), pages 63-65, and Samuel Sandmel in *Anti-Semitism in the New Testament?* (Philadelphia: Fortress, 1978), page 28, all point to the acceptability in first century Jewish thought of Jesus' saying about the Sabbath in Mark 2:27.

Around this Mark 2:27 core saying of Jesus it is likely that an anti-Jewish controversy story was developed in order to show how much superior Jesus was to the Pharisees, who were and remained within Judaism. As the controversy story developed, its most important purpose apparently became to indicate what is stated in the "punch line" (Mark 2:28) that "the Son of man is Lord also over the Sabbath." The dialogue of the account as it was developed presents the Pharisees in a particularly negative position in that they are depicted as objecting to the rubbing out of a few heads of barley or wheat (thereby "working" on the Sabbath) and not to what we might consider to be a more serious matter of eating someone else's grain. We should also note that "real" Pharisees would not have been walking in the grain fields on the Sabbath where they would see what disciples of Jesus would be doing. Only "literary" Pharisees, i.e., Pharisees in a literary composition developed by early Christians, would be in the grain fields on the Sabbath. In this account, Mark 2:23-26 functions as an extensive introduction to the saying of Jesus that is Mark 2:27. In Mark 2:23-26, the introduction to Jesus' saying, the "literary" Pharisees are refuted from their own Scriptures. The Markan Jesus is depicted as wise and the Pharisees are depicted as foolish.

Since there is no mention in this Mark 2:23-28 account that the disciples were hungry or that they ate the kernels, perhaps the symbolism of the account includes the idea of gathering people at the time of the harvest into the eschatological community and doing that even on the Sabbath in order to indicate the urgency of the end and to show that the Lord of the Markan community is indeed the Lord over the Sabbath and also by implication the Lord over the Jewish religious leaders.

The Mark 2:23-28 account, therefore, reveals much about the practices of the leadership within the Markan community and the pre-Markan tradition and actually relatively little about the life of the Jesus of history, apart from the very important saying by Jesus in Mark 2:27, "The Sabbath was established for the sake of people; people were not brought into existence so that they could observe the Sabbath."

The redactors who produced Matthew 12:1-8 and Luke 6:1-5 retained the introduction to this saying of Jesus (Mark 2:23-26) and they retained the anti-Jewish Christological statement "Therefore, the Son of man is Lord also over the Sabbath" that was developed by the writer and tradition of Mark and that we see in Mark 2:28, but they did not use the core saying (Mark 2:27) that Jesus himself had used, most likely frequently, whenever he was involved in a discussion about observance of the Sabbath. The redactors did not use the core saying of Jesus, the only Jewish element in the Mark 2:23-28 account, because it was "too Jewish" for them to use. Instead, they intensified the anti-Jewish material that was already in the Mark 2:23-26 introduction to Jesus' saying and in the Mark 2:28 conclusion after Jesus' saying. Because of this, and because they also made their accounts even more anti-Jewish by stating in Luke 6:1 that the disciples of Jesus ate the kernels of grain and in Matthew 12:1 that the disciples of Jesus were hungry and they ate the kernels, a trajectory of increasing anti-Jewish polemic can easily be traced as we read these accounts in the sequence of Mark to Luke and to Matthew in this segment of the tradition.

It would be helpful in our time if the words *hoi Pharisaioi* of Mark 2:24 would be translated as "some of the religious leaders" or as "some people." This would be a small step toward counteracting what was obviously an increasing tendency within the early followers of Jesus whose descendants became the Christian Church to clothe sayings of the Jesus of history in the form of controversy dialogues in which the scribes and the Pharisees are presented as sinister opponents of Jesus. Our Mark 2:23-28 text for next Sunday is one among many examples of this tendency among followers of Jesus in which they obscured sayings of the Jesus of history himself and developed and magnified their own anti-Jewish polemic. We have a responsibility to penetrate through this tendency that we can see in this text and in other similar controversy dialogues within the Gospel accounts in order to get back as much as possible to the sayings of Jesus himself, that here in Mark 2:27 and frequently elsewhere within the Gospel accounts are not anti-Jewish, but are actually "timeless," applicable in our time and in every time.

Next Sunday, as we read and use this Mark 2:23-28 text, it will be important to focus on Mark 2:27 and to proclaim with the Jesus of history — to paraphrase Jesus' statement — that "Although doctrines, customs, and rituals are important, people are always more important than doctrines, customs, or rituals, more important than even the most significant rituals and customs." We should have the courage to say this in appropriate ways next Sunday wherever we are, to speak as Jesus spoke, even though there was an obvious tendency within the developing Gospel tradition, as there is still today, to move away from the Jesus of history and to concentrate on other things.

2 Corinthians 4:5-12

This pericope is only a small segment of Paul's line of thought that we see in 2 Corinthians 2:14—6:13, all of which we should study if we wish to understand Paul's position. Paul was writing here about the ministry that he and his fellow leaders among followers of Jesus were bringing to the people as representatives of Jesus as the Christ. Paul wanted to emphasize that he and the others were not proclaiming that they themselves were the Lord; they were proclaiming that Jesus as the Christ is the Lord! Paul insisted that he and his fellow followers of Jesus as the Christ were only vessels, pottery containers, vehicles carrying the message. Paul's emphasis in this entire section was on the message. It is for this reason that we should concentrate next Sunday not on our ministry but on the message of the Jesus of history in Mark 2:27 about people. This place, here or on the Ninth Sunday after the Epiphany, depending upon whether Easter is early or late on our calendar in any given year, is the only place within our three-year cycle of texts in which this very important saying of Jesus is read.

The most significant reason that the Jesus of history was tortured and crucified by the Romans was because Jesus was a most courageous advocate for people, in his context for his fellow oppressed Jews of that time, giving to his fellow oppressed people hope that soon the Lord God would come and then only the Lord God would be ruling over them and the oppressive Romans would be gone! Jesus proclaimed that people are much more important than laws, rules, and doctrines, than customs, rituals, and ceremonies, whether promulgated by some of Jesus' fellow Jews or by the oppressive Romans who occupied the land of the Jews. This saying of the Jesus of history in Mark 2:27 is a message also for our time, for every time, and for every place!

Psalm 81:1-10

In this psalm the Lord God addresses the people to remind them that the Lord God has liberated their ancestors and them from bondage and warns them that no other god shall be permitted in their land. This is preceded by a call to worship. It is appropriate for us, as Christians, to adapt this psalm so that when we read and hear it we will think about our liberation from sin and death through our faith in God, whom we believe has raised from the dead Jesus as the Christ to be our Lord and Savior.

Deuteronomy 5:12-15

As in Psalm 81:1-10, the Israelites are reminded here that the Lord God liberated their ancestors from bondage in Egypt. Therefore, they are commanded to observe the Sabbath. None of them, nor their animals, nor their servants, nor their guests, shall do any work on the Sabbath. They shall remember their former servitude and provide a time for rest also for their servants and for their animals.

Although our observance of Sunday differs somewhat from what is commanded here, we can learn from this text how the Sabbath is perceived in the Torah. We should compare this perception of the Sabbath with the saying of Jesus in Mark 2:27 and discuss it, perhaps in a youth or in an adult Bible class. It would be helpful also to discuss this text with Jewish people in open dialogue.

Psalm 139:1-6 (13-18)

The psalmist is asking God for deliverance from the psalmist's enemies. In the portion of the psalm chosen for our use here, the psalmist expresses the belief that everything that the psalmist has ever thought or done is known to God, from the time of the psalmist's conception until the psalmist is dead and in the grave.

1 Samuel 3:1-10 (11-20)

In this account the young boy Samuel, given as a gift by God to Samuel's mother Hannah, and given back to God by Hannah to be a prophet of God under the care of the aged priest Eli, has a revelation from God during the night. The revelation that God was going to punish Eli put Samuel into a very difficult personal situation.

PROPER 5
ORDINARY TIME 10
THIRD SUNDAY AFTER PENTECOST

Sunday between June 5 and 11 inclusive (if after Trinity Sunday)

Mark 3:20-35

The dispute about exorcism and the charge that Jesus was possessed by Beelzebul in Mark 3:22-30 are particularly interesting because of the context into which these verses are placed in the Markan account. Instead of the exorcism that is included in the parallel accounts in Luke 11:14-23 and Matthew 12:22-32; 9:32-34, we read in Mark 3:20-21 the statement peculiar to Mark that "those from him," that is, Jesus' own family or his own relatives — probably defined more fully in Mark 3:31-35 as Jesus' mother and his brothers and perhaps his sisters — having heard about what he was doing, had gone out from Nazareth to bring him back to Nazareth, for they were saying that he had lost his senses by speaking openly about the time soon when the Lord God would be coming to rule over them instead of the oppressive Romans. In the Markan context of this account, therefore, Jesus is presented as facing conflict on two fronts, one with the scribes who had come down from Jerusalem and the other with his own mother and closest relatives.

An analysis of the Synoptic interrelationships that would see no more than a simple progression of development from Mark and "Q" material to Matthew and to Luke would probably lead to the conclusion that Jesus' mother and siblings did not understand what Jesus was doing and tried to stop him. Later Synoptic traditions, with their greater interest in Jesus' parents as God the Father and by the power of the Spirit of God the Virgin Mary as his mother, the conception and birth of Jesus as the divine Son of God, and their much

215

higher Christology than the Christology in Mark, with correspondingly diminishing emphasis on Jesus' humanity, suppressed the Markan tradition of misunderstanding on the part of Jesus' mother and brothers, retaining only Mark 3:31-35 in their renditions and rejecting Mark 3:20-21 outright.

Such an analysis may be a fairly accurate representation of what had occurred, but it is also possible that behind Mark 3:20-21 lies something more than — or other than — an historical reminiscence by Peter or by someone else within the tradition.

If community self-consciousness was an important factor in the shaping of the Markan account, it is possible that the complete controversy dialogue here includes not only the central portion (Mark 3:22-30), but the entire text of Mark 3:20-35 selected for our use next Sunday. If the complete controversy dialogue includes all of Mark 3:20-35, the Markan community may have been polemicizing not only against the scribes from Jerusalem, its principal antagonists in the Markan account, but also against those from Jesus' background who did not understand what the Jesus of the Markan community was doing and as "his mother and brothers" were attempting to suppress him. According to Mark 3:20-35, neither "the scribes from Jerusalem" nor "those from Jesus' own family background" were truly Jesus' mother and Jesus' brothers. Instead, whoever does the will of God (the Markan community gathered around Jesus as they perceived him) is Jesus' brother and sister and mother (Mark 3:33-35).

In the Luke 11:15-22 parallel, it is merely some people from the multitude who said that it was in the name of Beelzebul, the most prominent of the demons, that Jesus was casting out demons. Mark assigned to these objectors the identity of the scribes from Jerusalem and Matthew the identity of the Pharisees. Those who would try to separate Jesus from the ones who were sitting around Jesus in a circle (the Markan community) are not recognized (Mark 3:33) as Jesus' mother and brothers. Those who say that Jesus has an unclean spirit are said to be speaking against the Holy Spirit and do not have forgiveness ever. They are guilty of an eternal sin (Mark 3:29-30). The polemic of Mark 3:20-35 is probably directed, therefore, against both of these groups. The polemic is gentle and subtle against "those from Jesus" from Galilee, but it is intense and severe against the "scribes from Jerusalem." The warning and condemnation included in Mark 3:28-29 are separated by enough space in the account from the mention of the scribes from Jerusalem in Mark 3:22 that most readers of Mark 3:20-35 are probably not aware of how the complete controversy dialogue of Mark 3:20-35 is constructed. For a carefully reasoned discussion of this issue, see Raymond E. Brown, Karl P. Donfried, Joseph A. Fitzmyer, and John Reumann, *Mary in the New Testament* (Philadelphia: Fortress and New York: Paulist, 1978), pages 51-59. Consequently, most readers apply the warning against exclusion from fellowship with Jesus and against anyone who would speak evil of the Holy Spirit to themselves and to each other rather than to first century Jewish or to contemporary Jewish groups.

Therefore, we in our expository proclamation based on this text should also apply the warning against exclusion from fellowship with Jesus and against anyone who would speak evil against the Holy Spirit of God to ourselves rather than to Jewish groups of the past or present, even though anti-Jewish polemic was probably intended by the writer of Mark 3:20-35 when the literary "sandwich" of placing Mark 3:22-30 between Mark 3:20-21 and Mark 3:31-35 was formed.

2 Corinthians 4:13—5:1

It is in this text that the confident proclamation of the gospel is seen most clearly in the texts selected for this day.

Paul writes that he and his companions have the same spirit of faith as the Israelite psalmist (Psalm 116:10) who is said to have written, "I believed. Therefore, I have spoken." Since Paul and his companions have believed that God has raised Jesus from the dead, they have also proclaimed that God will raise them after they have died and that God will present them, along with their fellow-believers in Corinth, by the grace of God into a setting that, even though they cannot see it now, is eternal. Certainly that was Paul's proclamation in this text and certainly it should be our proclamation this coming Sunday. In the words of the Mark 3:20-35 text, it is the acceptance of this proclamation that makes us "Jesus' mother and Jesus' brothers." It is the acceptance of this proclamation that ties the Christian Church and people together within the "Body of Christ" throughout time and space.

Genesis 3:8-15

In traditional Christian identification of Messianic prophecies within the Hebrew Scriptures (the Older Testament), Genesis 3:15 is said to contain the first glimmer of the Christian gospel in its words regarding the "seed" of the first woman (Eve) bruising the head of the serpent. There can be little doubt that this verse was perceived to be "gospel" by the ancient Israelites, although their perception in the context of their experiences in a climate in which poisonous snakes were a common hazard did not extend beyond the realization that very alert people might be able to bruise or crush the head of a snake and that a snake can and did in many instances strike the heel of a person. (The ancient Israelites obviously did not wear thick, heavy Texas cowboy boots and carry a rifle to protect them against rattlesnakes!) Beyond that, there was likely a prediction or claim in this poetic form that although initially the Canaanites with their snake symbols had been bruising the heels of the nomadic

Israelites, eventually the encroaching Israelites would crush the head of the Canaanites and of their religious practices. We as Christians can obviously apply the "gospel" of this text to our time and to our particular situation, as in various Liberation theologies and wherever relevant.

Psalm 130

In deep agony caused by the psalmist's own sin, the psalmist cries out to the Lord for forgiveness. While the psalmist waits for mercy from the Lord, the psalmist calls upon Israel to have this same hope in the Lord. This applies to us as well. We too cry out and wait. For us as Christians, we have, along with psalms such as this, the model of Jesus dying on the cross and the belief that, by dying, Jesus, now perceived as the Risen Christ and as the Son of God, was bearing our sins.

1 Samuel 8:4-11 (12-15) 16-20; 11:14-15

The leaders among the people asked Samuel to appoint for them a king, so that they would be like the other nations around them. Samuel took this to the Lord in prayer and was told by the Lord to do as the people wished, but to let them know what the king would take from them. Samuel responds reluctantly and Saul becomes the first king over the people of Israel.

Psalm 138

Unlike earthly kings, the Lord as king has provided the help that the psalmist needed. Therefore, the psalmist acclaims the Lord as God over all of the kings on the earth and praises the Lord God for the steadfast love and mercy of the Lord God, for the love and mercy that will endure forever. This contrasts sharply with the depiction of earthly kings in the 1 Samuel 8:4-11 (12-15) 16-20; 11:14-15 text above. Who do we want to be our "king" over us?

PROPER 6
ORDINARY TIME 11
FOURTH SUNDAY AFTER PENTECOST

Sunday between June 12 and 18 inclusive (if after Trinity Sunday)

Mark 4:26-34

The hidden activity of God is a major theme within many of the most notable narratives within the Hebrew Bible (our Old Testament), for example, within the Joseph story in Genesis 37-50, in the book of Ruth, and in the story of the court history of David in 2 Samuel 6—1 Kings 2. In fact, in many of these accounts it seems as though the activity of God is hidden much of the time even from those who believe in God!

One of the most helpful ways in which to interpret and to understand parables, especially the parables of Jesus within our New Testament, is to see them as manifestations of the hidden activity of God. The parables of Jesus conceal. The parables of Jesus conceal messages of Jesus of hope and liberation for the oppressed followers of Jesus from the understanding of the oppressive Romans. The full meaning of these parables of Jesus, while intended to be understood by Jesus' oppressed followers, is often concealed from them as well. The refrain frequently used in conjunction with parables of Jesus within the Synoptic Gospels, "Let the one who has ears hear" is an indication of this.

The interpretation of the parables of Jesus is and remains a challenge for us, especially because we and our lifestyles constantly become more distant and different from the lifestyle of Jesus and of those with whom he worked. The more we can regain an understanding of the economic, political, social, and religious conditions of Jesus and of his fellow Jews in Galilee and in Judea during the third decade of the first century of the common era the better we will be able to understand the parables of Jesus.

The emphasis on the hidden activity of God is most apparent within the first of the two parables about the "kingdom" of God in this Mark 4:26-34 text. Just as we cannot see the process of the germination of the seed, the development of the root and of the sprout until the sprout penetrates the surface of the soil, we cannot see that the kingdom of God is taking root and is developing a sprout that will soon penetrate through the surface of the soil. That kingdom of God will replace the kingdom of the Roman empire and its oppressive rule over Jesus and over the other oppressed Jews in Galilee and in Judea. Just as the plant will grow rapidly if there is moisture under the soil and if there is adequate rain and sunshine, the Jews with whom Jesus was sharing his message will grow in faith in God and in confidence in the inevitable and ongoing activity of God. Just as within a few weeks and months the plant will extend its stalk, form the embryonic seeds that cannot be seen until the stalk opens to reveal the soft, moist seeds that harden into the precious grain, so also the hidden activity of God will result in the precious "harvest" of freedom from Roman rule.

The growth is great and the harvest must proceed at the proper time. The kingdom of God is concealed. The kingdom of God is revealed. Those who are oppressive and do not believe in God will see no activity of God until the harvest, when they will be cast aside to be plowed under or to be burned by those who are now oppressed but for whom God intends the harvest.

As we pray the Lord's Prayer, we pray that the kingdom of God will come. As we proclaim the gospel and as we interpret this parable analogy of Jesus in Mark 4:26-29 next Sunday, we are called to interpret the nature of God's kingdom. What is being revealed to us about that kingdom?

What will be revealed through us next Sunday about that kingdom?

The second parable analogy in our appointed text, Mark 4:30-32 and the summary statement in 4:33-34, bring in a somewhat different factor. While the father and sons of the family till the soil on the stone-terraced hillsides outside the village in order to produce grain for bread, the mother and daughters plant and tend the herb garden near their dwelling. The mustard seed, said to be the smallest of all of the seeds, grows within the herb garden to become a large bush, strong and thick enough to provide a place where the birds of the air can make their nests.

How will we use this mustard seed analogy parable next Sunday? Our situation is so different; and yet in many ways it is still the same. How is God at work here and now? How is the Church an expression of the work of God? How is the Church a participant with God in the sprouting, growth, and harvest of the kingdom of God?

Psalm 92:1-4, 12-15

Along with the writer of this psalm and with many others who have used Psalm 92, we find that our lives are more meaningful when we praise God day and night. We find that our lives are enriched when we realize that, as perceived by people within the Zoroastrian religion, the Jewish religion, Christianity, Islam, and all of the smaller groups derived from them, even though the "wicked" may seem for a time to be flourishing, those who by the grace of God and by their response to God are "righteous" will eventually outlast the wicked, in order to show that God is firm with love and with justice. The analogy in Psalm 92 of the righteous being like a palm tree, a cedar in Lebanon, planted in the "courts of our God," full of sap and green, bringing forth fruit even in old age, used so well here, is carried over into the Ezekiel 17:22-24 text in a somewhat different form in a different situation.

Ezekiel 17:22-24

The analogy of the tree is continued here with the image of a tender sprig of green cedar — the product of a single season of growth — rescued by the Lord God before the tree itself is destroyed. This sprig of new growth is then said to have been planted by the Lord God on the mountain height of Jerusalem. There it is said that it will flourish, bear fruit, and provide nesting places for all types of birds. (The parable in Mark 4:30-32 also to be used next Sunday of the mustard seed producing a shrub that is large enough for the birds of the air to build nests in it is an indication of familiarity with Ezekiel 17:22-24.) God will produce such wonders, as those who believe in God can perceive.

1 Samuel 15:34—16:13

If this text and the option of somewhat sequential readings from 1 Samuel, 2 Samuel, and 1 Kings during these summer weeks is taken, there will be many weeks in which little or no significant connection will be seen between the First Readings and the texts from the Four Gospels. For next Sunday in this account from 1 Samuel 15:34—16:13 about Samuel anointing the young shepherd lad David we may see a connection between the small mustard seed in Mark 4:30-32 developing into a large shrub and the smallest of the sons of Jesse being anointed by Samuel to grow up to become Israel's most complex king, the "father" of the nation. That connection, however, is a rather long "stretch," it seems to me. God, of course, is the most significant unifying factor in all of these texts.

Psalm 20

This psalm appears to be prayer to God that the king of Israel be victorious in a coming battle. It is designated as a psalm of David, appropriately, since David, said in 1 Samuel 16:1-13 to have been anointed by Samuel to be the future king to replace the hapless Saul, was a warrior king during the highly successful early portion of his reign.

2 Corinthians 5:6-10 (11-13) 14-17

In this text we move from analogies of the small seed becoming a huge shrub and the small boy David becoming a mighty king to a comparison by the Apostle Paul of this earthly "tent" (our body) in which we now sojourn to the heavenly home, our permanent residence that God in Jesus the Christ will provide for each of us. In this text, Paul makes it clear that he himself would prefer to depart and be with God in the heavenly home. Nevertheless, the decision of when to depart is not a decision that Paul will make. Here also the activity of God is in a sense hidden from our eyes.

Consideration of this text provides an opportunity for us to discuss the biomedical ethics issue of under what circumstances it may be appropriate to delay an inevitable death by use of "heroic" life-support systems.

PROPER 7
ORDINARY TIME 12
FIFTH SUNDAY AFTER PENTECOST

Sunday between June 19 and 25 inclusive (if after Trinity Sunday)

Our understanding of the Mark 4:35-41 Gospel account about Jesus stilling the storm on the Sea of Galilee is enhanced by the use in this lectionary of Psalm 107:1-3, 23-32 with it. Therefore, let us begin our consideration of the multiple texts offered for next Sunday in the Revised Common Lectionary with Psalm 107:1-3, 23-32.

Psalm 107:1-3, 23-32

After the introductory verses 1-3, the main body of this psalm is comprised of four self-contained strophes, each with its own refrain. Within each of these four sections, a different situation of peril is described. In each, those whose lives had been endangered call upon the Lord to save their lives. In every instance, the Lord delivers them from distress, and the people are urged to thank the Lord for the mercy that the Lord has had for them.

The first section (107:4-9) describes wanderers in the wilderness, the second (107:10-16) those who had been in prison, the third (107:17-22) the ill, and the fourth (107:23-32) those caught in a storm at sea. It is this fourth section, the longest and most fully developed that has been chosen to be used with the account of Jesus stilling the storm in Mark 4:35-41, for obvious reasons.

The principal theme of this psalm is belief in intervention by the Lord to rescue those who believe in the Lord from the four basic perils that, prior to old age and increasing senility, threaten our lives. It is the Lord alone, we believe, who ultimately has the power to deliver us from all of these situations of peril, and for that we are to give thanks and praise to God. Actually, of course, we are to give thanks and praise to God our Lord even when the Lord does not deliver us from these perils.

Mark 4:35-41

As in so many other instances in the Gospel accounts, Jesus as our Lord is said in Mark 4:35-41 to have done what in the Hebrew Bible (our Old Testament) is ascribed to the Lord God as the ancient Israelites perceived God and as Jews, with some modifications, continue to perceive God. Just as the Lord God is said in Psalm 107:28-29 to have stilled the storm after those in the ships had cried out to the Lord God in their distress, so also in Mark 4:38-39 Jesus as our Lord is said to have stilled the storm on the Sea of Galilee after his followers in the boat had cried out to him. Clearly Jesus as the Christ is portrayed as having the power that is ascribed to the Lord God also in Job 38:10-11, to stop the proud waves and to say, "This far you have come, and no farther!"

Regardless of whether the Mark 4:35-41 text depicts an event as it occurred on a particular evening during Jesus' activities in the region of the Sea of Galilee, or whether the Mark 4:35-41 account preserves a story formulated within early Christian circles to proclaim that Jesus as the Risen Christ is Lord for his followers just as the Lord God as perceived by Jews is for them, there can be no doubt that this Mark 4:35-41 account is a proclamation of the Lordship of Jesus, of the divine power of Jesus as the Risen Christ over all of the elements of nature.

Therefore, for our proclamation next Sunday certainly the emphasis should be on the proclamation of the Lordship of Jesus as the Risen Christ, the Risen Christ of faith who for us as Christians is one with God the Father as God for us. We should not put our primary emphasis on the reactions of the disciples, the turbulent nature of the Sea of Galilee, or on other unnecessary attempts to "shore up" the historicity of the account. The account is not primarily history. Instead, the account is primarily proclamation. Since the account is primarily proclamation, we should proclaim it. We should proclaim its message in terms that are meaningful and understandable in our own historical situation. Whether the Jesus of history actually caused a storm to cease on the Sea of Galilee nearly 2,000 years ago is not the primary issue. At least, it is not the primary issue for us. It may be the primary issue for an historian, one who is interested in historicity. But since we are pastors proclaiming the Word of God and not historians who are trying to determine historicity, our proclamation should be that we believe that Jesus as the Risen Christ, who we believe is one with God the Father as God for us, rescues us from the perils of our lives both now and forever. Even when everything seems to be out of control for us, we believe that nothing is not out of control for God. This is what we believe and this is what we should proclaim, even when our current situation in our individual, family, congregational, corporate, national, and international existence seems to indicate otherwise.

Job 38:1-11

In this magnificent section, the climax of the Job drama, in which the Lord answers Job out of the whirlwind, the Lord reveals that it was the Lord and not Job nor anyone else who "shut in the sea with doors," "prescribed bounds for it," and "set limits for its proud waves." This text is appropriate with Psalm 107:23-32 and with Mark 4:35-41.

2 Corinthians 6:1-13

There is a linkage between this segment of 2 Corinthians and the Mark 4:35-41 account of Jesus as the Risen Christ stilling the storm on the Sea of Galilee. We see this in the paraphrase of a portion of Isaiah 49:8 by the Apostle Paul in 2 Corinthians 6:2, "At a favorable time I have heard your call and on the day of salvation I have come to rescue you." What Paul used from Isaiah 49:8 may be said to have been used in a different way by followers of Jesus who developed and told their story about Jesus in the boat. Jesus as their Lord heard their call and rescued them. So also it is for us, by faith.

Paul wrote tenderly in this segment to the Corinthians revealing some of his deepest feelings to them about his experiences of suffering and of rejoicing. Then, in 2 Corinthians 6:13 he urged them to respond in a similar way, as follows: "I speak to you tenderly — reveal your deepest feelings in response to us." Here in this text we are in the presence of deep feelings of intimacy within the Church, which for Paul was depicted as the "Body of Christ."

It should be noted that this segment of 2 Corinthians comes near the end of the portions of the composite letter that are sometimes called the "fragrant" or "sweet smelling" portions of the document. These are the portions 2 Corinthians 2:14—6:13 and 7:2-4, which should be read in preparation for our message next Sunday, since they provide the context for our selection, 2 Corinthians 6:1-13. This "sweet-smelling" portion seems to have been inserted at some point from a different letter by Paul to the Corinthians, interrupting Paul's reference to his travels to Macedonia that is continued at what we know as 2 Corinthians 7:5, where Paul continues to write about his travels to Macedonia. (There appears to have been an insertion within this "sweet-smelling" portion of another insertion, an insertion within an insertion, specifically 2 Corinthians 6:14—7:1, Paul's comments about not recommending that followers of Christ marry non-believers.) Our text for next Sunday lies within the most precious, "sweet-smelling" section of the document.

1 Samuel 17:(1a, 4-11, 19-23) 32-49

We have here the basic portions of the story of the young man David with his slingshot stunning the giant Philistine warrior Goliath, who had been taunting the army of King Saul and of Israel, by hitting Goliath on his forehead with a stone. The most important part of this account, an account that is always a favorite of young boys, especially of young boys who are threatened and beaten by older and larger "bullies," and by others who are underdogs and/or who favor the underdogs in any contest, is the response of David within 1 Samuel 17:45, "You come to try to kill me with your sword, your spear, and your javelin, but I come to meet you in the name of the Lord of hosts." If and when we use this text, we must be aware of and sensitive to the reality that in our culture there have been young men, who, after being repeatedly bullied and ridiculed by others in their schools, have come to school with a pistol or a rifle and have shot and killed students in that school.

Psalm 9:9-20

The Lord is praised here as the avenger of blood, as the one who snares the wicked and sends them to their death. That is the point of contact with the 1 Samuel 17:1a, 4-11, 19-23, 32-48 David and Goliath story considered above. This psalm also has positive assurances for the poor, the needy, and the oppressed, and these are the portions that we should proclaim.

1 Samuel 17:57—18:5, 10-16

This text continues the story of David's rapidly growing popularity among the people of Israel, of the deep friendship of Saul's son Jonathan with David, of King Saul's envy, fear, and hatred of David, and of the initial attempts of Saul to kill David. This is a profound commentary upon human nature; it is not a very edifying story, however, for us as we seek to fulfill our call to proclaim the good news of the grace of God revealed in our lives.

Psalm 133

The point of contact between this psalm and the 1 Samuel 17:57—18:5, 10-16 text with which it is connected in our lectionary is obviously the acclamation in Psalm 133 of the joys that come when people live together as brothers peacefully and the deep friendship between Jonathan and David in the 1 Samuel text.

PROPER 8
ORDINARY TIME 13
SIXTH SUNDAY AFTER PENTECOST

Sunday between June 26 and July 2 inclusive

Mark 5:21-43

The introductory note in Mark 5:21 regarding Jesus crossing again in the boat to the other side of the lake should alert us to the interest in and the importance of "theological geography" in this section of the Gospel According to Mark. In Mark 5:20 Jesus was on the "Gentile" side of the Sea of Galilee. He was with the Gerasenes. He cast out the unclean spirit whose name was "Legion," and he permitted the thousands of demons to enter into the herd of swine, which then rushed down the steep bank into the sea where they were all drowned. What possible purposes could this rather bizarre miracle story have served for the Markan community?

If this constructive/destructive miracle story was put into written form during the war in Galilee and Judea between the Jewish patriots and the Roman legions during the years 66-72 CE, could the Markan writer and community by any chance have balanced the somewhat subtle polemic in the Mark 5:21-43 text we will be using next Sunday with the even more subtle polemic against the Romans in Mark 5:1-20? We know that direct, open polemic against the Roman oppressors within lands occupied by the Roman military was much too risky for the early followers of Jesus throughout the period in which the documents that would eventually become the New Testament were being formulated.

But perhaps Mark 5:1-20 is, among other things, a subtle anti-Roman cryptogram, a communication in the coded language of a strange constructive/destructive miracle of Jesus story that the members of the Markan community could use, particularly in this story within the ministry of Jesus "gospel" form, without the Roman oppressors suspecting anything, even if they would seize and read a copy of the Markan Gospel.

Why was the name of the unclean spirit said to have been "Legion"? A legion was the name used for a major unit of troops in the Roman army, a unit of several thousands of armed men who would sweep through an area. Could the approximately 2,000 swine in this story have been a cryptic representation of the hated Roman military presence in Galilee and Judea during the period when Jesus was a significant Jewish religious and political figure? Could the members of the Markan community have desired to depict several thousands of Roman military forces as rushing demonically within swine bodies down a cliff to be drowned in the sea, depicting them doing this in a way that the members of the Markan community would understand, but which the Roman military leaders would suspect nothing? Even if Romans or the few of Jesus' fellow Jews who cooperated fully with the Romans might accuse the leaders of the Markan community of directing this story against them, the Markan followers of Jesus could say that they were not talking and writing about the Romans; they were writing about pigs! There were, after all, herds of swine in the area mentioned in this text, swine grubbing in the soil, growing to the size at which they could be herded into Roman ships and sent to Roman markets.

Although the interpretation and explanation of Mark 5:1-20 in the Church over the centuries has been that this text describes something that Jesus actually did and that it was a demonstration that the life of one man is far more valuable than is the commercial worth of 2,000 hogs, possibly the original purpose of the Mark 5:1-20 account when it was developed was somewhat along the lines described above.

As we turn from the possibly very subtle anti-Roman polemic in Mark 5:1-20 to what may have been somewhat subtle anti-Jewish polemic in the Mark 5:21-43 text appointed for us for next Sunday, we see that, among other purposes, this account was clearly demonstrating the superiority of the wonder-working Jesus the Risen Christ, the Lord of the Markan community, over the Jewish religious leadership of that time. According to this miracle story, the "daughter" of one of the "rulers of the synagogue" was at the point of death. This miracle story indicates that a ruler of a synagogue who is wise will come to Jesus with such a critical problem as the mortal illness of his daughter, a problem that presumably could not be handled by the religious leaders within the Jewish synagogue.

The inserted account of the woman who had the uncontrollable flow of blood to form a typical Markan "sandwich" account (Mark 5:21-24a / 24b-34 / 35-43) is an additional indication of the great healing potency ascribed to the Lord Jesus by his followers. It may also have been originally an indication of the way in which the members of the Markan community believed that there would continue to be a hemorrhaging of Jewish blood until each Jewish person would turn to Jesus the Risen Christ and touch his garment. We note the possible symbolism in the flow of the woman's blood for twelve years — a Jewish number symbol.

In Mark 5:36 the ruler of the synagogue was told not to continue to be afraid, but to believe constantly. The message intended is that if the elders of the synagogue would only be wise enough to do as this ruler of the synagogue had done, if only they would accept the superiority of Jesus the Risen Christ and come to him for help, setting aside their fears and believing in him, their "daughter," their offspring, would live again and be fed.

When we turn from this to our use of these texts within our life situation, we see that our proclamation should be that God, whom we believe raised Jesus from the dead, works through Jesus the Risen Christ to restore life and to provide salvation also to us and to all who believe in Jesus our Lord, who restores to life Jairus' daughter in Mark, Matthew, and Luke, the widow's son at Nain in Luke, and Lazarus in John. We note the progression to greater miracles of restoration to life in the later Gospels Luke and John, for in them the man had been dead for a day at Nain and another for several days at Bethany were restored to life. We have been called to study the Scriptures within their life situation contexts and then to proclaim them and their messages from God in our life situation contexts. Let us do this boldly!

2 Corinthians 8:7-15

It would be much more effective to read with the other texts appointed for next Sunday a different text from Paul rather than this one about the gathering of the offerings in Corinth to be taken to the followers of Jesus in Jerusalem. A much better choice for next Sunday would be 2 Corinthians 6:1b-2, a portion of our reading from the previous Sunday, in which Paul wrote, "We urge you not to receive this grace of God in vain. For it says (in Isaiah 49:8), 'At a favorable time I have heard your call and on the day of salvation I have come to rescue you.'" This choice would provide a text from Paul that is much more in accord with the theme of the other texts chosen for next Sunday.

2 Samuel 1:1, 17-27

We have here a high-quality elegy expressing grief by David over the death of Saul, and especially of Jonathan, in battle against the Philistines. In it, David is said to have experienced love from Jonathan that was wondrous, greater than the love that David had received from women!

Psalm 130

This psalm can be considered here to be an expression of grief over the death of loved ones, such as the grief expressed by David in his elegy over Saul and of Jonathan in the 2 Samuel text with which it is intended to be read in our lectionary. It is also a cry for help from God, for redemption for the individual, as well as for the nation, in situations of great distress.

Wisdom of Solomon 1:13-15; 2:23-24

It is interesting to note that, in the opinion of the writer of the Wisdom of Solomon document, God had created all things to be immortal. It was ungodly men who had invited death and the devil as friends, to relieve them of their agony. This provides for us another perspective of sin and death, the general topics for consideration next Sunday.

Lamentations 3:22-33

In dire distress the writer proclaims the steadfast love that the Lord God has for the person who is in need and waits for God to come, for God's mercies, God's faithfulness that will never end, and God's loving compassion. Certainly this is always appropriate for us to hear and to embrace.

Psalm 30

The faith in God expressed in this psalm is similar to what we read in Lamentations 3:22-33. It is a comfort to us at all times. It is good that his Psalm was selected for use four times within our three-year cycle of texts in the Revised Common Lectionary.

PROPER 9
ORDINARY TIME 14
SEVENTH SUNDAY AFTER PENTECOST

Sunday between July 3 and July 9 inclusive

Mark 6:1-13

Within the Gospel of Jesus Christ (Mark) this text is one of several in which the Jesus of history is close enough to the surface that some of his human limitations and frustrations are depicted. "He was not able to do any mighty deed there, except for placing his hands on a few people who were sick and healing them," we read in Mark 6:5. Here as elsewhere the Matthean and Lukan redactors removed the human limitations and frustrations of the Jesus of history from their editions of this account in Matthew by changing Mark's "He was not able" to "He did not do" and in Luke by omitting this portion of Mark's account entirely.

We have, therefore, an opportunity next Sunday to emphasize the human limitations and the frustrations of the Jesus of history as depicted in this Markan text, and by doing this to make the distinction for the congregation between the Jesus of history who had human limitations and frustrations and our Christ of faith whom we believe that God has raised from the dead and is one with God the Father and one with God as Holy Spirit within our Christian theology. This distinction makes it possible for us to identify closely with the human Jesus of history and at the same time to pray to and to worship the divine Christ of faith. Jesus as the Christ is for us, as Martin Luther wrote in his explanation of the second article of the Apostles' Creed, "true God, begotten of the Father from eternity, and true man, born of the Virgin Mary — our Lord." He is a carpenter given wisdom, a prophet rejected in his own land. It is such that we shall be able to proclaim him next Sunday, as depicted in this text.

Since our American Civil Religion Fourth of July celebration of the anniversary of the Declaration of Independence will occur during this week, it might be helpful to suggest that when our Declaration of Independence was declared the people in the thirteen colonies had many limitations of power and frustrations. Later, especially within our American public school system, many of these limitations and frustrations were edited out and largely removed much as the Matthean and Lukan redactors edited out most of the limitations and frustrations of the Jesus of history. We need, however, to be aware of the human limitations of each, since we ourselves have human limitations and since we are becoming aware that our nation has some serious limitations and frustrations as well.

2 Corinthians 12:2-10

Paul was well aware of his own human limitations and frustrations, as he indicated many times in his letters that we have in the New Testament. It is not surprising, therefore, that when he was somewhat "carried away" in his claims of spiritual experiences in his attempts to counteract the boastings of the "spirit-filled" Christian enthusiasts of Corinth, he was reminded of his human limitations, of his "thorn in the flesh" as he called it. All of us also have our human limitations, of which each of us is painfully aware. But God's word — especially God's word of forgiveness, of resurrection, and of salvation — is proclaimed nevertheless, for as Paul wrote (2 Corinthians 12:9), "The Lord has said to me, 'My grace is sufficient for you, for my power is perfected in your weakness.' " For us also, in spite of everything that may happen to us, God's grace is perfected in our weakness. God's grace is sufficient for us. Shall this not be the message that we must proclaim next Sunday? Shall not our message next Sunday reach its climax with this expression of the "Gospel According to Paul"?

2 Samuel 5:1-5, 9-10

In this text the young man David was anointed to be the king of Israel, to reign over all of Israel and Judah for 33 years. It is said that David increased more and more in strength, because the Lord, the God of power and might, was with him.

There are plenty of other texts, however, that are indications of the sins, weaknesses, and human limitations of David as king, texts that depict David as not being with the Lord, as a failure as a husband and as a father. These texts are reminders to us that all of us sin, in spite of the grace of God and the blessings of God. Together with the need that David had for the grace of God, our need for the grace of God continues and is multiplied by our sins.

Psalm 48

This psalm of celebration of the magnificence of Jerusalem and of its temple expresses the positive outlook of 2 Samuel 5:1-5, 9-10 at the beginning of the reign of David as king. We know, however, that just as David later failed and fell as a husband and as a father, so also the city of Jerusalem and its temple later would fall. The theme of human limitations stands, therefore, like a shadow over this text.

Ezekiel 2:1-5

In this segment of the fascinating "call" of Ezekiel accounts, the human limitations of the people of Israel are described in great detail. They are said to be a rebellious people, stubborn and impudent, refusing to hear the commandments of the Lord. Even the prophet Ezekiel, receiving and transmitting the Word of God, is portrayed as limited, as being a person whom most of the people will neither hear nor heed.

Psalm 123

In this brief lament, the psalmist is depicted as extremely limited in comparison to God. The psalmist is said to be like a humble male servant who is totally dependent upon the male servant's master and like a female servant who is in every way inferior to the woman who has complete control over her. The only thing that the psalmist can do is to beg for mercy from the Lord God. So also is it for us in our human condition today. We believe that our "salvation" is dependent upon the life, death, and resurrection of Jesus, the human who became divine for us.

PROPER 10
ORDINARY TIME 15
EIGHTH SUNDAY AFTER PENTECOST

Sunday between July 10 and July 16 inclusive

Mark 6:14-29

According to the portion of Mark that precedes this text, a portion that we used last Sunday, the proclamation of Jesus that his fellow Jews should ask God for forgiveness whenever they had cooperated fully with the oppressive Romans who were occupying the land of the Jews had been extended to Jesus' twelve disciples. That proclamation had been validated by the casting out of demons and the healing of many who were ill.

The text designated for our use next Sunday begins with the information that Herod Antipas, a son of Herod the Great, was told about the success that Jesus and his followers were having in proclaiming their message that soon the Lord God rather than the Romans and their supporters such as Herod would be ruling in Galilee and in Judea. Many of the Jews who had been cooperating with the Romans and with Herod Antipas were no longer doing this; the "demons" that had been in them when they submitted to the Romans and to Herod had been cast out. The "diseases" that they had when they had cooperated with the Romans and with Herod were being healed.

Herod Antipas is then portrayed as accepting the suggestion that some of his advisors made that the success that Jesus was having was an indication that Jesus was actually a reincarnation of John the Baptist, whom Herod had ordered that he be beheaded while being held in a dungeon as ordered by Herod. There is a tremendous message in these verses. Herod, even with the support of the Roman empire and its military power behind him, is portrayed here as weak and powerless to withstand God, who has the power to bring back to life John the Baptist, whom Herod had killed. The oppressed, who most of the time have little or nothing to laugh about, are given the pleasure of laughing at powerful rulers such as Herod, who in the presence of God and of Jesus the Risen Son of God are powerless. What follows in our text is a description of the despicable events that had occurred when the half-drunken Herod had foolishly made an almost unrestricted promise to the young daughter of Herod's hateful wife Herodias.

What are we called to proclaim when we use this text next Sunday? What guidelines for how we should live our lives are provided by this account? What from this text is applicable for us today? What is happening in our time and place that is somewhat similar to what is provided in this text? Where in this text are we and the people whom we serve? With whom in this text and in the text that precedes it are we identified? How is this text related to the other readings and to the psalms selected for our use next Sunday? The challenge to us is great. Yet it is to this that we have been called.

Ephesians 1:3-14

In the Greek New Testament these twelve verses are all presented in one single sentence, a magnificent Greek sentence in which the principal verb of the sentence is implied but not expressed. The verb implied is the indicative or the imperative form of the verb "to be." Blessed is the God and Father of our Lord Jesus Christ, or May the God and Father of our Lord Jesus Christ be blessed! When we translate the rest of this Greek sentence into English, we must break it up into at least six English sentences for our readers.

In order to connect this text with the Mark 6:14-29 Gospel account, we may see that this text is a way, our way of responding with a blessing to God, who is to be blessed for being active in our history, confounding the powerful and providing a meaningful life now and eternally for us. Indeed, we want to bless God and bless God as God is revealed in Jesus the Risen Christ in our lives.

2 Samuel 6:1-5, 12b-19

The still youthful King David is presented here as celebrating in a sort of liturgical dance as he brings the sacred ark of the covenant into the city of Jerusalem, a city that his soldiers have conquered. While David celebrates and provides burnt offerings and peace offerings to the Lord, David's wife Michal, the daughter of Saul, despises David. Since the power of God is thought to be concentrated in the ark, symbolically David is bringing the power and the presence of God into the new capital city of the developing nation. David is presented in a positive light in this text, Michal in a negative one. What a difference it might have made had David continued to bless and to celebrate the power and presence of God rather than to turn from God as David later does. Was Michal despising what David was doing, or what David would soon be doing? How do we celebrate and respond to the power and to the presence of God as we attempt to bring that power and that presence into our lives?

Psalm 24

I personally have precious memories of the use of this psalm when I was very young. Before we would go to our various Sunday school classes, the Sunday school superintendent would lead all of us in a brief opening worship. Psalm 24 was one of the psalms used on alternate Sunday mornings in this way in order to prepare us for our study of the Bible within our various age groups.

In ancient Israel, this psalm was most likely one of several that were used as the people together came into the holy place of study, instruction, and worship. If we use this psalm next Sunday, how can we use it most effectively and creatively as we as a congregation enter into our study and worship of God? We do not always have to do the same things, and we should not always do things in the same way each Sunday that we come together. What we do and how we worship should be guided by the texts and what is included in the texts selected for our use in our study and in our worship. If we use this psalm next Sunday, it should be used as in a way a "liturgical dance" as our choirs and other worship leaders enter the sanctuary.

Amos 7:7-15

There is a sharp contrast between the condemnation in this text of the economic, political, social, and religious practices of the people in Bethel in the Northern Kingdom, Israel, and the message of peace and blessing from God on the people to whom Psalm 85:8-13 is presented. The proclamation in Psalm 85 is good news to the people who turn back to God; the proclamation in Amos 7:7-15 is bad news to those who have turned their backs to God.

Psalm 85:8-13

Amos 7:7-15 is directed against people who are like Herod Antipas and those who were with him. Psalm 85:8-13 is provided for the people who are like John the Baptist, the Jesus of history, and followers of Jesus who turn toward serving only the Lord God. We are called to be like the people in ancient Israel for whom Psalm 85 was prepared, to be like John the Baptist, like Jesus and like those who were following him. We are not to be like those in Bethel in the Northern Kingdom, nor like Herod Antipas and those around him. This we must proclaim.

PROPER 11
ORDINARY TIME 16
NINTH SUNDAY AFTER PENTECOST

Sunday between July 17 and July 23 inclusive

Mark 6:30-34, 53-56

These verses have preserved in summary fashion typical events and occurrences during the time when the Jesus of history was serving so well in meeting the needs of large numbers of his own Jewish people. In many ways he was like a shepherd for them, and that shepherd was later killed by the enemy (the Roman governor Pontius Pilate and the Roman occupational forces in Jerusalem). For us as Christians, that shepherd Jesus perceived as the Risen Christ lives as our Lord and Savior, one with God forever. When we gladly share Jesus the Risen Christ with persons and groups of people who are not with us and when we offer the joys and gifts of Jesus as the "Good Shepherd" with them, many of them join with us in the Church, the "Body of Christ."

Ephesians 2:11-22

In this text the writer was commenting on and celebrating the coming together during the previous decades of Jewish background followers of Jesus with the growing and by that time far larger number of non-Jewish background followers of Jesus. That trend and those demographics accelerated and continued after that time. After Jesus had been crucified by the Romans, when many followers of Jesus moved from their admiration of the Jesus of history to adulation, veneration, and deification of Jesus as the Risen Christ, very few Jews identified with the groups of followers of Jesus who proclaimed him as the Son of God, and even as God the Son.

Increasing numbers of people who were not of Jewish background, however, were attracted to and identified with various groups of followers of Jesus who perceived him as their Risen Christ and Lord, groups that offered a religion with an impressive Savior figure, hope for the physical resurrection and a glorious eternal life for each person, good ethical teachings, and no requirements of men having to be circumcised and of families having to follow Jewish dietary restrictions. New people continue to be added to the Church today when we offer these same benefits.

2 Samuel 7:1-14a

This text in which the promise of God to build a house, a dynasty of descendants of King David who will reign forever, was a source of reassurance for Israelites until the day when the city of Jerusalem and the temple in it were destroyed by the Babylonians. After that, this promise became problematic for Israelites and remained problematic for Jews for whom, obviously, there was no kingdom, no independent nation, and no throne with a descendant of David sitting on it.

Although there is no evidence that the Jesus of history had aspirations or ambitions or any desires of becoming a political ruler over a revived political nation Israel, some of the followers of Jesus, after they came to believe that Jesus who had been crucified by the Romans had become the Risen Christ their Lord, developed the idea that Jesus' ancestry could be traced back to King David and that, as the Risen Christ, Jesus was now their king, the king over a "New Israel," one of their favorite names for the Church. Even today, we as Christians, especially during our Advent and Christmas seasons, proclaim Jesus as the Son of David, our King, and we invite others to join with us in accepting and in proclaiming Jesus the Risen Christ as King.

Psalm 89:20-37

The psalmist poetically depicts in Psalm 89 the everlasting covenant that is presented in 2 Samuel 7:1-14a as having been made by God with David. The intention in this psalm is to remind God of that covenant and to urge God to deliver the king from his powerful enemies in accordance with that covenant.

How do we perceive the "New Covenant" that we believe that God through Jesus the Risen Christ has made with us? Do we think that because we have entered into the "New Covenant" with God as Christians we will always be successful in everything that we do? What promises with regard to this "New Covenant" do we make to potential new members of this "New Covenant"?

Jeremiah 23:1-6

The Jeremiah tradition in Jeremiah 23:1-6 expresses total dissatisfaction with the leadership of the Israelite kingdoms during the final years of Israel's existence as a nation (just prior to 721 BCE) and the last few years of Judah's national life (just prior to 586 BCE). The political and religious leaders of Israel and of Judah are blamed for the destruction of Samaria and of Jerusalem and for the scattering of the Israelite people.

The historical Jeremiah, whose life influenced the Jeremiah traditions, functioned as a "peripheral" prophet outside the royal court circles, but still within Jerusalem. Jeremiah was highly critical of the political and religious leadership in Jerusalem. Aware of the virtually complete annihilation of the people of the Northern Kingdom Israel who had fought against the mighty armies of the great world power Assyria, Jeremiah used every means at his disposal to try to prevent the Southern Kingdom Judah from forming an alliance with Egypt and rebelling against the military power of the Mesopotamian Babylonian empire, the great world power of the time of Jeremiah. Apparently Jeremiah thought that if the Southern Kingdom would rely upon Egypt for military support and revolt against Babylonia, the Southern Kingdom would suffer the same fate that the Northern Kingdom had experienced a century and a half earlier, and the remaining inhabitants of Jerusalem would perish from the earth.

When the political leaders in Jerusalem did rebel against Babylonia, and when the city was destroyed and much of its population had been deported to Babylonia, and only a small remnant remained with an Israelite consciousness, partly in Babylonia, partly in decimated Judah, and partly in Egypt, Jeremiah and his disciples in Egypt and in Judah longed for the time to come when the Lord God would gather remnants of the people from these various places and bring them back to Jerusalem. They longed for the time when the Lord God would again cause them to be fruitful and to multiply under new political and religious leadership that would care for them so well that none of them would be missing. In Jeremiah 23:5-6 the tradition becomes even more specific, looking forward to the time when a descendant within the lineage of David would be raised up by the Lord God as a new shoot from the Davidic stump, a new branch on the Davidic family tree, one who would rule wisely and cause justice and righteousness to flourish within the land. This new king who was anticipated is even given a symbolic name, "The Lord is our righteousness," in order to do everything that a prophetic tradition could do to cause this to occur.

What we see in this text is, of course, one of the many Messianic expectations through which the Israelites would express their hopes that the Lord God would act decisively to restore their nation to independence, peace, and prosperity. These texts do not refer specifically to Jesus, the Jewish religious and political figure of the first century of the common era who had no intention of encouraging military

247

means to remove the Roman occupation forces from Galilee and Judea, even though he was crucified by order of the Roman governor in Jerusalem as a person who was giving hope for freedom from Roman rule to his fellow oppressed Jews.

Our Christian tradition as it developed claimed that Jesus was and is the Christ (Messiah) through whom God acted and acts to bring peace, justice, and righteousness not to the Jews as such but to the world. Our Christian tradition has every right to make this claim. With all due respect, however, we must observe that for us as Christian people, just as for the Jews who have survived with us to our time, the establishment of peace, justice, and righteousness is still a future hope. It is a future hope for which Jews, Christians, Muslims, in fact, for which all people of the world still wait. There are moments when we realize that we should work together and wait together, rising above our selfish interests and our cherished differences. For more on this subject, with special reference to the Middle East, see my book, *Blessed to Be a Blessing to Each Other: Jews, Muslims, and Christians as Children of Abraham in the Middle East* (Lima, Ohio: Fairway Press, Revised edition, 2010).

Psalm 23

Within the context of this particular series of texts, we should probably understand Psalm 23 corporately rather than individually and read it together in our congregation next Sunday changing the singular pronouns "I," "my," and "me" to "we," "our," and "us." Psalm 23 is a beautiful expression of our hope that someday the Lord God will provide for all of us (especially for all Jews, Christians, and Muslims, but not in any way limited to these three groups) perfect peace and security and that the Lord God will protect and feed all of us forever. The shepherd analogy continues to be unsurpassed, even during this age of high technology.

PROPER 12
ORDINARY TIME 17
TENTH SUNDAY AFTER PENTECOST

Sunday between July 24 and July 30 inclusive

John 6:1-21

This text in which Jesus is portrayed as feeding 5,000 men with five barley loaves and two fish and as walking on the water of the Sea of Galilee begins a section in which the Fourth Gospel follows the pattern established in Mark (compare John 6:1-25 to Mark 6:32-56) more closely and for a more lengthy time than anywhere else prior to the extended Passion of Jesus account that begins with Mark 11:1 and John 12:12. Various possible reasons for the similarities that we see between the First and the Fourth Gospels include the following:

1) The persons who wrote both Gospels were inspired by God in a more similar way at some points in their writings than in others.

2) The writers of both Gospels utilized a similar strand of written and oral materials in some places more than in others.

3) The writers of the Fourth Gospel had access to a brief early edition of Mark that contained the series of texts that begin with Mark 6:32 and Mark 11:1, and from this brief early edition of Mark the more fully developed Markan Gospel and the more fully developed Johannine Gospel were formed.

4) The writers of the Fourth Gospel had access to a rather fully developed Markan Gospel (and perhaps to early editions of Matthew and of Luke as well) but chose to use only a few portions of the Synoptic material because they preferred to present their message in their own way.

Regardless of which of the reasons outlined above appears to explain the similarities here most satisfactorily, in most places the Fourth Gospel was developed quite differently from the development of the Synoptics, and the Fourth Gospel was not substantially modified to make it conform closely to the Gospels According to Mark, Matthew, and Luke at a later date when people within the Fourth Gospel tradition obviously had access to fully developed copies of the Synoptics. There is much evidence from a careful comparison of the texts of the Four Gospels to indicate that the writers of the Fourth Gospel chose to develop their account quite differently from the way that those within the Synoptic Gospels tradition had done. This makes it even more noteworthy that here in John 6 the Johannine tradition did not depart extensively from the Synoptic pattern.

Where there are differences between Markan and the Johannine accounts of the feeding of the 5,000, the Fourth Gospel tradition adds that the Passover feast of the Jews was near (John 6:4), that Jesus went up on the mountain (John 6:3), that Jesus knew what he would do to provide food for the multitude (John 6:6), specific names of the disciples (Philip in John 6:5, 7 and Andrew and Simon Peter in John 6:8), that Jesus, having given thanks, distributed the loaves to the multitude (John 6:11), and that, since Jesus knew that the people were planning to come to seize him in order to make him their king, he withdrew to the mountain by himself alone (John 6:15). Many of these additions bring the Johannine account much closer to the covenant ratification ceremonies depicted in Exodus 24:1-18 than is the Markan account.

Ephesians 3:14-21

This Pauline prayer intended for some early Christian audience during the second half of the first century is appropriate also for us today. We are in need of "the love of

Christ that surpasses all human knowledge" just as much as the people were for whom this document was first written.

The prayer is concluded with a model doxology that deserves more widespread use: "And to God who is able to do infinitely more than all that we ask or think through the power that God has activated within us, to God be glory in the church and in Christ Jesus for all generations forever and ever. So let it be!"

2 Kings 4:42-44

This text is a brief story about a man bringing twenty barley loaves and other grain in a sack to Elisha. Although the man considered the food that he had brought to be very inadequate to feed the 100 men who were there and were hungry, Elisha commanded that the loaves be used to feed the men, saying that the Lord has said that they shall eat and there will be some left. They ate and, as had been said by the Lord, they were filled and had some bread left. Since this account is not well-known by most Christians, it is good that it is designated at this place in our lectionary to be read as the First Reading together with the Johannine account of Jesus feeding the 5,000. Although this 2 Kings 4:42-44 account is not well-known in the Church during our time, it was almost certainly known to the Markan writer and community when the account about Jesus feeding the 5,000 was recorded in what is for us Mark 6:30-44 and was used also in the later Gospels According to Matthew, Luke, and John.

Psalm 145:10-18

In this beautiful psalm that is so important in Jewish daily devotional piety even today we read that the Lord gives food to all who look to the Lord. The psalmist wrote here that the Lord satisfies the desire of every living thing, that the Lord has compassion over everything that the Lord has made, and that the Lord keeps the covenant. This psalm has many points of contact with the John 6:1-15 and the 2 Kings 4:42-44 texts selected for our use next Sunday. Psalm 145 is also especially precious to me personally, because my father used a paraphrase of portions of it as one of his table prayers in our family when I was a child. Much later, when I was an overnight guest in the apartment of Conservative Jewish Rabbi/Dr. Sol Bernards and his wife Ruth, Sol Bernards used Psalm 145 within his table prayers before we ate our evening meal together.

2 Samuel 11:1-15

It seems to me that for next Sunday the semi-continuous selections of 2 Samuel 11:1-15 and with that text Psalm 14 are much less edifying than are the 2 Kings 4:42-44 and Psalm 145:10-18 selections considered above. Nevertheless, the story about King David's adultery and his order to his field general Joab that are in this 2 Samuel 11:1-15 account and in the semi-continuous reading of the continuation of the story of 2 Samuel 11:26—12:13a on the following Sunday are texts that we should have to consider. These texts are realistic portrayals that people, including people who have very important and powerful positions, often attempt to cover up one sin by committing another. When that happens, many people, including the sinner, are hurt terribly.

Psalm 14

The "fool" depicted in this psalm is not merely ignorant and "brainless." The fool here is morally corrupt and despicable. It is easy to see the reason that Psalm 14 is paired here with the account in 2 Samuel 11:1-15 about King David's sin with Bathsheba and David's unsuccessful attempt to cover up his sin of adultery with the sin of ordering events that will result in the death of Bathsheba's husband, the valiant Uriah the Hittite, a gallant hero in David's army.

PROPER 13
ORDINARY TIME 18
ELEVENTH SUNDAY AFTER PENTECOST

Sunday between July 31 and August 6 inclusive

Exodus 16:2-4, 9-15

In story form this account is a testimony that the Lord provides and has provided "bread from heaven" for the people in response to their call for food. Moses and Aaron are depicted as silent in the face of the murmuring of the people against them. The Lord does not seem to object to the complaints of the people. Instead, the impression is given that the Lord was actually waiting with the bread from heaven and with the quail so that they could be provided whenever the people would need them. It is said that the Lord would provide the bread and the quail so that the people would survive in the desolate wilderness and realize that it was the Lord who had brought them out of the land of Egypt (Exodus 16:6, 12), that they might see the glory of the Lord (Exodus 16:7), and so that the Lord would test them to see whether they would conduct themselves in accordance with the Torah, whether they would be capable of following the commandments of the Lord (Exodus 16:4). There was to be no doubt that the bread had been provided by the Lord; it was not something that the people themselves had earned. The people had merely been in need and had expressed their need, even though it had been done in a childish manner. The bread and the quail had been a gift of the unmerited grace of the Lord God.

Psalm 78:23-29

Here within an extended psalm in which many mighty deeds of the Lord God in behalf of the people are recited, the rather prosaic story form of Exodus 16 is expressed poetically.

Here in this psalm it is said that the Lord "commanded the skies," and "opened the doors of heaven." The Lord "rained upon them manna to eat," and "provided the grain of heaven," "the bread of the angels." The Lord "rained flesh upon them like dust," sent "winged birds as numerous as the sands of the seashores." The people "ate and were filled," for the Lord "gave them what they craved." Within this segment of Psalm 78 there is no hint of complaint or disgust on the part of either the Lord or of the people.

John 6:24-35

This text is a short commentary on the Exodus 16 and Psalm 78 texts that was developed in John 6 into an extended dialogue of reflection over the same feeding of the multitude story that had been incorporated into the Mark 6 account. Johannine studies during the past century have helped us to see that the extended dialogue in John 6 is also in many ways a recapitulation of the story of the development and experiences of the Johannine community, of its increasingly high Christology, its struggles with Jewish groups, and its determination of its own destiny. The John 6:24-35 text, therefore, is best understood as much more autobiographical of the Johannine community than it is biographical about Jesus.

In retrospect, we may wish that the extended commentary on Exodus 16, the story of the development of the Johannine community and of its increasingly high Christology would have been done without the anti-Jewish polemic that is included in our gospel text for next Sunday. The anti-Jewish polemic in John 6:24-35 becomes more intense and bitter later in the John 6 dialogue where the Jews are represented as murmuring against the Johannine Jesus because he claims to be "the bread of life" and they do not believe in him. The anti-Jewish polemic becomes even more intense and bitter in chapters 7-9 in the Gospel According to John, especially within John 8.

We are called to proclaim next Sunday that Jesus is indeed "the true bread from heaven," the "bread of life," and to declare that whoever comes to Jesus will never hunger and whoever believes in Jesus will never thirst. At the same time, we realize, however, that in spite of the activities of Jesus during the first century of the common era and in spite of our faith in God and in Jesus as the Risen Christ, we and others still become hungry, and we still become thirsty. Millions of people each year die after suffering from hunger and thirst. The life that is provided is eternal life, at least within the context of this Fourth Gospel. We see also that Christian hymns such as "O Bread of Life from Heaven" are to John 6:24-35 what Psalm 78:23-29 is to Exodus 16:2-4, 9-15. At the same time, we who are relatively well fed have a responsibility that is much greater than the responsibility of those who developed our biblical traditions, a responsibility to work to develop food sources and to oppose those whose greed and oppression cause so many people in our time to suffer and to die because of lack of food and of good water to drink.

Ephesians 4:1-16

The two groups of people, that is, the followers of Jesus who were of Jewish background and followers of Jesus who were of non-Jewish background, whose coming together with one Lord, one faith, and one baptism into the one "body of Christ" is celebrated and encouraged in Ephesians 4:1-16, are not the two predominant groups in the current composition of the Church. In our life situation, however, there are other groups that should be brought together more closely within the Church. It is our calling to identify the groups within our life setting and to apply this text to our situation. Unity of the Spirit of God and much greater cooperation and fellowship within the Church are essential without, however, demanding uniformity and conformity where respect for diversity is needed.

2 Samuel 11:26—12:13a

The semi-continuous reading of the accounts of the David and Bathsheba relationship continues in this text with the "mourning" of Bathsheba for her valiant husband Uriah, David "graciously" taking Bathsheba as one of his wives, and Nathan the prophet adroitly confronting David with the parable of the one little ewe lamb. The powerful king is maneuvered into confessing the magnitude of his sins.

Psalm 51:1-12

This widely used call upon God for mercy and forgiveness is traditionally associated with what David may have said after the events portrayed in the 2 Samuel 11-12 texts when David and Bathsheba's relationship became public knowledge. We should note that although David is presented in 2 Samuel 12:13 as having said to Nathan, "I have sinned against the Lord," and although in Psalm 51:4 the sinner (David or every one of us) as saying to God "against you and you only have I sinned," David in the 2 Samuel 11-12 account sinned first against the valiant warrior Uriah, and David and/or each of us sin against other people and at the same time ultimately against God. In our didactical and in our homiletical use of this David and Bathsheba account this should be discussed and reflected upon.

PROPER 14
ORDINARY TIME 19
TWELFTH SUNDAY AFTER PENTECOST

Sunday between August 7 and August 13 inclusive

John 6:35, 41-51

Within the similarities and differences between this account in John 6:35, 41-51 and the Mark 6:1-6a account describing activities of Jesus in his hometown, we can see the distinction between "the Jesus of history" and "the Christ of faith." In the Mark 6 account there is still a recollection of Jesus, the Jesus of history, as a son of Joseph, as a first-century Jewish religious and political figure whose father Joseph and mother Mary had been known to other Jews in the village of Nazareth. In John 6:35, 41-51, however, and throughout the Fourth Gospel, Jesus is the Christ of faith, the Son of God who is said to have pre-existed before the foundation of the world was laid, who was the Logos, the "Word" by which the world was called into being. As the Christ of faith in John 6, Jesus is presented as having an exclusivistic claim to God as Father, as one who comes from God and has seen God. It is affirmed that no one can come to Jesus as the Christ unless God the Father draws that person to Jesus as the Christ, and that Jesus as the Christ of faith will raise such a person from the dead on the last day. The person who "eats" of this "bread from heaven" will not die. Jesus the Christ as this "bread from heaven" is far superior to the manna that the fathers of the first-century Jews had eaten in the wilderness, for although they ate they still died. According to John 6, the bread that the Johannine Jesus as the Christ of faith will give for the life of the world is the flesh of the Christ of faith, the Lamb of God who in Johannine terms "takes away the sin of the world."

When this John 6:35, 41-51 text is read and when it forms the primary basis for the worship service, we have an obligation to the people of the congregations in which we serve to say something about the theological development that occurred between perceiving Jesus as the Jesus of history, one among several sons of Joseph and his wife Mary, and Jesus as the Christ of faith, the only-begotten Son of God. If we do not indicate this development and show that we are aware of this distinction, we shall be propagating the longstanding and non-productive anti-Jewish polemic that is associated with this text. If we do not share some of our understanding of this theological development and of this distinction in perceptions of Jesus, we shall simply be promulgating supersessionistic anti-Jewish polemic without helping the thinking people within the congregations in which we serve to come to a better understanding of the process in the development of their Christian religion as the impact that the Jesus of history had made on some of his followers was shaped by the inspiration of God into belief in Jesus as the Christ of faith, one with God, through whom salvation and eternal life is offered to all of us.

Ephesians 4:25—5:2

Here in Ephesians 4:25—5:2 we have the *parenesis*, the guidelines of how we should respond to the proclamation that Jesus as the Christ provides eternal life for us. As among those who as the "Body of Christ" are "in Christ," we should put aside all bitterness, anger, and slander and replace them with kindness and forgiveness. Then we will not grieve the Holy Spirit of God. We are exhorted to be imitators of God and to conduct ourselves in a life that is characterized by love, just as Christ loved us and gave himself for us as a fragrant offering and sacrifice to God. We see that by the time that this section of the epistle "to the Ephesians" was written much reflection had occurred within the thoughts of some of the followers of Jesus about the significance of Jesus' life, of his death, and of his resurrection as the Christ of faith. In some ways this Ephesians 4:25—5:2 text is similar to that of the Fourth Gospel and of the Epistle to the Hebrews, all of which may stem from approximately the same period in the development of the early Church.

1 Kings 19:4-8

The food that the Lord provided for Elijah in this Elijah story was so nutritious that it sustained Elijah during his journey of forty days and forty nights to the mountain of God at Horeb. It is said that Elijah would have preferred to die under the broom tree, but the Lord would not permit that to occur. Instead, the Lord permitted Elijah only to sleep, and then through the intermediary of an angel in this story twice touched him and told him to eat the freshly baked cake and the jar of water provided for him so that he would be strengthened. This story about Elijah obviously has a message for us also in our discouragement and in our need.

Psalm 34:1-8

This Individual Hymn of Praise and Thanksgiving is appropriately used in conjunction with the Elijah story in 1 Kings 19:4-8. It is a poetic, hymnic rendition of the Elijah story situation. The psalmist cried unto the Lord, and the Lord heard the psalmist. The angel of the Lord is said to camp around those who fear the Lord in order to deliver them. "O taste and see that the Lord is good" can be understood metaphorically, or almost literally with reference to the freshly baked cakes of the Elijah story in 1 Kings 19:4-8 or of the bread and wine of the Christian Eucharist.

2 Samuel 18:5-9, 15, 31-33

The situation depicted here is most understandable to those who have participated in war and battle conditions in which the combatants are conditioned to do everything possible to destroy the enemy and to preserve one's own life and the lives of one's buddies. David as king confounds his general and the men who are engaged in the horrible conditions of battle in behalf of David and of the nation in his desire to spare the life of his own son Absalom who has rebelled against David. We are torn as we read and hear this story between identification with David as a father trying to save his son from death and with Joab and the soldiers under Joab's command who are being killed or injured because of the horrible civil war that was caused by David and by David's son. Perhaps this text should be used in high school and adult Bible study sessions rather than in a worship setting, so that we will be able to share and discuss our feelings. The story provides a good opportunity for those who have been involved in the horrors of military combat to talk within a supportive congregational setting about their experiences and their feelings.

Psalm 130

Out of the depths of despair the psalmist cries for help from the Lord. The psalmist waits for the Lord to come, for the Lord to rescue the psalmist and to rescue the people of Israel. Although the situation depicted in this prayer is not specifically a situation of war and of the horrible conditions endured during battle conditions, the psalm certainly can be associated with war, as it is when the reading of this psalm is linked to the 2 Samuel 18:5-9, 15, 31-33 reading.

PROPER 15
ORDINARY TIME 20
THIRTEENTH SUNDAY AFTER PENTECOST

Sunday between August 14 and August 20 inclusive

John 6:51-58

This text selection continues to advance the claims of the Johannine Jesus to be the true bread from heaven that is incorporated into the earlier portions of John 6. In some congregations and denominations the words in John 6:53, "Jesus said to them, 'If you do not eat the flesh of the Son of man and drink his blood, you do not have life in yourselves,'" have been interpreted legalistically, resulting in the denial of Christian funeral services to persons who have not participated in the Eucharistic action as frequently as had been stipulated by the leadership of the congregation or by the synod of which the congregation is a component. Such legalism has been applied without the recognition that this kind of legalism with regard to John 6:53, if consistently applied, would require also the denial of a Christian funeral for children who die before they attain the age at which the congregation and synod would permit them to participate in the Eucharist.

Obviously, the words of the Johannine Jesus in this text should not be applied legalistically, nor should they be interpreted only literally. If they are interpreted literally, we would be proclaiming to the world that we as Christians are indeed cannibals. It should be recalled that it was for this reason that the charge of cannibalism was leveled against followers of Jesus by some outsiders early within the history of the Church.

This text provides for us a non-Pauline opportunity to emphasize the concept of the Real Presence of Christ in the Eucharist and to show how the Real Presence terminology has been helpful in ecumenical discussions. We can also draw upon elaborations of the Real Presence of Christ concept within books, papers, and articles published within recent years that describe the Eucharistic action as a reactualization of the life, death, and resurrection of our Lord. There is no longer the necessity for Lutheran Christians and for Christians who are in any other Christian group to think and to claim that they alone have the "correct" understanding and interpretation of the words of John 6:51-58 and of related texts. It should be sufficient to state that many Christians have found and are finding the Real Presence terminology to be helpful, meaningful, and desirable within the Church and fully in accord with texts such as John 6:56, "The one who eats my flesh and drinks my blood abides in me, and I abide in that person."

Ephesians 5:15-20

This brief text provides considerable insight into the conduct and lifestyle expected of Christians during the last decade of the first century. There is no specific mention of the impending parousia of Jesus, but the days are described as evil, because persecution and the threat of persecution by the Romans continues. The followers of Jesus then and now are encouraged to share in the singing of psalms, hymns, and spiritual songs, to make melody to the Lord with their entire being, and to give thanks to God for everything, always in the name of our Lord Jesus Christ. We can hardly improve on this, but we can emphasize the beauty of this type of conduct and lifestyle.

Proverbs 9:1-6

It is interesting to see in this text that the Wisdom of God personified invites even those who are simple to come to her feast, to eat of her bread, and to drink from the wine that she has prepared for them. By the juxtaposition of the texts selected for our use next Sunday, we are urged to perceive that the Wisdom personification of God in the Israelite literature and the Johannine Jesus personification of God in the Fourth Gospel of the Christian literature in similar ways invite people to come to them and to partake of their treasures.

It is difficult to think about the use of these texts in anything other than in a Eucharistic service in which there will be at least some expression of fellowship, of oneness within the Church as the Body of Christ in the world.

Psalm 34:9-14

Long before the development of the Fourth Gospel, an Israelite psalmist sang this song that became so popular that it became one of the top 150 for the Jews who hundreds of years later canonized the Psalter. The psalmist proclaimed that those who seek the Lord and respect the Lord lack nothing that is important in their lives. The psalmist sang that the Lord looks favorably upon people who are just and fair in their relationships with each other and who not only seek peace but also pursue it.

We see how similar the expressions of faith in Psalm 34:9-14 are to the words of Ephesians 5:15-20. According to these texts, adequate faith and right living are both important for happiness, now and forever.

1 Kings 2:10-12; 3:3-14

The combination of adequate faith and right living expressed in Ephesians 5:15-20 and in Psalm 34:9-14 is evident in 1 Kings 2:10-12 and 3:3-14. Appearing in a dream to Solomon soon after Solomon had been acclaimed as king, the Lord asks Solomon what he wants to receive from the Lord. Solomon asks for an understanding mind to govern the people wisely. The Lord provides such a mind for Solomon in great abundance and, in addition, gives to Solomon riches and honor and a long life.

Can we proclaim this without also being aware and sharing with our congregations that in later chapters of 1 Kings, Solomon is depicted as falling short of the wisdom and understanding given to him by God? Can it be possible then or now for political leaders to have great power and, when they have that, not fall short of the wisdom and understanding given to them by God? We are intrigued to think that it might be possible, especially since there have been a few people who have had such power and have not significantly fallen short of the wisdom and understanding given to them by God. What examples of this can we identify?

Psalm 111

May the beautiful words of this hymn of praise to the Lord be our words and the words of our religious and political leaders, not only of ours but also of the religious and political leaders of all other people throughout the world, now and forever!

PROPER 16
ORDINARY TIME 21
FOURTEENTH SUNDAY AFTER PENTECOST

Sunday between August 21 and 27 inclusive

John 6:56-69

In this segment of the John 6 "bread from heaven" discourse, there is no fully developed covenant and naturalization ceremony comparable to what we see in Joshua 24. This is not surprising, since Christianity did not become a civil religion, a state religion, the religion accepted and imposed upon all who live in the territory controlled by a state or nation until the fourth century — nearly two and one half centuries after the composition of this text. There is, however, a call for a decision in the words of the Johannine Jesus, "Do you also wish to go away?" The Greek construction of the negative and the indicative mood indicates that a negative answer to Jesus' question is expected. The phrase in John 6:67 could be translated into English as "Perhaps you also wish to go away?" with an emphatic "No!" being expected, or "You do not wish to go away also, do you?"

Although it is difficult to decide which translation into English is the most satisfactory, any exposition of this text should include an explanation that the Greek construction indicates that a negative answer is expected. The particular translation that we make or use will have a heavy impact on how Jesus is perceived in this text. (Ideally, we should all learn Greek and not translate this sentence at all!) In Greek, English, or any other language, the inflection of the voice as John 6:67 is read is crucial. In this particular setting in the Fourth Gospel, with the always-confident Johannine Jesus as the speaker, possibly the best translation we could make would be to render John 6:67 as an affirmation, "Perhaps you also wish to go away," rather than as a question. (The

Johannine Jesus is presented as knowing everything and has no need to ask anyone for information.)

At any rate, Peter's response is decisive. "No! There is no one else, Lord, to whom we can go! You have the words of eternal life! And we have decided to believe and to accept that you are the Holy One of God!"

Ephesians 6:10-20

The author of Ephesians 6:10-20 is also very decisive, urging those who read or hear this text to be empowered with the strength of the Lord. They are instructed to put on the full armor of God that includes truth as a belt around their waist, righteousness as a breastplate to protect their heart and lungs, the gospel of peace as sandals for their feet, faith in God as their shield, salvation as their helmet, and the Spirit, which is the Word of God, as their sword. Thus armed, they are to be engaged in every situation in earnest prayer and supplication in the Spirit of God.

Joshua 24:1-2a, 14-18

The use of Joshua 24:1-2a, 14-18 with John 6:56-69 is an indication that those who selected our Series B texts for next Sunday desired that our emphasis this coming weekend should be on a call for a decision. Within this Joshua 24:1-2a, 14-18 text there is a call for a decision to serve the Lord God as the Israelites perceived the Lord God. In John 6:56-69 it is a call to believe in and to remain with the Lord Jesus. Each of these two texts is in capsule form representative of decisions to be made for people to join into what was in each instance a relatively new religion.

Joshua 24:1-2a, 14-18 is evidence that the Israelite religion and the Israelite nation were comprised of people who at an earlier time had worshiped other lords and gods (or had worshiped God by other names). After the heads of families and tribal groups had been asked to listen to a public recital of the ways in which the Lord God of the Israelites had rescued the forefathers of the first Israelites from bondage in Egypt, led them in the wilderness, and established their children in the land of Canaan, these heads of families and of tribal groups were required to renounce their allegiance to other gods and to other nations and to accept the Lord God of Israel as their Lord and their God in this land. This text in Joshua 24 is an indication that a clear and unambiguous decision of allegiance to the Lord God of Israel and a renunciation of loyalty to other gods and nations was demanded each time this covenant ceremony was utilized. It is likely that this covenant ceremony was repeated in some form whenever new groups from related tribes entered the land and were incorporated into the Israelite nation and its religion. We see here, therefore, a glimpse of the development of the national, civil religion of Israel in its land and of the questions asked during the periodic ceremonies of naturalization of new groups of people as they settled within the borders of the land and of the covenant renewal for those who were already participants in the land. The ceremonies that we have developed and use when we receive new persons into our nation and into our congregations are similar to these.

Psalm 34:15-22

This concluding portion of the Psalm 34 Individual Hymn of Praise forms a most fitting concluding statement of faith. It is a beautiful expression of what we believe that the Lord does for those who have right relationships with God and with other people. Since Psalm 34:15-22 is in many respects a creedal statement, it can best be used as a creedal statement in our worship services, which for many of us usually comes after the sermon or homily.

It would be appropriate and effective to schedule the beginning of a church membership class, or the conclusion of such a class and a ceremony of reception into membership of a group of persons on the day when this series of texts is used, and/or when there is a service of baptism of adults.

1 Kings 8:(1, 6, 10-11) 22-30, 41-43

In 1 Kings 8 we have a depiction of the bringing of the ark of the covenant into the temple that King Solomon had designed and authorized and of the dedication of the temple with appropriate ceremonies and speeches. What do we have in our nation and in our congregations that is somewhat comparable to this? Would it be feasible to have a dramatic reenactment of this text in some way within our worship services when this text is used? Perhaps a youth or adult Bible study group within the congregation could prepare and share a dramatic reenactment of this text for the congregation.

Psalm 84

This psalm was obviously selected for use with the 1 Kings 8 text because in this psalm the temple is praised and great appreciation for the experiences of the worshiper within the temple is expressed. Even the sparrows and the barn swallows that build their nests, hatch, and feed their young have a home in the place where the Lord dwells and is worshiped. What experiences that we have had in our church buildings can others and we share when this text is read?

PROPER 17
ORDINARY TIME 22
FIFTEENTH SUNDAY AFTER PENTECOST

Sunday between August 28 and September 3 inclusive

This is one of the relatively few occasions within use of the Revised Common Lectionary in which there is, strictly speaking, no "gospel" in the Gospel selection chosen and not much "gospel" in the other texts either. Mark 7:15 is a wisdom saying that may be from the Jesus of history, "There is nothing outside of a person entering into the mouth of the person that causes the person to be considered profane. It is some of the things that come out of the mouth of a person that cause the person to be profane." The extended introduction in Mark 7:13 to this saying of Jesus has all of the characteristics of polemic developed among followers of Jesus. The materials in Mark 7:16-23 provide elaborations and explanations of the Mark 7:15 wisdom saying.

In this selection from Mark 7 and in most of the other texts chosen for our use next Sunday the emphasis is on appropriate human ethical behavior, and the "gospel" of the grace of God is perceived and expressed only indirectly. The suggestions that follow here are intended to assist in bringing out the "gospel" that is perceived only indirectly within these texts.

Mark 7:1-8, 14-15, 21-23

The most significant initial step in bringing out the "gospel" that is perceived and expressed only indirectly within these texts would be to adjust the Mark 7 reading to Mark 7:14-23, using instead of the anti-Jewish polemic in Mark 7:1-8 that continues in Mark 7:9-13 the more earthy explanations of the Mark 7:15 wisdom saying that we have in Mark 7:17-23. The anti-Jewish polemic of Mark 7:1-

13, one of the most extensive expressions of anti-Jewish polemic in the Gospel According to Mark, distracts from the "gospel" as anti-Jewish polemic always does. The quotation from the Septuagint version of Isaiah 29:13 in Mark 7:6-7 has little actual connection with the content of the question that is said to have been raised by the religious leaders in Mark 7:1-6, and as a response to that question can best be described as overkill. For a detailed discussion of evidence for the development of this controversy dialogue among followers of Jesus, see Arland J. Hultgren, *Jesus and His Adversaries* (Minneapolis: Augsburg, 1979, pages 115-119). If we are serious about application of statements such as that by the Division of Theological Studies, Lutheran Council in the USA, that "Christians should make it clear that there is no biblical or theological basis for anti-Semitism. Supposed theological or biblical bases for anti-Semitism are to be examined and repudiated," in "Some Observations and Guidelines for Conversations between Lutherans and Jews," forwarded to LCUSA member churches in 1971 and printed in *Speaking of God Today: Jews and Lutherans in Conversation*, edited by Paul D. Opsahl and Marc H. Tannenbaum (Philadelphia: Fortress, 1974), page 165, we will not use Mark 7:6-8 and preferably not any of Mark 7:1-8 on this occasion.

If we use Mark 7:14-23 in our sermon or homily next Sunday, it would be helpful to mention that the wisdom saying in Mark 7:15 and the elaboration of that statement in Mark 7:18-23 are observations in the realm of theology, ethics, and anthropology rather than in the realm of biology and of health, since we are all aware that certain foods, liquids, and drugs if taken by mouth into the stomach will certainly "defile" a person. Perhaps the most that we can do in our explication of Mark 7:1-8, 14-15, 21-23 is to remove impediments so that the implied "gospel" in the saying of Jesus in Mark 7:15 will at least not be hidden because of the unnecessary distractions of anti-Jewish polemic in Mark 7:1-8, nor by concerns raised by our awareness of important factors in biology and health that impede our acceptance of the statements in Mark 7:15-19 that nothing that we eat or drink into our bodies can harm us, can "profane" us.

James 1:17-27

The "gospel" in this portion of the Epistle of James document is expressed in the statements in James 1:17-21 that every good action and every perfect gift has been provided by God from above, by God who spoke the creative and redeeming word that saves our lives. Our response to the "gospel," therefore, is to receive that word of God not merely as hearers but as doers of it by providing care for those who are in need, especially for orphans and for widows, and by keeping ourselves unspotted by the evils of the world, restraining our tongues from speaking evil.

Deuteronomy 4:1-2, 6-9

For the people of God in ancient Israel, it was life giving to live in accordance with the statutes and ordinances that the Lord commands. There was and is life in the Torah, that is, the Torah provides the guidelines that are necessary for a person to live in responsive interaction with God. While the primary emphasis is on the commandments and ordinances that are in the Torah, the stories about the responsive interaction with God and often of the lack of responsive interaction with God of the people as portrayed in the Torah are also vitally important. We can and should point this out as "gospel" next Sunday. We should also note that, at their most profound level, the letters written by the Apostle Paul that are included in our New Testament do not disagree with this expression of the "gospel" that is in Deuteronomy 4:1-2, 6-9.

Psalm 15

It is asserted in Psalm 15 that the person who does what is just and right, who speaks truth and does not slander others, is graciously accepted into the presence of God. This is "gospel" in Psalm 15, in which the grace of God is proclaimed within a life that is lived well. For us as Christians, the life of the Jesus of history is the best example of such a life, and we should seek to learn as much as we possibly can about the Jesus of history. There have been and are, of course, many other examples of the grace of God in lives that are lived well, including examples within our times.

Song of Solomon 2:8-13

The "gospel" is proclaimed here in a song of a bride hearing the voice of her beloved as he is bounding over the hills like a graceful young antelope in the springtime, coming to her and calling her to come with him. The winter is past. The flowers spring up from the earth. The time for singing has come.

Psalm 45:1-2, 6-9

The "gospel" in Song of Solomon 2:8-13 of the joyful song of the bride is carried over in Psalm 45:1-2, 6-9 in the words of a court poet, preparing and singing a lyric poem to be used in a royal wedding. God is said to have anointed and blessed this new king with glory and honor as the king stands with his bride, the queen, at his right hand.

PROPER 18
ORDINARY TIME 23
SIXTEENTH SUNDAY AFTER PENTECOST

Sunday between September 4 and September 10 inclusive

As if to compensate for the paucity of direct proclamation of the gospel in the texts that were used last Sunday, those who selected the readings for this lectionary have provided clear expressions of the gospel in the texts selected for next Sunday. As we read these texts, it is as if we are in Eden in an orchard filled with many varieties of fresh fruit that is ours for the picking! From among these rich resources we can pick as much as we can use and give away this week and next Sunday.

Isaiah 35:4-7a

It is after long periods of bad news or of no news at all that good news is most appreciated. Certainly the Israelite exiles whose parents and grandparents had been deported from Jerusalem to Babylon and had lived there against their will among people who had dominated them and despised them for so many decades welcomed this message that the Lord God — now perceived as not merely the God of the nation Israel but the Creator and Ruler of the universe — would soon be coming with resolute strength and determination to rescue them. The overall theme of the extensive Isaiah traditions is clearly expressed in this text. Here as elsewhere in the Isaiah document this theme is "Do not give up! God will fight for you! It is not by your strength but by God's power and strength that you will prevail." Therefore, we read in this text, "Be strong! Do not be afraid!" Human infirmities of all kinds will be removed when the Lord comes. The eyes of the blind will be opened, the ears of the deaf will hear, the lame will leap, and those who cannot talk will sing for joy! When the Lord God comes, it will be natural to assume that the all of the limitations of nature within Israel will be removed. Dry, barren, useless desert land will become well-watered, useful, productive soil for the growing of fruit trees and crops and the grazing of cattle. The land and the people will be even better and more productive than they had been before at the height of their productivity during the reigns of David and of Solomon. This enthusiastic message of joyful expectations was certainly needed by the exiles in Babylon. We are happy to hear it also today, whatever our conditions may be.

From our historical perspective, we realize that neither the Israelite people nor the land was refreshed to the extent proclaimed here when the small groups of exiles trickled back to Jerusalem after Babylon had fallen to the Medes and to the Persians. In part, there has been fulfillment theologically for those of us who are Christians in the Gospel According to Mark 7:24-37 text appointed for this occasion and for Jews in the extensive irrigation projects that have turned substantial desolate areas of the land of Israel into productive farms. For both Christians and Jews, however, the complete fulfillment of the enthusiastic prediction of Isaiah 35:4-7a is still to come. As Christians and as Jews together we stand in need of this good news and of its still future total fulfillment. We stand together in faith in God who alone can make these things occur. Until that day, we praise the Lord God for what has been done, as in the words of the beautiful Psalm 146.

Psalm 146

It is to the Immortal, Just, and Gracious God rather than to mortal, unjust, and transient human beings that we should turn with our thanks and praise as Jews, Christians, Muslims, and all others. Though less specifically tied to the return of the Israelite exiles from Babylon to Jerusalem, the hopes expressed in this psalm are quite similar to those of Isaiah 35:4-7a.

Mark 7:24-37

Here, as in so many other texts in "the Gospel of Jesus Christ" (Mark) and in related texts within the other Gospels in our New Testament, followers of Jesus during the second half of the first century of the common era were claiming that within the life, death, and resurrection of Jesus as the Risen Christ the expectations of the writers of Isaiah 35:4-7a, Psalm 146, and many other texts from the Old Testament had been fulfilled. The geography of the Mark 7:24-37 account (Tyre, Sidon, and the Decapolis) suggests that the fulfillment was perceived to have occurred not only within Israel geographically and theologically, but among non-Jews and beyond the land of Israel as well.

From the vantage point of our Christian faith, we have no reason to question the fulfillment of these expectations within the life, death, and resurrection of Jesus perceived as the Risen Christ. We can note, however, that within the context of the early followers of Jesus the fulfillment of the expectations of the Isaiah 35:4-7a tradition, Psalm 146, and other similar texts from the Old Testament within the life, death, and resurrection of Jesus was necessary in order to support the claims of followers of Jesus during the latter decades of the first century and later that Jesus as the Risen Christ is indeed the Son of God, the Representative of God, the Lord God Incarnate. Anything less than accounts such as Mark 7:24-37 of Jesus' healing power would have been inadequate. And so we proclaim this Mark 7:24-37 account today and next Sunday, with added appreciation to God for the healing powers that God makes available for us during our lifetimes through medical healing, surgical healing, psychiatric healing, and the healing power of faith.

James 2:1-10 (11-13) 14-17

This text reminds us of the importance of our faith being actively demonstrated and used in actions of love for other people. This is as important and essential today as it has ever been. These actions of love for other people should always be done in grateful response to God who provides every gift. Faith by itself, if it is not put into practice, is useless according to the writer of James 2:17. Would the Apostle Paul have agreed? What do you think? Is not a creative tension between the importance of faith in God and an appropriate response to God in what we do better than either faith alone without good works or good works alone without faith? This creative tension is what we see when we look at the entire biblical account rather than at merely a portion of it.

Proverbs 22:1-2, 8-9, 22-23

The wisdom expressed here is that a good name is far more valuable than are great riches and that those who are affluent should share their food with the poor, and those who are rich and powerful should not rob and crush those who are weak and in need. God is the Creator of the rich and the poor, and when both die they will meet together for whatever their Creator will do to them and for them.

Psalm 125

As presented by the psalmist, those who trust in the Lord are established as firmly as is the bedrock on which Jerusalem is built. The Lord God, rather than their enemies, is camped around the city of Jerusalem to protect God's people as long as they trust in the Lord God. The Lord God is asked to do good things for those who do whatever is good, for those who avoid evil and are upright and righteous. For all who trust in the Lord, this is indeed good news. For those who do not, they have every reason to be afraid.

PROPER 19
ORDINARY TIME 24
SEVENTEENTH SUNDAY AFTER PENTECOST

Sunday between September 11 and September 17 inclusive

In each of these texts selected for use in our worship services next Sunday there is a model that the hearer is urged to follow. Let us look at these models more closely in preparation for our proclamation and for our parenesis next Sunday. How will these models be helpful to us and to the people with whom we serve as we prepare this week for the message that we will be called by God to share during the worship services next Sunday?

Isaiah 50:4-9a

Within the context of the Suffering Servant songs of the Isaiah traditions near the end of the exilic period we hear this voice, we have this testimony, we perceive this model. It is the voice and the model of a prophet, perhaps of an ideal prophet or of the best elements of Israelite prophecy. Eventually within the ongoing Israelite and Jewish interpretation of this portion of the Suffering Servant songs with the addition of the word "Israel" in Isaiah 49:3 the voice and model became the voice and model of Israel itself. For the followers of Jesus during the embryonic period in the development of the Christian Church, in retrospective reflection over the life, suffering and death, and resurrection of Jesus as the Risen Christ of faith, it also became the voice of Jesus, the one now perceived within the developing Church as the Suffering Servant par excellence who suffered and died on the cross for all of us.

Perhaps we should say that for us today it is not a matter of whether it is Israelite prophecy at its best, Israel itself, or Jesus who is the Suffering Servant. The inspired prophets of ancient Israel, the people of Israel, and Jesus as the Risen Christ all have suffered for us. Can we and all other Christians accept the sharing of the Suffering Servant role with Israel and the Jews? After Auschwitz, do we have any other choice? Was the suffering of the Jesus of history, of Jesus the Jew, on the Roman cross for a few horrible hours greater than the suffering of a million Jewish babies and children torn from their mothers and thrown over the heads of their mothers into the packed gas chambers by the Nazis? If Jesus the Jew had been born to Mary the Jew in Germany, Poland, or elsewhere in the lands occupied by the Germans during the Holocaust, would his life have been spared? Of course it would not have been spared.

In this Isaiah 50:4-9a Suffering Servant model, therefore, the suffering of Jesus the Jew can no longer be separated from the suffering of other Jews and from the suffering of others as well who are oppressed even today in the Sudan, China, and in many other places. Do we have the call and the courage to share this realization in some way as we use this Isaiah 50:4-9a model in our message next Sunday? If we lack the call and the courage to share it, let us remain silent next Sunday and not merely mouth our old, oft-repeated clichés that separate the suffering of Jesus from our time, from twentieth and twenty-first century suffering. With this Isaiah 50:4-9a Suffering Servant model, neither should we retain without any attempt at repudiation the most vicious anti-Jewish expressions within our New Testament that contributed to the situation in Europe that made the success of the Nazi war against the Jews and against other powerless people in Europe possible.

Perhaps there are times when we must say with the Jesus of Matthew 5, "It is written, but I say..." or with Paul in 2 Corinthians 3:6 that "the written record condemns and kills, but the Spirit makes us alive." Cannot we permit the Spirit of God to "make us alive" today? Is the Lord God of revelation silent or even perhaps dead among us? Has God said nothing new for the past eighteen centuries? Cannot we be inspired individuals today? Of course we can. To the glory of God, we can and must.

Psalm 116:1-9

It is basic to this Individual Hymn of Praise and Thank-offering genre to testify to everyone who is present concerning the seriousness of the problem that the psalmist has faced, the wisdom of turning to the Lord for help, the nature of the deliverance, and the necessity of offering thanks and praise to the Lord. As a result, the person offering the testimony automatically becomes the model to be followed. Even though we have many of these Individual Hymns of Praise and Thankoffering within the biblical accounts, many of us have been conditioned within our tradition to refrain from offering ourselves as a model of this sort. Perhaps we should ask some respected mature persons within our congregations who have been in distress, have called upon the Lord, have been relieved from the distress, and praise God for that relief to share their experiences within the worship service next Sunday in order to provide contemporary counterparts to the psalmist's song. Every congregation at any given time has several persons who have had such experiences and probably will be glad to tell about them if asked.

Proverbs 1:20-33

Here, as in many other places in the collection of the Writings that we call the book of Proverbs, wisdom is personified as a woman crying out in the street, offering to help those who are simple and who foolishly turn away. The wisdom of God is the model here, warning those who reject her moral guidelines that they will realize their need for the wisdom that God provides only when it will be too late for them to respond.

Psalm 19

At the conclusion of this Hymn of Praise to God as the Creator of the universe and as the one who graciously provides the Torah, the model for us to follow is that of the person who rejects sin and acts of evil, calls upon God as one's rock and redeemer, and asks that the person's words and meditation be acceptable in the sight of God.

Wisdom of Solomon 7:26—8:1

The model to follow here is the person who lives with wisdom, with the wisdom that God so freely and graciously provides. Such a person is truly loved by God. How could anyone be so foolish as not to be and not to live like the person depicted in this model, the person who is attracted in this way to God?

James 3:1-12

The writer of this document urges the reader and hearer to understand the importance of controlling the person's own tongue, what the person says. The tongue of a person, though it is a small portion of the person's body, is like the mouth of a horse, for the horse will go in the direction of its mouth, a huge ship will be guided by a small rudder, and a little fire can cause a huge forest to burn. The person who can control that person's tongue is the model to be followed here. No human without the power that God provides is strong enough and disciplined enough to provide that model for us to follow. Not here in this portion of the Epistle of James, but beyond it in the portion of the Gospel According to Mark selected for next Sunday will we see this model.

Mark 8:27-38

The model that this text provides within the context of the other readings selected for our use next Sunday is the model, of course, of Jesus suffering on the cross, and here in Mark 8:27-38 we are urged to take up our cross and to follow after Jesus. Jesus is depicted here as the Christ, not a military Messiah who leads his followers boldly into battle against his enemies, but a Messiah who is the Suffering Servant of the Lord, the Christ who dies on the cross. Jesus, as this Messiah, at first cautions his followers to tell no one about his identity in order that he may tell as many of his fellow Jews as possible what he believes, that the Lord God is coming very soon to remove the Roman oppressors, that at that time only the Lord God will be ruling over them and the Romans will be gone from the land. Jesus, as this Messiah, tells his followers to worship and accept the absolute claims of authority only of the Lord God and no longer to submit to the absolute claims of authority of the Romans. He tells his followers not to talk with outsiders about his identity as a Messiah figure, because he wants to reach as many people as possible with his message of suffering resistance before he dies on the cross.

The Theology of this Mark 8:27-38 text and the dominant Theology of the entire New Testament tradition is a Theology of the Cross, a Theology of Jesus as the Christ crucified and risen from the dead. According to this Theology of the Cross, God did not intervene to prevent the death of Jesus on the cross, but God vindicated and validated him as the Christ by raising Jesus from the dead.

What then is our task this week and at all times? We are urged to develop, to apply to our own lives, and to proclaim a Theology of the Cross that is adequate and appropriate for our time and place. What does this mean? It is our task to follow the role model of Jesus crucified and raised from the dead. We are no longer passively to endure needless and meaningless suffering in ourselves and in other people, but instead to join vigorously and fearlessly to oppose needless suffering, to do everything that we possibly can to overcome poverty, hunger, oppression, exploitation, abuse, disease, and death. It is our task to "go to the wall," if necessary, for the sake of others. Is this not what is meant by the biblical injunction to "participate in the sufferings of Christ"? What a model to follow! What kind of example are we as pastors and worship leaders and members of our congregations providing? Is the priestly role of building up a congregation of power, prestige, and wealth the only role appropriate for us?

There are many in the Church who proclaim and who live not a "Theology of the Cross," but instead a "Theology of Prosperity," a "Theology of Success," a message that says that if you, like us, accept Jesus into your hearts and no longer sin, you will be as happy and as successful as we are! The "Theology of Prosperity" is appealing to many people, to many who are poor and have no prosperity, as well as to many who have become wealthy and prosperous. It is not the Theology, however, of these texts, of Paul and the Four Gospels, of our biblical tradition.

For a well-written and very understandable biblical "Theology of the Cross," amply illustrated with examples from his own experiences, see Philip L. Ruge-Jones, *The Word of the Cross in a World of Glory* (Minneapolis: Fortress, 2008).

PROPER 20
ORDINARY TIME 25
EIGHTEENTH SUNDAY AFTER PENTECOST

Sunday between September 18 and September 24 inclusive

Since Mark 9:30-37 is comprised of two loosely connected pericope units, most of the other texts selected for our use next Sunday branch out from Mark 9:30-37 in two different directions. Jeremiah 11:18-20, Psalm 54, and Wisdom of Solomon 1:16—2:1, 12-22 with their emphasis on threats to life and deliverance from evil, provide a backdrop for the second Markan passion-resurrection prediction in Mark 9:30-32, and James 3:13—4:3, 7-8a provides wisdom elaborations of the Mark 9:33-37 discussion of the problem of jealousy and greed among the early followers of Jesus. There are no significant direct linkages between the Proverbs 31:10-31 text extolling the virtues of an ideal housewife and Psalm 1 that compares and contrasts the good that will come to the person who delights in living in accordance with the guidelines provided in the Torah to the wicked person who will perish, unless these latter texts are seen to point out the contrast between the righteous people and people who are jealous and greedy.

Jeremiah 11:18-20

In this personal lament of Jeremiah, which is followed by five additional laments in Jeremiah 15:10-21, 17:14-18, 18:18-23, 20:7-13, and 20:14-18, Jeremiah claims to have been shown by the Lord that Jeremiah's enemies have plotted to slaughter him, to destroy him and his message, and to blot out his name from the earth. Jeremiah is depicted as confident, however, that the Lord, to whom Jeremiah has committed his cause, will deliver Jeremiah and take vengeance upon the enemies of Jeremiah.

We can see that within the early traditions of followers of Jesus it was perceived that if the prophet Jeremiah had been told by the Lord that his life was in danger, certainly Jesus as the Son of God must have been told by God the Father when and where Jesus would be crucified. If Jeremiah had been confident of deliverance, so also Jesus must have been confident that the Lord God would deliver Jesus, if not in the avoidance of death, then certainly in the overcoming of death in the resurrection of Jesus from death to eternal life. The justice of God as judge is "gospel" within this text.

Psalm 54

The "gospel" is expressed more clearly here than in the Jeremiah 11:28-20 text. Particularly in Psalm 54:4 we see this in the claim that "God is the one who comes to rescue me; the Lord upholds my life!" The proclamation of the gospel continues in the words of Psalm 54:6b, "Your name, O Lord, is good," and in Psalm 54:7a, "You have delivered me from every distress." Even though the form of this Individual Hymn of Thanksgiving may have caused the psalmist to exaggerate somewhat, the message of good news is abundantly clear in this psalm.

Wisdom of Solomon 1:16—2:1, 12-22

The ungodly, who have no hope of immortality, abuse and torment the righteous, testing them to see whether God will help and protect them. The righteous, however, know the hidden purposes of God, that God has a prize for those who are blameless, to give them an eternity of life with God.

Mark 9:30-37

As in Jeremiah 11:18-20, Psalm 54, and Wisdom of Solomon 1:16—2:1, 12-22, there is bad news and there is good news in Mark 9:30-32. The bad news is that Jesus will be tortured and crucified by the Romans; the good news is that three days later God will raise Jesus from the dead. It is the good news of the resurrection of Jesus as Christ for us and as Redeemer of the world that is of the greatest interest to us. Because Jesus as the Risen Christ lives, we too shall live! This is the essence of the gospel as we who are Christians proclaim it.

Mark 9:33-37 is an indication that during the time of the Jesus of history and in the decades after his death there were problems of jealousy and greed among the followers of Jesus. The problems of jealousy and greed were undoubtedly greatly increased as various groups of followers of Jesus were formed, as this text and the text that we shall have the following week indicate. The solution to that problem during the first century, as well as now, lies in service to others rather than in the exercise of power over them. How frequently we are tempted to exercise the power that we have because of our position rather than for us to find fulfillment for our lives in service to God and to other people! The Jesus of history demonstrated service to God and to other people in a remarkable way. It is probable that Mark 9:37 is a statement of the Jesus of history only moderately embellished. Perhaps the Jesus of history took a child into his arms (probably on many similar occasions) and said something such as "Whoever takes care of a child such as this takes care of me, takes care of the whole world, and takes care of God!" (This text provides an excellent example for a "children's sermon" and as an object lesson during a Service of Baptism.)

James 3:13-4:3, 7-8a

This "wisdom" text is certainly "wisdom" also for us. Have we not found that life is just as it is depicted in this text? The parenesis here can be applied to individuals, to groups, to nations, to all of humanity. What is taught in James 3:16—4:2 is similar to the basic teachings of many other great religions of the world, especially of the Buddhists. It is not unlike the teachings within the Hindu religions. We shall lose nothing by recognizing that these ideas are shared freely among the best of all of the other great religions of the world. At the same time, we can make this parenesis to be Christian parenesis by presenting it as appropriate that in response to the gospel of God's grace shown in the life, death, and resurrection of Jesus Christ we can control and overcome our jealousy and our greed and can work and live in peace.

Proverbs 31:10-31

The opposite of a life that is tainted by jealousy and greed is depicted in this portrait of an ideal wife. From the perspective of the rabbinical tradition, she does everything that is needed within the home and household so that her husband can study the Torah at all times. How do we respond to this portrayal of an ideal life? Would the women in the congregations in which we serve want to be like this wife? Would the men want a wife like that? How would we portray the ideal wife and the ideal husband in our own context?

Psalm 1

With a wife who is as resourceful as the ideal wife depicted in Proverbs 31:10-31, her husband can, as it is expressed in Psalm 1:2, meditate day and night on the Torah that is revealed by God. There is no jealousy and there is no greed in such a household and in such a marriage.

Although few of us would expect any woman to be as industrious as the ideal wife depicted in Proverbs 31, our study of Proverbs 31:10-31 together with Psalm 1 can be very helpful for men and for women in our congregations. Should these and other texts be studied by men apart from women and by women apart from men, or is it more productive for men and women to study them in one group together? How are the Bible study groups arranged in the congregations in which we serve?

Whether studied by men apart from women, women apart from men, or men and women together, Psalm 1 is of primary importance in any study of the Psalter. It was placed where we have it in the collection of psalms for good reasons. As Denise Dombkowski Hopkins expresses it in her *Journey through the Psalms*, rev. ed. (St. Louis: Chalice Press, 2002), page 66, "The context for praying, singing, or preaching the rest of the psalms is set by Psalm 1 and its declaration of the Two Ways and the joy of the Torah. Psalm 1 serves as our guidepost at the entrance to the Psalter; it helps us to keep our bearings through life's journey because it tells us that Torah articulates God's intentions for us."

PROPER 21
ORDINARY TIME 26
NINETEENTH SUNDAY AFTER PENTECOST

Sunday between September 25 and October 1 inclusive

Mark 9:38-50

It is clearly stated in this pericope that all evil and all evil impulses in a person's life must be opposed by each person. In order to accomplish this, criticism of one's self must be incisive, "cutting," and complete.

The core saying in Mark 9:40, "Whoever is not against us is for us," as with other core sayings of Jesus in Mark, was probably remembered by his followers because it had been stated by the Jesus of history on so many occasions. It should be noted that the Matthean and Lukan redactors in contexts that are somewhat different from that in Mark turned the saying of Jesus "inside out" to present Jesus in Matthew 12:30 and in Luke 11:23 as saying that "The one who is not with me is against me." According to this Mark 9:38-50 text, however, other people who oppose evil in Jesus' name are to be supported even if they are in a different group.

Mark 9:38-50, therefore, does not require that there be unity in organization or uniformity in practice within the Church. Cell division into a multitude of denominations in the Church to permit and even to encourage diversity and to provide a multitude of opportunities to live and to serve has biblical sanction in the core saying of Jesus in this text. Without opportunities for diversity, rapid growth of the Church is not likely to occur. What are the implications of this for those who have difficulty in accepting into participation and leadership positions in the Church persons whose lifestyles are different from those of the majority of the people in the established Church? Why is it so important for us to note the distinction in this text between self-criticism that is supported by Jesus and criticism of others that is rejected by

Jesus? Why are we often quick to criticize others and slow to criticize ourselves?

James 5:13-20

The writer of this epistle is directive throughout most of the document, and these final eight verses are not an exception. In the many and diverse situations of life, all persons are directed to pray for themselves and for each other. They should always help each other and ask God to guide them in the right path.

Numbers 11:4-6, 10-16, 24-29

The Spirit of the Lord is said to have rested also upon the two men, Eldad and Medad, who had not gone out with Moses to receive from the Lord some of the Spirit of God that had previously been only upon Moses. When Joshua complained about this to Moses and asked Moses to silence these two men, Moses responded with the famous words, "I wish that all of the people of the Lord were prophets! I would be greatly pleased if the Lord would put the Spirit of the Lord upon every one of them!" The saying of Jesus in Mark 9:40 is consistent with this.

Furthermore, *Formgeschichte* (form study) analysis of this text indicates that the account functions among other things as an etiology that provides an explanation of the origin of prophecy in Israel. Apparently many of the Israelites were opposed to some of the expressions of prophecy in Israel, especially when, as in this case, the prophecy did not coincide with the wishes of some of the people. God is said, however, in this account, to have validated prophecy in Israel with the words spoken through Moses in Numbers 11:29. In a way that is similar to the validation of the Torah through Moses in the "burning bush" account in Exodus 3:1—4:17. In Numbers 11:24-29 prophecy in Israel is validated through Moses as a legitimate extension of the

Torah. The implications of this are considerable for Israel, both theologically and historically. According to Numbers 11:24-29, the Lord God will not be limited to revelation given directly through Moses. In this text, the Lord God uses Moses in order to authorize an ongoing process of revelation. The implications of this extend also to us today. We believe that God continues God's ongoing process of revelation through each of us in the Church and not only in the Church.

Psalm 19:7-14

The revelation of the Lord God in the Torah is acclaimed beautifully in this psalm. Although prophecy is not mentioned as such in this psalm, we can see in this psalm that when the psalmist proclaims the merits of the Torah to the people the psalmist is speaking prophetically in the basic sense of prophecy, which is to proclaim something for God to the people.

Esther 7:1-6, 9-10; 9:20-22

In the context of the other texts selected for this day, these portions of the story about Esther provide a validation of a festival that is not mentioned or included anywhere in the Torah. Along with the validation of the festival of Purim, a celebration of the rescue of the Israelite-Jewish people from a decree of death to the Israelites-Jews issued by a cruel and vindictive oppressor, the Esther story is also validated as authoritative for Israel.

Psalm 124

This is one of numerous psalms celebrating the actions of the Lord God in rescuing Israel and its people from death and annihilation. It can be applied here to the rescue of the Jewish people in the Esther story. It can be applied, of course, also to the rescue of Jews in many other times as well, and to the rescue by God of Christians and of other people.

PROPER 22
ORDINARY TIME 27
TWENTIETH SUNDAY AFTER PENTECOST

Sunday between October 2 and October 8 inclusive

The unifying factor within the first three of these selections is obviously "the family," more specifically "the ideal family" or "the family as it should be."

Genesis 2:18-24

This text, the second half of the "Jahwistic" folk tradition "creation" account that we have in Genesis 2:4b-25, is evidence for the belief among the ancient Israelites that the Lord God instituted marriage, arranged the first marriage, provided the participants in the first marriage, and brought them together into a single monogamous unit.

Mark 10:2-16

In this text, we have the teaching of the Markan community regarding family life as it should be, the Markan community ideal! Possibly this was also the teaching of the Jesus of history regarding family life, regarding divorce, regarding remarriage, and regarding the place of children within a family. Let us look more closely at this text.

The framework for this teaching of the Markan community regarding marriage, divorce, remarriage, and the place of children is a controversy dialogue between the Markan Jesus and the Markan Pharisees who have come to the Markan Jesus "in order to try to cause him to fall." The Markan Pharisees are the typical opponents of the Markan Jesus here, and their motives are labeled as sinister by the Markan writer and community. As Eduard Schweizer in *The Good News According to Mark*, trans. by D. H. Madvig (Atlanta: John Knox, 1970) page 202, observed, real life

Pharisees would hardly have asked such a radical question as "Is it in accordance with the Torah for a man to divorce his wife?" since for the Pharisees divorce was regulated by Deuteronomy 24:1-4, legislation designed to protect the wife and to guarantee for her a measure of freedom. At the most, real life Pharisees might have asked the Jesus of history what, in his opinion, should be the attitude of first-century Jews in Galilee and Judea in view of the expectation of Jesus and of many other Jews in that area at that time that God's rule would soon be experienced in a new, more direct manner. The radical question is included in Mark 10:2, probably because the Markan community, in establishing its own identity, was impelled to raise questions such as this. It needed to provide authoritative answers within this "Gospel," its evolving compilation of Jesus' teachings as guidelines for the people of the Markan community.

Since, as the Markan community self-consciously was establishing its own identity, it was doing this for the most part over against its Jewish antecedents, it is not surprising that it tended to be comparatively strict, similar to the Qumran community in this respect. The Markan writer obviously rejected the Jewish Torah legislation of Deuteronomy 24:1-4 in favor of the "two as one flesh" ideal descriptions in the Genesis 1:27 and 2:24 creation accounts. Probably perceiving the Genesis 1 and 2 accounts to have priority over Deuteronomy 24:1-4 both in time (as earlier than Moses) and in scope (for all people, not merely for the Israelites), the Markan writer chose to base the teachings of the Markan community upon Genesis 1-2 and accused the Markan Pharisees of hardness of hearts (Mark 10:5) stating that because of such hardness of hearts Moses provided some possibility of a certificate of divorce.

In our translation and use of Mark 10:2-16, it is important that we recognize and emphasize that in the theological opinion of the leadership of the Markan community divorce was not permitted. They, or at least the writer of the Gospel According to Mark, used the technique of controversy dialogue to clarify their own position and to show that it had priority over the position of the Pharisees on that subject. Since the controversy dialogue itself has relatively little value for us today, the controversy dialogue should be treated as secondary in our own proclamation and teaching, just as it was secondary in their situation. Our primary interest is in the position of the Markan community — which became sacred Scripture for us — as we reflect upon the issues of marriage, family life, divorce, and remarriage as possibilities under certain circumstances, and the place of children today.

Accordingly, it would be advisable for us to translate the word *Pharisaioi* in Mark 10:2 as "some religious leaders," which is, of course, what Pharisees were at that time, and to express the text of Mark 10:5b in English as "He wrote this commandment to our ancestors and for you because of human intransigence." Just as the new Markan community of followers of Jesus found it to be necessary to define the concept of "family" and related matters for itself, so also followers of Jesus in each new period of time since then find it to be necessary to define these concepts for themselves in relation to their own traditions.

The narrow issue here (divorce) is negative — much too negative to be the focal point in our message next Sunday. The bigger, broader, and better issue is "family," and for that Genesis 2:18-24, Mark 10:2-16, and to a lesser extent, Hebrews 1:1-4; 2:5-12, are all helpful.

In our homiletical application, the ideal family situation should be lifted up as the model for which to strive constantly and conscientiously, with the full realization and recognition that we must also be non-judgmental and compassionate regarding less-than-ideal situations and that every "real" situation is to some extent less-than-ideal.

Hebrews 1:1-4; 2:5-12

These portions of the Epistle to the Hebrews, which is the longest sustained argument within the Newer Testament, depict the person and work of Jesus the Christ as perceived by the inspired writer who composed it. The portions of this document that have been selected for our use next Sunday may have been chosen because of the emphasis on family relationships in Hebrews 2:11b-12 and 2:13b-14. These portions of the document have a rather tenuous connection to the Genesis 2:18-24 and Mark 10:2-16 readings appointed for this occasion.

Psalm 8

Perhaps the reference in Psalm 8:2 to the mouths of babies and infants praising God and extolling the greatness of God with sounds that we as adults cannot understand is the reason that this beautiful psalm was selected for use on this occasion. God, who is said to have established the moon and the stars with God's own fingers, has given to us responsibility to manage and to protect life on the earth. How majestic, how awesome, therefore, is the name of the Lord!

Job 1:1; 2:1-10

Job is presented in this literary drama as the ideal man, with supposedly the ideal wife and family, perhaps with the ideal friends. He and his faith in God will be stretched, however, to the limit when first his wife and later his friends test his patience. Perhaps the message is that within this life there is no place in which the ideal man and the ideal family can be seen. Nevertheless, we are to live and to keep our relationship of faith in God, regardless of what may happen to us.

Psalm 26

This psalm could be considered to be an expression of the thought of Job as he suffered physically and mentally and yet maintained his integrity and his faith in God. Are there men and women in the congregations in which we serve whose situations are similar in many ways to the situations of Job and of this psalmist as both are presented here?

PROPER 23
ORDINARY TIME 28
TWENTY-FIRST SUNDAY AFTER PENTECOST

Sunday between October 9 and October 15 inclusive

Most of our attention both exegetically and homiletically in preparation for next Sunday should probably be focused on Amos 5:6-7, 10-15 and Mark 10:17-31. These two tests provide similar prescriptions for life. "If you wish to live," they both say, "seek the Lord God, who is good, for the Lord God gives life!"

What are some of the implications of this for us here and now? An answer is clearly expressed. "Show respect for life, for marriage, for the property of other people, and for your parents," they say, and beyond that, "Protect and provide for the poor. No longer exploit them. Instead, help them. Do more for them than is required by the civil legal system of the land."

Let us examine the social and political situation in which each of these two texts originated, and then look at our own in preparation for our message for next Sunday.

Amos 5:6-7, 10-15

Socially, it is apparent that many of the rich and prosperous residents of the Northern Kingdom Israel were severely exploiting the poor people of that land economically. Government policy permitted those who were rich to expand their wealth greatly at the expense of the poor. Politically, there was little effective opposition to the policies and practices of the rich men and women who controlled the government and the economy of that land — except for the prophet Amos, a visitor from the Southern Kingdom Judah. After Amos had proclaimed the message that he was called and inspired by the Lord God to proclaim, the social, political, and religious leaders of the Northern Kingdom — through Amaziah, the priest at Bethel — "advised" Amos to flee away to his own land of Judah, to eat his bread there, to prophesy there if he wishes, but never again to prophesy at Bethel (Amos 7:10-15).

The text suggests that God had revealed to Amos that soon the Northern Kingdom would be destroyed. Perhaps Amos himself perceived this because of his awareness of the international political situation. Certainly by the time that the Amos traditions had been fully formed, the "house of Joseph" and its people had been utterly destroyed by the Assyrians and only a few refugees remained, most of whom were poor and many of whom had been sustained only by sheep and goat herding in barren areas. Within this social and political situation the message of the prophet Amos was expressed and eventually recorded.

Mark 10:17-31

Socially, politically, economicly, and religiously during the lifetime of the Jesus of history the Jews in Galilee and in Judea were a heavily oppressed people within their own land. They had none of the autonomy that had been enjoyed by the wealthy people of the Northern Kingdom who had been condemned by Amos. The only Jews in Galilee and Judea during the time of Jesus who were relatively prosperous were those few who cooperated fully with the Roman occupational forces as priests managing the Temple, as tax collectors, and as business contractors. Even these lived in a precarious position, subject to the wishes and whims of the Romans and endangered by the actions of Jewish revolutionaries, the Zealot guerrilla forces, primarily teenage boys whose daring attacks on isolated Roman guards were always met by severe Roman reprisals. Under the conditions in which the Jews in Galilee and Judea lived during the time of Jesus, it is apparent from Mark 10:21 and similar texts that the Jesus of history advocated direct assistance to poor and destitute Jews by the few Jews such as the man depicted in this Mark 10:17-22 account who through full cooperation with the Roman occupational forces managed temporarily to have significant possessions.

Formgeschichte (form study) analysis of the Mark 10:17-22 account indicates that, as in the somewhat similar account in Mark 12:28-34, it is likely that much of the Jesus of history level is still discernible in this Mark 10:17-22 account, even though there had been additions and probably many deletions during the development of the account throughout the reminiscences of followers of Jesus level and the pre-Markan level to the Markan level of development. A careful reconstruction of a scenario during the Jesus of history level provides something similar to the following dialogue.

A fellow Jew, relatively prosperous because he "did business" with the Romans, after hearing Jesus express Jesus' belief that soon only the Lord God would be ruling over them, approached Jesus and asked for Jesus' opinion.

"My good man," he said, "what do you think that I should do so that I may receive God's gift of eternal life?"

"Why do you address me as your 'good man'?" Jesus replied. "No one is truly good except God alone! You know the commandments: 'Do not ever murder anyone, nor commit adultery, nor steal nor defraud anyone. Honor your father and your mother.' "

And the man said to Jesus, "Sir. I have carefully observed all of these commandments from the time that I was young."

Jesus looked at him with compassion and said, "One thing is lacking with you. Go! Sell what you have accumulated and give to the oppressed poor people in our land. Then you will have treasures in heaven!"

The man was dismayed about this reply and went away looking very sad and depressed, for he was a man who had accumulated many possessions.

Jesus looked at those who were with him and said, "How difficult it is for people who have accumulated wealth by cooperating fully with the oppressive Romans to let God and only God rule in their lives. I think that it must be easier for a camel loaded down with a heavy burden to go through the eye of a needle than for a man such as that, who has accumulated wealth by cooperating fully with the oppressive Romans and making it easier for the Romans to oppress the rest of us, to let only the Lord God and not the Romans rule that person's life."

Those around Jesus then said, "Who then will be saved?"

Jesus said to them, "People with their selfish attachments and limitations are not able to be saved, but God has no such limitations. All things are possible for God!"

The social, political, economic, and religious situations in which we live are different from those of the time of either Amos or Jesus, but probably in most instances closer to the situation at the time of Amos than at the time of Jesus. Much of what Amos apparently condemned could rather easily be condemned among us.

Each of us should analyze the social, political, economic, and religious situation in which we live and in which we are called to proclaim the message from God next Sunday. The prescriptions for life derived from these two texts remain valid today and will remain valid for all of us in this life. The implications of this for us also remain valid. The message that we will proclaim next Sunday will hardly be living, dynamic "Word of God" unless we apply it boldly and courageously to the particular social, political, economic, and religious situation in which we live and work. That is our prophetic call.

Hebrews 4:12-16

In the context of Amos 5:6-7, 10-15 and of Mark 10:17-31, the words of Hebrews 4:12-13 are incisive:

> "For the word of God is living and active, sharper than the sharpest two-edged sword. It penetrates until it separates one's psyche from one's spirit. It slices into the places where one's bones are joined together from the marrow in one's bones. It exposes a person's most intimate fantasies and speculations. No person whom God has created is invisible to God. All are stripped bare and exposed to God's eyes, to God, to whom we are fully accountable."

The writer continues in Hebrews 4:14-16 to assure the reader and the hearer that since we have Jesus as the "great, supreme priest, the Son of God," we can "with courage and confidence approach God's throne of grace, in order that we may receive mercy and find grace to rescue us and to sustain us in our hour of need." That is certainly what we need.

Psalm 90:12-17

These concluding verses of Psalm 90, though not originally intended directly for us, certainly are applicable also to us as we "approach God's throne of grace" with our people next Sunday.

Job 23:1-9, 16-17

Near despair, the character Job in this poignant drama searches for God, wanting to present his case, to reason with God in the presence of God, but cannot find God. For him, God is the Hidden God, like Martin Luther's concept of *deus absconditus*. How can we help those for whom God is experienced only as the Hidden God? How can we maintain our faith in God when God is *deus absconditus* from us? We need more of the Job drama than these eleven verses to be touched by God here.

Psalm 22:1-15

The emotions expressed in this portion of Psalm 22, best known to us because the Markan writer and the Matthean redactors suggest that these were the emotions of the Markan Jesus and of the Matthean Jesus on the cross, are almost identical to the words of Job 23:1-9, 16-17.

If we use Job 23:1-9, 16-17 and Psalm 22:1-15 within our worship services next Sunday, we have the responsibility to explicate and interpret them. If these readings express the emotions of even one or two persons within the worshiping congregations in which we serve, we must not fail to stand with them.

PROPER 24
ORDINARY TIME 29
TWENTY-SECOND SUNDAY AFTER PENTECOST

Sunday between October 16 and October 22 inclusive

Psalm 91:9-16

It is obvious that the people in ancient Israel among whom this psalm was developed and sung lived in situations in which life was a struggle for survival. They lived with "scourge near their tents," "lions," "adders," "serpents," "sharp stones," and other constant threats to their existence. The inspired psalmist spoke and sang to assure them that because they have faith in the Lord God they will be delivered from the perils cited, protected from all manner of evil, and assured of long life. This was the hope provided for them in this psalm.

Within the daily struggles of our lives there are moments and sometimes days and months and years in which we suffer from illness and injury. Disease and death threaten us at all times. Even though we believe in God and believe that God has been active in Jesus our Risen Lord and Savior, we are not shielded from all evil in this life. Nevertheless, it is our hope that ultimately God will rescue us and give us life eternally.

For us it is Jesus who is Lord, even as for the Israelites among whom this psalm was first sung it was the Lord God of Israel who was Lord for them. For the ancient Israelites, for Jews, for us, for Muslims, Hindus, and many other people, it is God who is beyond us and beyond our limitations to whom we turn for help, to God best known by us through Jesus the Risen Christ and in other ways by them.

In the explanatory stories (*midrashim*) in Matthew 4:6 and Luke 4:10-11 about how Jesus was tempted by "Satan" to try to help his fellow oppressed Jews in Galilee and in

Judea by cooperating fully with the Romans who occupied the land and thereby perhaps reduce the Roman oppression, portions of Psalm 91 are said to have been quoted by Satan. This should be a reminder to us that it was not Jesus to whom originally this psalm was spoken and that texts from our Scriptures can be and often are manipulated for nefarious purposes. Like every other text, Psalm 91:9-16 should be studied first in its own setting for its own sake. Then, after we have seen how the text has been used by people who believed in God in the past, we listen to and apply its message of hope for us. And that message of hope comes to us even though at the moment and for days and months and years we too may still suffer from pain and disease and will eventually experience death.

Isaiah 53:4-12

In this poetic climax and conclusion to the fourth "Servant Song" of the Isaiah tradition we see features that can be applied to various persons and groups. These features can be applied in part to the great Israelite prophets within a "larger than life composite figure" that was most likely the original intent, in part to the nation and people of Israel to which these features were later applied, and still later in part to Jesus by followers of Jesus who perceived Jesus after his death as the one who suffered and died for us and for all people and who lives again. Perhaps we shall be true to this text and to God best if we see all of these features, all of these interpretations and applications in it, and do not try to limit its applications to any one of these three. It is said in the text that it was the will of the Lord that the "Servant" should suffer, but that it is through the suffering of the "Servant" that we have hope.

Hebrews 5:1-10

A priest who is selected to serve as the high priest can try to be non-judgmental while serving people who are sinful, since the high priest is also a sinner. Such a high priest must offer sacrifices, however, for the priest's own sins in addition to offering sacrifices for the sins of other human beings. Jesus as the Risen Christ has been tested and tempted in every respect as we have been but, unlike other priests, without ever succumbing to sin (Hebrews 4:15). During the suffering that Jesus experienced in human form on the earth (Hebrews 5:8-10), Jesus became perfectly submissive to God's will and, as the Christ, the source of eternal salvation to all who accept him as their ruler-priest, a ruler-priest similar to, but obviously greater than Melchizedek was said in Genesis 14:17-20 to have been. This is a portion of the argument made by the writer of the Epistle to the Hebrews to try to persuade Jewish background followers of Jesus to remain among followers of Jesus as the Christ and not return to their previous Jewish beliefs and practices.

Mark 10:35-45

The suffering to be endured is described in this text as "a cup to drink" and as "a baptism with which to be baptized." This is to be experienced by James and John as well as by Jesus; each of them shall suffer and each of them shall die. The difference, however, is that Jesus' suffering and death shall have redemptive significance in a way that the suffering and death of James and of John will not. Because of Jesus' suffering and death, many will have hope. If Jesus as "the Son of man" came not to be served but to serve, how much more should Jesus' followers serve if they wish to be great!

These four texts (Psalm 91:9-16, Isaiah 53:4-12, Hebrews 5:1-10, and Mark 10:35-45) provide a biblical basis for a most serious consideration of the subject of suffering, of what makes suffering redemptive, and of how God is perceived as providing hope through suffering and in spite of the suffering and death of people throughout history and in our own time. Although the suffering and death of Jesus provides the basic Christian model of redemptive suffering, perhaps we as Christians should also perceive that God has been and continues to be active and alive to provide hope through the suffering and death of other people as well. Our study of Psalm 91:9-16, Isaiah 53:10-12, and other texts should keep us open to that possibility.

Job 38:1-7 (34-41)

The long-anticipated and long-awaited response and answer of God to Job in this protracted Job drama finally comes for us in the voice of God speaking from the whirlwind in Job 38:1—42:6. Instead of expressing sympathy and empathy with Job whom God has made to suffer so greatly in order to prove to Satan, the adversary of God, that Job is a blameless and upright man, God points out in great detail how great God is and how inconsequential Job is in comparison to God. Therefore, we have in this Job drama the most profound and extensive theodicy that we see in our entire biblical tradition. How does this help us as Christians to appreciate and to praise God?

Psalm 104:1-9, 24, 35c

We have in these verses in Psalm 104 expressions of the greatness of God as the Creator of the heavens and of the earth that we see more extensively in Job 38:1—42:6, but with humans urged to bless God, to say good things about God, rather than with God stating as in the Job drama how inconsequential even the most blameless and upright humans are. Does this help us as Christians to appreciate and to praise God more or less than the Job text does?

PROPER 25
ORDINARY TIME 30
TWENTY-THIRD SUNDAY AFTER PENTECOST

Sunday between October 23 and October 29 inclusive

Following the emphasis this past Sunday on struggling and suffering, we have in the first three texts to consider for next Sunday the cry to God, "Have mercy on me!" expressed or implied directly to God or to God through Jesus. The prayers for mercy are prayers of communities of faith in the two Old Testament texts and is a prayer of an individual in Mark 10:46-52.

Psalm 126

Severe economic depression and drought appear to be the reason for the prayers for mercy in this psalm. The situation depicted is primarily agricultural. The Lord, who has restored the fortunes of Zion in the past, is urged to act now to deliver the people from sadness and starvation.

Those of us who live close to the soil, who have sowed and waited for the needed rains and have hoped for the harvest that is always uncertain, have the greatest understanding of the plea for mercy in this psalm. Lack of moisture, disease in the crop, destruction by insects, and hail from the skies constantly threaten the livelihood and survival of the grain farmer. No rain means no grass for the cattle. There is no regular paycheck here, only a heavy investment of time and resources and a plea for mercy to God.

Jeremiah 31:7-9

The prayer "Have mercy on us" is declared to have been answered in this text. The return of the exiles in large numbers of all ages and physical conditions is said to be accomplished even though it has not yet occurred. The blind and the lame come, assisted by those who can see and who can walk, in this prophetic declaration. We should not be surprised if there is some exaggeration here, with Jacob described as the chief of the nations and the parade depicted as a great multitude. The theological point to be made is that the Lord has shown mercy abundantly. After many years of waiting and of suffering, the Lord has saved the people who belong to the Lord.

Mark 10:46-52

"Have mercy on me!" the blind beggar Bartimaeus cries out repeatedly when he hears that Jesus of Nazareth is passing by. Bartimaeus refuses to be silent even when many people rebuke him. He states his request and he receives his sight. Instead of going away, he follows Jesus in the way.

Comparison of this account with the redacted texts in Matthew 20:29-34 and in Luke 18:35-43 indicates how freely the Matthean and Lukan writers changed this story. The sequence of events is basically the same in all three accounts, but in Matthew instead of one beggar named Bartimaeus there are two blind men sitting along the path where Jesus was walking and in Luke the blind man was encountered as Jesus was entering the city of Jericho rather than as he was leaving it. This is consistent with the other redactions of Markan material by the Matthean and Lukan writers.

The Matthean redactors often magnified the Markan stories, doubling the number of blind men given sight here, doubling the number of animals on which Jesus rode into Jerusalem, and increasing the speed and magnitude of the miraculous.

The Lukan writer often "pruned" some of the details from the Markan accounts and added other details. Our analysis of the changes made in the redactions from Mark to Matthew and from Mark to Luke indicate that it is very likely that even greater changes would become apparent if we would be able to reach back beyond Mark to the pre-Markan level of oral and written development of this and of other accounts.

The point of this Mark 10:46-52 text, of course, is not in the number of blind men who were given sight or in whether they called upon Jesus as he was entering the city of Jericho or as he was leaving it. The point of these accounts is that those who are blind called upon Jesus to have mercy on them and that Jesus, with the power of God, had mercy on them. That is the message of this Mark 10:46-52 account for us also.

Hebrews 7:23-28

Continuing the persuasive argument used throughout most of the document, the writer of Hebrews states in 7:23-28 that unlike all other priests who are mortal, Jesus as the Christ remains the ruler-priest forever, able for all time to save those who come to God through him, since as the Christ he lives forever to appeal to God in their behalf. Christ is the wonderful high priest who is holy, entirely good, morally pure, differentiated from those who are sinful and raised to heights greater than the heavens.

Job 42:1-6, 10-17

After God has spoken to Job, clearly separating God's almighty and everlasting self from Job's human weakness and limitations, Job repents "in dust and ashes." Then, after Job intercedes with God in behalf of Job's friends, God restores to Job his family and flocks, twice as much as he had before. Job dies in peace as an old man, and the prolonged literary drama is ended.

Psalm 34:1-8 (19-22)

The psalmist testifies that he had cried out to the Lord, and the Lord has delivered him from all of his afflictions. He blesses the Lord with praise and thanksgiving and invites the young men to listen to him, "to taste and see that the Lord is good!"

PROPER 26
ORDINARY TIME 31
TWENTY-FOURTH SUNDAY AFTER PENTECOST

Sunday between October 30 and November 5 inclusive

As we near the conclusion of another Church Year, we see that the texts selected for us for next Sunday emphasize priorities for our lives. The major texts, Deuteronomy 6:1-9 and Mark 12:28-34, boldly proclaim that God is and must be Number One in our lives and that we must remember this at all times. These two texts, in which the most important of the 613 commandments of God in the Torah for Israelites and all Jews and for the Jesus of history as a Jew are highlighted, are used only this one Sunday in our three-year series in the Revised Common Lectionary.

It is unfortunate that in many congregations, other than Roman Catholic congregations and perhaps Episcopalian congregations, All Saints Day is celebrated on the first Sunday in November rather than on November 1 and the texts selected for All Saints Day are used instead of Deuteronomy 6:1-9 and Mark 12:28-34. Also, some Lutheran congregations still celebrate Reformation Sunday on the last Sunday in October and use "Reformation" texts rather than the texts of Proper 26. If we cannot succeed in bringing our congregations together on a weekday on November 1 this year, or on a weekday on October 31 for those of us who are Lutheran Christians, I strongly urge that we use the powerful texts Deuteronomy 6:1-9 and Mark 12:28-34 on the Sunday between October 30 and November 5 this year and call the day "All Saints" Day and, if Lutheran, "All Saints" Day and "Reformation Sunday" as well if we wish. These Deuteronomy 6:1-9 and Mark 12:28-34 texts are strong enough to carry double or even triple emphases! If we must have All Saints Day and Reformation Day as primary emphases, let us schedule worship services this year on November 1 and, if Lutheran, also on October 31, if these are weekdays, and hold meaningful worship services with the people, even if they are few in number, who come on these weekdays to worship God with us.

Deuteronomy 6:1-9

This powerful text speaks specifically to the ancient Israelites, and to all Jews since antiquity, to urge them to remember that God, the Lord God of Israel, the God of their Fathers, is and must always be Number One in their lives. In addition, since the Hebrew word *echad* that is used in Deuteronomy 6:4 is both a cardinal and an ordinal number, God is and has been proclaimed joyously by all Jews every day to be both "One" and "Number One." All Jews, as well as all of us as Christians, Muslims, Hindus, Sikhs, Baha'is, and others, are urged in Deuteronomy 6:5-9 to respond with complete and unconditional love to God, to teach our children these things about God, and to teach them to love God with no reservations, with their total being. Deuteronomy 6:4 is the great confessional statement, "Listen, Israel! The Lord our God, the Lord is Number One!" that in terms of priorities — if not in every respect in terms of terminology — remains the primary statement of faith for all of the religious groups mentioned above, well over half of the people who are living on this planet earth. If we use this text next Sunday, it will be a day in which we can joyously invite our Jewish, Muslim, Hindu, Sikh, Baha'i, and other monotheistic friends to worship God in our congregations with us.

Psalm 119:1-8

The theme of this entire extensive hymn is that those who conduct their lives in accordance with the Torah, the "Word of God," will be blessed. The Torah as "Word of God," therefore, is to have priority in their lives. And it is through the Torah that that the Lord God is known. For us as Christians, God is known through the scriptures that reveal God's love and grace, especially in the life, death, and resurrection of Jesus as the Christ.

Hebrews 9:11-14

For the writer of the Epistle to the Hebrews, and for us, Jesus as the Christ, by entering once and for all into the Holiest Place of all and offering his very own blood accomplished an eternal redemption for all of us who draw near to God through him. Consequently, it should obviously be the top priority for us as Christians to draw near to God through Jesus as the Christ.

Ruth 1:1-18

The obvious connection to the other texts selected for next Sunday of this text in the story of Ruth is the statement to her mother-in-law Naomi by Ruth in 1:16 that "Your God, Naomi, will be my God." If God is indeed perceived as the one and only God, as we see in Deuteronomy 6:4 in our Bibles, the change in the faith and in the religion of Ruth was perhaps not as major as we may have thought. If there is indeed only one God, Ruth was changing her name for the one God, but not her basic faith in God. What implications does this have for us today in terms of "conversion" terminology, especially within Christianity?

Psalm 146

This beautiful "Halleluia!" psalm is an expression of praise to God as the Creator of the heavens and of the earth and as the One who is Active in Our Lives, doing in us and with us what we ought to do, establishing justice for the oppressed, providing food for the hungry, and lifting up those who are bowed down. The psalmist urges all who will listen to trust in the Lord and not to put their trust entirely on human rulers who all too often support the wicked rather than the oppressed and who themselves soon die.

Mark 12:28-34

Because the careful study of this text and of its parallels in Matthew 22:34-40 and Luke 10:25-28 provide for us some of the best access we have to the Jesus of history, let us analyze them exegetically. Comparison of these accounts within the Synoptic Gospels indicates that quotations by Jesus of Deuteronomy 6:4-5 and of a portion of Leviticus 19:18 are the central core of these texts. Each of the three Synoptic Gospels' traditions has a different introduction (Mark 12:28, Matthew 22:34-35, and Luke 10:25) to the central core saying of Jesus (Mark 12:29). Neither the Matthean nor the Lukan redactors use Jesus' quotation of Deuteronomy 6:4, "Listen, Israel! The Lord our God, the Lord is Number One!" most likely because this statement was considered to be too Jewish to be used in the extended Markan communities in Antioch and Ephesus when the Matthean and Lukan redactions were made. It is important to note also that the Matthean and Lukan redactors did not use the pleasant exchange of theological insights between the Jewish scribe and Jesus that we have in Mark 12:32-34ab, probably because these redactor-writers and their communities were no longer themselves having pleasant theological conversations with Pharisees and other Jews who were continuing to be thoroughly Jewish and not joining these developing Christian communities. Therefore, they did not wish to portray Jesus as they understood Jesus as having the pleasant theological conversations with another interested and intelligent Jew as Jesus had been portrayed in Mark 12:32-34ab. We see also that the Lukan writer reshaped the materials from the Markan account to make them serve a different purpose, as the Lukan writer's introduction to the Lukan parable of the Good Samaritan.

With regard to genre, Rudolf Bultmann in his *The History of the Synoptic Tradition*, trans. by J. Marsh (New York: Harper & Row, 1963), page 51, called Mark 12:28-34 a "pure scholastic dialogue" (*Schulgespräch*) and noted that Matthew and Luke transformed the genre of the account into a "controversy dialogue" or "conflict story" (*Streitgespräch*). Actually, with additional study, we today can say that already in the Markan account when the Markan writer added the adversarial introduction (Mark 12:28) and the very adversarial conclusion, "After that, no one dared to ask him any more questions" (Mark 12:34c), which is certainly a very strange conclusion to provide after a very pleasant conversation between Jesus and another interested and intelligent Jew, the Markan account is in a transition from a pleasant *Schulgespräch* to an adversarial *Streitgespräch*. At the pre-Markan level of development, basically the central body of the text in Mark 12:29-34ab, the material was still a pleasant *Schulgespräch*. Earlier in the development of the tradition, the material had been an important reminiscence by followers of Jesus in Galilee of what Jesus had said many times about the most important commandments in the Torah during pleasant and respectful conversations with a variety of other interested and intelligent Jews. Still earlier, during the lifetime of the Jesus of history as we can reconstruct it from this and from similar texts, the genre of the material was "a discussion about the most important and basic commandments in the Torah."

Parenthetically, we may postulate that it is likely that many of Mark's other controversy dialogues, especially in the series of such conflict stories that we have in Mark 2:1—3:6 and in Mark 11:27—12:37 and parallels in Matthew and in Luke, originated in discussions that the Jesus of history had with other intelligent and interested Jews about the commandments in the Torah. Many of these were repeated as followers of Jesus after his death reminisced about what

Jesus had said. Increasingly, these followers of Jesus came to see Jesus as their teacher and they as students (disciples) of Jesus. If we are interested in the reminiscences of followers of Jesus after his death and in what the Jesus of history said, we will focus our attention on the "pure scholastic dialogue, the *Schulgespräch* preserved and accessible to us in the main body of the text in Mark 12:29-34ab.

When we focus our study on the main body of this text, Mark 12:29-34ab, we can identify three interrelated themes.

1) God is Number One (vv. 29-30). Every other person and one's self are number two (v. 31), and by implication, all other things, even our most important religious rituals and practices, are number three.

2) Good theology (that God is Number One) and good ethics (loving one's neighbor as one's self) are more important than religious rituals (vv. 32-33).

3) When themes 1 and 2 (i.e., that God is Number One and that good theology and good ethics are more important than religious rituals) are affirmed, a person is "not far from the kingdom of God" (v. 34ab). In other words, then a person is not far from being ready to let God rule that person's life. These themes provide the basic materials from this text that we can use for personal, pastoral counseling, didactic, and homiletical applications, on applications that are firmly grounded in this text.

PROPER 27
ORDINARY TIME 32
TWENTY-FIFTH SUNDAY AFTER PENTECOST

Sunday between November 6 and November 12 inclusive

First Kings 17:8-16 and Psalm 146 both, though in different ways, describe how the Lord God provides what is needed by the poor and oppressed and most of all for the widow and the fatherless. Mark 12:39-40 is a warning against the scribes who are said to act as if they are very religious, while secretly they are taking possession of the houses of poor widows whom they evict. Mark 12:41-44 has Jesus acclaim a poor widow who puts her last two small copper coins into the temple treasury, trusting that God will provide for her, and God will give everything that she needs to her just as she has given everything to God. In Hebrews 9:24-28 the argument of this document continues that Jesus as the Christ has made the once-for-all sacrifice of himself to overcome sin and announces that Jesus as the Risen Christ will appear again in order to save those who are waiting for him. These texts bring us one more step closer, therefore, to the end of the Church Year.

1 Kings 17:8-16

This story is most of all an expression of faith that the Lord God provides what is necessary, even for the most needy person that one can imagine, a poor widow with a dependent child during an extended famine. Elijah, the "man of God," is a rather passive figure in the story. The widow is a hero of faith because she believes the "man of God" when he tells her that the Lord, the God of Israel, will continue to supply grain and oil until the famine is ended.

We, who live in a much less precarious situation than that of the poor widow, should certainly believe, as she did, that God will provide also for us. Therefore, we should share our resources with others who are in need and trust in God, just as the widows do in both the 1 Kings 17:8-16 and in the Mark 12:41-44 accounts.

Psalm 146

This joyful "Halleluia" psalm considered also last week amply illustrates that praise of God is our most appropriate response to God. The psalmist praises the Lord God as the faithful in Israel perceive God, as the Creator of heaven and earth and the Provider of everything that is needed by those who remain faithful to their covenant with the Lord.

With the wisdom gained from experiences during a lifetime of faith in the Lord, the psalmist urges all who will listen not to trust human rulers, who all too often support their friends who are greedy and oppressive rather than provide help for the oppressed. Such rulers soon die. The psalmist calls upon all people to praise the Lord who will live forever. The older we become the more we appreciate the wisdom expressed in this psalm.

Hebrews 9:24-28

This text is packed full of Christian faith in the significance of Jesus' life and death. The writer summarizes a vast amount of theological reflection by followers of Jesus over the value to be found in Jesus' painful crucifixion by the oppressive Roman occupational forces. Then the writer gives this theological reflection a new twist in this document by depicting Jesus as the great high priest entering the holy place once and for all to offer his own blood as the totally efficacious sacrifice for sin. In this depiction of the death of Jesus we see Jesus totally in control of the situation, even more than in the depiction of Jesus as in control of the situation within the Fourth Gospel. The text of Hebrews 9:24-28 concludes with the statement that Jesus as the Risen

Christ will appear again not to die this time but to provide salvation for those who are eagerly waiting for him.

Mark 12:38-44

If one of the primary criteria for an event to be newsworthy is that it be unusual, the event here of the poor widow giving her last two small copper coins to the Lord in this Mark 12:41-44 account certainly qualifies. Total commitment to God is unusual and newsworthy. The issue here is not how much could be accomplished for herself or for others with her small offering or whether her decision was a rational or an irrational act. The issue here is the significance of her trust in God. Her offering of everything that she had to God is comparable to the total commitment of the poor widow in the 1 Kings 17:8-16 account and even in some respects to the total commitment of Jesus as the Christ in the Hebrews 9:24-28 account used with this text.

Can such a commitment be expected also of us? Can we ourselves model such a commitment to God, and can we then urge others to make such a commitment to God?

Ruth 3:1-5; 4:13-17

In these two excerpts from the story of Ruth we see the "hidden hand" of God at work in the success of the bold actions of Ruth as directed and guided by her mother-in-law Naomi. Whatever the methods, the result was good. Naomi has a son "born" to her!

Psalm 127

The son "born" to Naomi through her daughter-in-law Ruth and the good man Boaz became the foundation of the "house" of David. It was to be a house built by the Lord God of Israel. According to Psalm 127, unless the Lord God builds a house, it cannot be constructed; if we try to build it ourselves, it will crumble.

PROPER 28
ORDINARY TIME 33
TWENTY-SIXTH SUNDAY AFTER PENTECOST

Sunday between November 13 and 19 inclusive

Daniel 12:1-3

The composer of this apocalyptic text that we call Daniel wrote in this portion that "At that time, there will be great trouble and anxiety!" As we read this, it is important that we realize the writer was describing events of his own time, not of our time nearly 2,200 years later. Whether we are reading apocalyptic texts such as Daniel, or the Apocalypse (the book of Revelation) in the New Testament, or any other text in our Bibles, we are reading about events that were occurring during the time in which the biblical texts were written. They were not written specifically about anything that is happening now. Do we, no matter how inspired we may be, speak, teach, and preach about events that will occur 2,200 years into the future? We speak, teach, and preach about events within our time, just as they spoke, taught, and preached about events within their time.

Therefore, we should be reluctant to accept unquestioningly what people say when they try to tell us that something written in the Bible was written with specific reference to someone or to something in our time and place. In our study and use of biblical texts we must always begin with learning as much as we can about the setting in which the texts were formulated. When we have done that, then it is necessary to bring what we have learned over into our time and place and make the appropriate applications. That is what we are called to do.

The Daniel traditions were formed by devout Jews who were living during the oppressive rule of the Seleucid dictator Antiochus Epiphanes within the years 167-164 BCE. That

Syrian ruler apparently thought that the Hellenistic culture he had embraced was far superior to any other culture and that the culture and lifestyle of the small minority of people called Jews was so hopelessly inferior that for the good of his realm and even for the good of the Jews, Hellenistic culture should be accepted by everyone. Therefore, it was a period of great trouble and anxiety for Jews who wanted to remain Jews within that situation.

What do we have in our situations that is comparable to what is depicted in the Daniel traditions? What is there in our situations of economic, political, social, and religious catastrophes that can be compared to what is depicted in Daniel? What people and groups today are in situations that are somewhat similar to the situation of the Jews whose survival as a people was uncertain at the time Daniel 12:1-3 was written?

It is the hope and prediction of the writer of Daniel 12:1-3 that soon the Jews, the people of God, will be delivered from this threat to their lives and culture. This is expressed in terms of a return to life even of some who "sleep in their graves." They will awake, some to a condition of eternal life and some to one of eternal contempt. It is not clear whether this expectation was intended to apply to the return to life of the Jewish people as a whole, in groups, or as individual Jews. Perhaps at first it was intended to apply to the Jewish people as a whole; then later to groups of Jews (the easier concepts), and finally to individual Jews (the most difficult). At any rate, there is evidence that the hope of the return to life of individual Jews became the hope of some Jews, but not of all Jews, during what we as Christians call the intertestamental period.

This is the milieu in which the Jesus of history lived. It is the milieu in which Christianity was developed and formed. It is the hope for the return to life of individuals that has made Christianity and later Islam attractive to so many people. Certainly we are called to proclaim with personal conviction this hope in the resurrection to life of individuals. We are called to proclaim this hope with our lives and in the message that we share next Sunday and every day.

Psalm 16

The psalmist remains faithful to the Lord and the Lord provides guidance, security, and a meaningful life for the psalmist. In the presence of the Lord the psalmist has complete satisfaction and joy.

This was a good arrangement for the psalmist, and it is a good arrangement for us. For us, of course, the Lord is God as we perceive God, as Father, Son, and Holy Spirit. Each of us perceives God in a special, unique way, as special and as unique as we ourselves are as individuals within the diversity of the Church, the "Body of Christ" in the world.

Hebrews 10:11-14 (15-18) 19-25

Our emphasis in our application of Hebrews 10:11-14 (15-18) 19-25 should be on Jesus as the Risen Christ sitting at the "right hand" of God and waiting until his enemies will be placed as a footstool under his feet. Part of our job will be to explain, if necessary, that the language of Hebrews 10:12-13 is taken from what was known at the time of the composition of this text about how ancient monarchs ruled from their thrones above the people with their closest subordinates seated on either side of the monarchs to give the orders and to do the "dirty work" that was necessary so that the monarchs could retain their power and authority. Then, perhaps we should use some other descriptive language more appropriate for our time to depict and to proclaim what is proclaimed in this text. It is important that we emphasize that the descriptive language used by the writer of the Epistle to the Hebrews is descriptive, vivid language. It is, in a sense, "art" work. We should not necessarily expect in the life to come to see God the Father seated on a throne and Jesus as God the Son seated on a lesser but still ornate chair with his feet on a footstool comprised of his enemies and mimicking the practice of ancient potentates and their closest subordinates.

Mark 13:1-8

This introductory portion of the Mark 13 "Little Apocalypse" is most likely a mixture of statements that the Jesus of history had made on various occasions about catastrophes that would occur soon, both those that would involve phenomena in nature such as earthquakes and famine and those that would be political disasters such as wars and the destruction of Jerusalem and of the temple within it, and experiences of Jesus' followers after he had been crucified. The experiences of Jesus' followers, including events that were occurring during the revolt against the Roman occupation by Jewish nationalists in 66 CE and the suppression of that revolt during the seven years that followed it, were incorporated into what Jesus himself had said. If the Gospel According to Mark was initially written among followers of Jesus who had fled among other refugees from Galilee and Judea as Roman armies were converging upon those areas to suppress that revolt, they could easily have added vivid historical details from reports that they received about the Roman siege of Jerusalem and of the destruction of the city and of its temple. We cannot, therefore, use the details about the destruction of Jerusalem in Mark 13 to determine the precise dating of the composition of Mark's Gospel.

What is obvious from our study of these texts is that the Markan writer and community considered the tumultuous times in which they were living to be analogous to the times described in the Daniel traditions, and like those who had compiled the Daniel traditions two and a half centuries earlier, they hoped for relief from the horrible afflictions imposed upon them by the world power of their time. Like those who had compiled the Daniel traditions, these followers of Jesus could not safely write directly against their oppressors or identify them by name. They could not safely mention the name of the currently reigning Roman Caesar any more than the writers of the Daniel tradition could mention the name of Antiochus Epiphanes during their time.

1 Samuel 1:4-20

This portion of the 1 Samuel document provides the backdrop for the reading of the Song of Hannah in 1 Samuel 2:1-10 that is used with it. The oppression here is caused by the situation of barrenness of Hannah and by the initial inability of her husband Elkanah and of the priest Eli to help her to deal with her affliction. When Eli finally understood the reason for her weeping and blessed her, her affliction ended as she conceived and bore a son, who would become the great religious leader in Israelite life and politics, Samuel.

1 Samuel 2:1-10

The Song of Hannah, along with the Song of Mary (the Magnificat) in Luke 1:46-55 that is modeled upon it, is essentially a thanksgiving to the Lord God for the reversal of fortune as God breaks into pieces the military power of the oppressors and raises up from the dust the poor and oppressed. Such exaltation is understandable given the conditions of oppression experienced. From the perspective of many of us for whom oppression is much less severe, we may hope that conditions of oppression could change without a complete reversal of fortunes. We are aware that oppressed people who come into power sometimes become oppressors themselves when they possess power.

PROPER 29
ORDINARY TIME 34
LAST DAY AFTER PENTECOST
(REIGN OF CHRIST or CHRIST THE KING)

Sunday between November 20 and November 26 inclusive

John 18:33-37

We have in John 18:33-37 a combination of historical recollection that the Jesus of history had been tortured and crucified by the Roman governor Pontius Pilate as a political leader, a potential "King of the Jews," and consequently a potential threat to the Roman occupation of Galilee and Judea, and of theological reflection of the role of the Johannine Jesus within the Johannine community. In this text the Roman governor is depicted as confused and frustrated but trying to be just and fair. The "Jews" are portrayed as the evil people and nation to whom Jesus was handed over and who in turn handed Jesus over to Pilate for condemnation and crucifixion. The Johannine writers and community have their Jesus admit finally that he had been born to be a king and that he had come as a king to testify to the truth, but his kingdom was not derived from this world. The kingship and the kingdom of the Johannine Jesus are given to him by God, not through human earthly authority. The theological reflection and claims of the Johannine community take us far from the life of the Jesus of history.

As we celebrate Christ as the King next Sunday, it will be essential that we emphasize that having Jesus the Risen Christ as our king is as much or more our future hope than it is our present reality. We should also be aware that the Jesus of history would probably be uncomfortable with our Christ the King emphasis. The Jesus of history would most likely identify with the oppressed people of our time and die with them rather than identify with our Christ the King emphasis.

In the English language there are a variety of single syllable words such as "sing," "cling," "ring," and "wing" that rhyme with "king." This has made the use of the designation of Jesus Christ as king a favorite for writers of English language hymns, especially during the Christmas, Epiphany, Lent, and Easter seasons. It has often been observed that the hymns we sing have as much or more impact on the thinking of many Christians than the actual biblical texts have. As a result of the rhyming of these word endings and our heavy use of these hymns, our Lord Jesus Christ is designated as king in our thinking within the English language far more frequently than Jesus is designated as "the King" in the Greek New Testament.

Revelation 1:4b-8

According to this text, oppressive people in all of the tribes of the earth (in the New Testament and especially in the book of Revelation this means within the Roman Empire) will wail and beat their breasts in grief because of the coming of Jesus the Christ in the clouds. However, by contrast, those who have remained faithful within the Johannine community are said to be loved by Jesus Christ, the Ruler over the kings of this world, i.e., over Caesar and his subordinates who rule in the provinces that Rome governs and from which it draws its economic resources. The Johannine Jesus with his divine power has freed those who have been cleansed of their sins by the blood of this Lamb of God and has provided for them a kingdom in which they will serve as priests of God, Christ's Father. Here, as elsewhere in the Apocalypse, Jesus the Christ is said to be powerful but subordinate in power to the Lord God, the Alpha and the Omega, who is, and was, and is to come, the Almighty.

Daniel 7:9-10, 13-14

The attempts to interpret the symbolism inherent in the words "one like a son of man" in Daniel 7:13 are innumerable, but within the context of Daniel 7 it is most likely that the person who wrote this verse intended the words "son of man" to be a personification of the righteous people of Israel, the perfect image of the righteous people within Israel, Israel at its best, and hope for a fulfillment that will be experienced by Israel at some time in the future. All peoples, nations, and languages will some day serve this "son of man," this righteous people so long oppressed, and by their service to this "son of man" they ultimately will serve the Lord God.

The interpretations given above, along with the concept of the "son of man" as the ideal messianic king, have remained for the most part the principal interpretations of the "son of man" symbol within Jewish use of this text. Christians, until recently becoming interested in a rediscovery of the original significance of the son of man image, have generally considered Daniel 7:13-14 to be a prediction of the visible return of Jesus to the earth as Christ the Triumphant King at the end of time. As we who are Christians serve Jesus as the Triumphant King, we also ultimately serve God. Jesus as the Christ, in this instance as Christ the King, has become for many Christians much of what Israel at its best has been for Jews. It is important for us to recognize this and to share these interpretations in the congregations within which we serve. If we do this, we can use Daniel 7:13-14 on Christ the King Sunday with an adequate awareness of what we are doing.

Psalm 93

The terminology of this psalm is obviously political, drawn from human experiences with kings, royal courts, and the exercise of political power. Many anthropomorphic terms are utilized in an effort to demonstrate that although from all appearances the world is ruled by the leaders of the great world powers who controlled the Ancient Near East, actually only the Lord God who transcends time and space in power and majesty is the King of the Universe who increasingly came to be addressed as such in Jewish prayers. We as Christians continue that practice, with some modifications caused by specifically Christian theological developments regarding Jesus as the Christ, as Christ the King, one with God perceived as Father and God perceived as Holy Spirit.

2 Samuel 23:1-7

This hymn of praise, presented in 2 Samuel 23:1 as the last words of David the king, represents poetically what David as king could and should have been and done.

Psalm 132:1-12 (13-18)

This psalm also depicts what David as king could and should have been and done rather than what David as king actually was and did. What we have here that is not in 2 Samuel 23:1-7 are the references to David as king desiring to build a house for the Lord, a dwelling place for the Mighty One of Jacob.

ALL SAINTS

November 1 or the First Sunday in November

John 11:32-44

The message of this text is that the Johannine Jesus has the power of God to raise from the dead a beloved friend who had been dead for four days and already was decomposing! This is a very powerful message that we treasure, since we fully realize that we too will die and decompose as Lazarus was said to have been decomposing in this account. What is proclaimed here in John 11:32-44 is not merely a resuscitation; it is fully a resurrection of the body. This proclamation is reassuring for us, as we receive it by faith, so that we do not think that only Jesus (who was and is obviously far superior to us) was or will be raised from the dead. This account is an indication that other people, ordinary people like ourselves, who love Jesus and are loved by him will be raised from the dead.

Since the account is a theological message, a message that is an expression of faith, to be received by faith, we should not ask of it questions about Lazarus' experiences during the four-day interval, what he did with his life after Jesus had raised him back to life, or whether he died at a later date like everyone else. Neither should we speculate about these things, nor should we try to provide answers to such questions within our proclamation of this text. It is enough (and best) for us to proclaim the message of this text and to state that we believe the message that God will raise us also from the dead, for that is the message that we believe and that is the message that has made Christianity what it is.

Revelation 21:1-6a

In the highly symbolic language of apocalyptic eschatology, this text is a beautiful proclamation of our

Christian hope. As we, like the writer of Revelation 21:1-6a and the people for whom this text was written, grow weary, suffer great pain and loss, we, like them, long for a time and a place where there will be no more pain and grief, where there will be no more death. This is what we hope for the "saints" who have died, and this is what we hope for ourselves. Every day, but most of all on All Saints' Day, we must proclaim this message of Christian hope. It is for this that we are called.

Wisdom of Solomon 3:1-9

This text is an expression of faith that those who have died are in the hands of God and at peace. God watches over them with grace and mercy. Although this expression of faith is made within the context of the Greek concept of the immortality of the soul, it can be brought together, as it has often been done, with our Christian concept of the resurrection of the body and of life everlasting within the "Body of Christ" that has no limits.

Isaiah 25:6-9

Although there is nothing specifically about the life, death, and resurrection of Jesus as the Christ in this text from the Isaiah traditions, the belief expressed here that God will "swallow up death forever," that the Lord our God will "wipe away tears from all faces," and that we should "be glad and rejoice in the salvation God provides" can not only be shared with our Jewish, Muslim, Hindu, Sikh, and Baha'i friends, and with other theists; it can and also should be brought into our Christian expressions of faith, especially during our All Saints' Day celebrations.

Psalm 24

Within the context of our Christian observance of All Saints' Day, the saints redeemed by God in Christ are, in the words of this Israelite psalm, those who with "clean hands and a pure heart" are receiving the blessing of the Lord. What the Israelite psalmist required for satisfactory worship of God in this world is basically what we as Christians anticipate will be the condition of those who in the presence of God worship God in the world that is to come.

THANKSGIVING DAY

Fourth Thursday in November (United States)
Second Monday in October (Canada)

Our seminary experiences and our work as pastors may have provided for us relatively few resources for use as leaders in the celebration of national holidays such as Memorial Days, Independence Days, Veterans' Days, and National Days of Thanksgiving. We may be urged by members of the congregations in which we serve to combine national holidays with Sunday Worship Services or even at times to replace Christian Worship Services with the celebration of national holidays within our congregations. Many of us respond to these requests by attempting, therefore, to include the celebration of national holidays within our Christian Worship Services several times each year, often with mixed results that for the people whom we serve confuse rather than clarify the distinction between civil religion and ecclesial religion and between church and state.

We are qualified leaders in ecclesial religion, but not in civil (state) religion. The national level of religion is prominent and is mingled with ecclesial religion with less than desirable results in much of the Old Testament. The national level of religion became prominent and was mingled with Christianity also in the Church after Christianity became essentially the state religion of the Roman Empire and of many of the nation states that evolved out of remnants of it, but within the New Testament the national religion of the Roman Empire was the principal oppressor of the developing Church, torturing and killing many of its most prominent leaders.

Even the most appropriate of biblical texts, therefore, such as the four selected for our use on Thanksgiving Day in Series B, do not address our situations of religious pluralism within constitutional democracies such as we have in the United States and Canada. As a result, we most often observe national days of thanksgiving only minimally within our separate ecclesial structures. Our most significant celebrations are usually only in our individual homes enjoying expansive family dinners and watching football games on large TV screens. Rarely do we come together as a total community to express our thanks to God within a civil religion setting.

Thanksgiving to God for life, sustenance, health, and other blessings should be for us a constant activity every day of our lives. If as the people of a particular nation we wish to specify a particular day near the conclusion of an ecclesial year or of a secular year, or during a season of fresh fruits, vegetables, and grain harvests as a day of thanksgiving as the people of a nation, perhaps we should be led in such thanksgiving events not by religious leaders of particular ecclesial religions but by the elected or appointed leaders of the state and nation, from executive, legislative, and judicial levels of government. Then there would be the possibility that all of the people of our communities and nations might participate fully and freely in thanksgiving to God. In such a situation, leaders at the various levels of government should not function as members of a particular ecclesial religion, but should address God in the name of all of the people of the community, state, or nation.

There are resources for doing this within the literature and national patriotic hymns of each nation, state, and community. With proper preparation national, state, and community leaders can do this well. They, rather than ecclesial ministers, pastors, priests, rabbis, imams, etc., should provide the leadership on such occasions, not only on national days of thanksgiving but also on other public occasions such as meetings of units of government, dedications, public athletic events, graduation ceremonies in public schools, etc. This would eliminate or at least alleviate many of the problems that we have over the issue of ecclesial prayers and of ecclesial worship activities within the public schools.

If, however, we do come together ecclesially within our various individual Christian communities or as groups of congregations planning ecclesial worship together on national days of thanksgiving, the texts selected here for us can be used, with some adaptations to our particular situations.

Joel 2:21-27

This text from the Joel traditions is very relevant in agricultural and ranching areas in which, after one or more "lean" years of drought and famine, during the current year the amounts of rainfall have been adequate and have come at the times when they were most needed. It is not an appropriate text to use during a year in which the grass is brown or the land has been flooded. It is also not directly relevant in situations in which the people are affluent and urban and buy most of their food and eat in restaurants supplied with fresh food purchased from world markets.

This text is a prime example of the limitations of using lectionaries prepared in advance to be used in specific occasions where it cannot be known years earlier what conditions will prevail when a text will be used. It would be helpful for those of us who use lectionaries if in situations such as this in which the purpose is to give thanks to God for a bountiful harvest this text could be one option among others so that we could choose the one that is most appropriate. During years of drought and economic recession, for example, we need to use texts in which we are encouraged to believe in God no matter how adverse the economy and how barren the crops may be. An alternate text from the same Joel tradition for use during "bad" years could be Joel 1:10-14; 2:12-17. If our texts and our worship of God based on our texts are relevant, people will be helped and will come. If our texts and our worship of God based on our texts are not relevant, people will not be helped and they will leave.

Psalm 126

The range of situations in which use of Psalm 126 is relevant is much broader than is the Joel 2:21-27 text considered above. Conditions described here are less specific than in the Joel texts. The people are reminded of what the Lord God has done for them in the past, and they call upon God to bring joyful conditions to them again now.

1 Timothy 2:1-7

This text, while not entirely appropriate for use in a civil religion celebration of thanksgiving, is a good choice for use among Christians. Requests, prayers, intercessions, and thanksgivings to God should certainly be made on a national day of thanksgiving and on every other day as well. We should ask God to guide "kings" and others who are in prominent positions over us so that "we may live an undisturbed and quiet life in all godliness and holiness." What the writer of 1 Timothy 2:1-7 urged followers of Jesus to do within the oppressive conditions imposed by the leaders in the Roman Empire can and should be done today. It should be supplemented for us who live within constitutional democracies with responsibilities to use our resources in church and state to provide assistance in health care, education, and lifestyle for all who need such assistance in our land and throughout the world.

Matthew 6:25-33

After followers of Jesus are urged not to be unduly concerned about securing lavish food and clothing for themselves, the key verse is the "bottom line" in Matthew 6:33, "First, strive for letting God rule your lives and for

334

doing what is the right thing in all of the relationships of your lives. Then all of these other things will be provided for you." This verse sums it all up very well, on Thanksgiving Day and on every day!

SPECIAL DAYS (A, B, C)

February 2
Presentation of the Lord

Malachi 3:1-4

It is somewhat of a stretch to apply this text, a text that anticipates the coming of the Lord God to the temple of the Lord, a coming that will refine with fire and purify with a caustic soap the Israelite people, with the presentation of the infant Jesus in the temple within a ceremony of the purification of his mother after the birth of her son. Nevertheless, it can be done. The Lukan writer did it and so can we.

Psalm 84

The joy of coming to the place where the gathered community worships the Lord God and remaining there is articulated beautifully in this psalm. The Lukan writer was apparently fascinated by the focus on the temple by many of the ancient Israelites and consequently portrayed the Lukan Jesus as brought to the temple as an infant by Mary and Joseph and as seeking out the temple as a twelve-year-old boy.

Psalm 24:7-10

This is a call that the gates and doors of the temple be opened so that the people will be able to enter bearing the ark that symbolizes the presence of the Lord so it may be brought into the temple and put into its appointed place. For the Lukan writer, the infant Jesus, far more than the ark, symbolized that presence of the Lord and was the presence of the Lord in human form.

Hebrews 2:14-18

Although it is not likely that the Lukan writer was familiar with this expression by the author of the Epistle to the Hebrews that Jesus as the great High Priest entered into the holiest place in the temple in order to offer himself as the supreme sacrifice for the sins of the people by experiencing and overcoming death, the Lukan writer accomplished much of the same purpose, alone among the authors of our four canonical Gospels, by having Jesus enter the temple as an infant carried by his mother.

Luke 2:22-40

Through the voices of the aged man Simeon and the aged woman Anna, the Lukan writer expressed the belief that the infant Jesus would be the means by which God would "accomplish salvation" and "redeem the people from oppression." It is in the "bottom line" summary of this text that the Lukan writer articulated it best, with the words, "And the child Jesus increased in size and became strong, filled with wisdom, and the grace of God was obvious in his life." May the same in other ways be said about us, and about our children and grandchildren on this day.

March 25
Annunciation of the Lord

Perhaps the most appropriate way that I can introduce these brief reflections over the texts appointed for our observance of the Annunciation of the Lord on March 25 this year is by quoting the Prayer for the Day for this occasion from *Evangelical Lutheran Worship* (Minneapolis: Augsburg Fortress, 2006), page 55, "Pour your grace into our hearts, O God, that we who have known the incarnation of your Son, Jesus Christ, announced by an angel, may by his cross and passion be brought to the glory of his resurrection; for he lives and reigns with you, in the unity of the Holy Spirit, one God, now and forever. Amen."

Isaiah 7:10-14

When, after the death of Jesus, some of his followers searched within the Torah and Prophetic traditions for texts they could use in support of their contention that Jesus had indeed been and continued to be "God among them," Isaiah 7:14, isolated from its own context, quickly became one of their favorites. And so it has remained until this day.

Nevertheless, as we as Christians use this text on March 25 this year, it is important that we realize when we look at Isaiah 7:14 in its own context that Isaiah 7:10-17 was and still is a poetic way someone within the Isaiah tradition was saying that within 12-15 years King Ahaz will have to face a foe, the king of Assyria, whose armies will destroy both Syria and the Northern Kingdom Israel.

The use by the Lukan writer of the Septuagint Greek translation of the Hebrew Bible, in which the Hebrew word for any woman capable of bearing a child had been rendered by a Greek word that specified a virgin woman, made the use of Isaiah 7:14 as proof of the "prediction" of the birth of Jesus to a virgin feasible. We should remember on this day and always that the birth of Jesus to a virgin is a theological construct, a very important theological construct for us, not a historical construct. As leaders in Christian worship, we proclaim theological constructs. That is our call and our task. We should not depreciate the theological constructs we proclaim by attempting foolishly to claim that they are merely historical constructs.

Psalm 45

Much to be preferred as a choice for a reading from the psalms on this occasion would be Psalm 40:5-10 rather than this "flowery" acclamation in Psalm 45 of a king in ancient

Israel on the occasion of his marriage to a Phoenician princess. Comparisons of the king acclaimed here with Jesus, our Lord and Savior on this day when we celebrate the annunciation of his birth by an angel are difficult, to say the least! It can be done, of course, by concentrating on the desire of the ancient Israelites that their king and his bride will rule together with grace, justice, and righteousness and stating that what the ancient Israelites hoped for in their king, we as Christians believe is manifest in Jesus, our Risen Lord and Savior.

Psalm 40:5-10

What the grateful psalmist proclaimed in this psalm about the "wondrous thoughts and deeds" of the Lord God and of the "steadfast love and faithfulness" of the Lord God in delivering the psalmist from grave distress we as Christians can and should say about Jesus our Lord and Savior, the annunciation of whose "conception" we celebrate on this day.

Hebrews 10:4-10

This reading is linked to Psalm 40:5-10 by the paraphrase of portions of Psalm 40 regarding God's desire that people do God's will rather than sacrificing animals and offering material gifts while disregarding the will of God. It is interesting to note that the writer of the Epistle to the Hebrews designated Christ as the one who said what the author of Psalm 40 had written.

The writer of the Epistle to the Hebrews used this consistently to state once more that because Jesus as the Christ came to do the will of God "we are forgiven and sanctified through the offering of the body of Jesus Christ once and for all, for all people and for all time." This we celebrate as we read the Lukan writer's story about the annunciation to the Virgin Mary of the "theological" conception of Jesus.

Luke 1:26-38

As this dramatic announcement is made to the Virgin Mary that she will become pregnant and bear a son whom she shall call Jesus, she responds not in disbelief but only with a question about the process by which this will occur, since she does not yet have a husband. When the angel Gabriel explains to her that this will happen when "God the Holy Spirit will come to you and when the power of God the Most High will cast a shadow over you," Mary replies that she will do whatever the Lord says, and affirms, "May all of this happen to me just as you have said." Mary as presented here is certainly a prime role model for each of us as Christians. For some Christians she is, of course, this and much, much more!

May 31
Visitation of Mary to Elizabeth

1 Samuel 2:1-10

This "Song of Hannah" is notable for us as Christians because it was obviously the primary model used by the Lukan writer in the formulation of the "Song of Mary," the "Magnificat," in Luke 1:46-55. It is actually one of many poetic expressions added to and used with sections of prose in Hebrew narratives. In some instances, of course, such poetic expressions may have antedated the narrative sections or have been composed at the same time as the composition of the narrative, as was most likely done by the Lukan playwright in composing Luke 1-2.

It is often noted that only in the reference to "the one who had been barren has given birth to seven" in 1 Samuel 2:5 is the content of the "Song of Hannah" closely connected to her condition as portrayed in the narrative. There is, of course, the expression of faith in 1 Samuel 2:9 that the Lord will guard the feet of the faithful ones that can be applied to Hannah, as well as to Mary in the Lukan account.

Psalm 113

This psalm is used appropriately with the 1 Samuel 2:1-10 and Luke 1:39-57 texts. It has a connection with Hannah's situation in the statement in Psalm 113 that the Lord God gives to the woman who had been barren a household as a joyous mother. It expresses the belief that the Lord lifts up the poor and needy, different in this respect from the "Song of Hannah" and the "Song of Mary" in which God is said to have put down the mighty from their seats.

Romans 12:9-16b

What Paul wrote in this section of his letter to the followers of Jesus in the house churches in Rome about the warm affection and devotion that they should have for one another is illustrated by the Lukan writer in how the relationships between Mary the mother of Jesus and Elizabeth the mother of John the Baptist are depicted in Luke 1:39-57 as they rejoiced together and prepared for the birth of their sons. They were, as Paul urged his readers in Romans 12:11 to be, "boiling over with the Spirit, serving the Lord." So also we should be at all times.

Luke 1:39-57

Elizabeth during the final three months of her pregnancy and Mary during the first three months of hers sharing their experiences of pregnancy and anticipating their responsibilities and joys as mothers is a bonding activity that no man can ever know. There is nothing in this text about Zachariah or about Joseph during this time, not even the suggestion that Joseph traveled with Mary to protect her as she traveled from Nazareth in Galilee to and from the city in the hill country of Judea where Elizabeth was living.

These were entirely presented as experiences of women. It is because all of the segments in the conception and birth of Jesus accounts in Luke 1:26—2:38 are presented from the perspective of Mary and because throughout the Gospel According to Luke and Acts of Apostles women are depicted with much more prominence than anywhere else in the New Testament that many of us think that Luke and Acts may have been written by a woman or at least by a man who was very sensitive to the perspectives of women. All of this makes us even more amazed and saddened that in the denominations of the Church in which the majority of Christians live women are prevented from serving as ministers, pastors, and priests and both men and women in those denominations are denied the ministry that women are providing with such diligence in the other denominations.

September 14
Holy Cross Day

Numbers 21:4b-9

It is, of course, because the writers of the Gospel According of John in John 3:14-15 wrote that "just as Moses lifted up the serpent in the desolate place, thus also it is necessary for the Son of man to be lifted up in order that everyone who believes in him may have life eternally" that this rather strange text from Numbers 21:4b-9 was selected to be read together with John 3:13-17 on Holy Cross Day.

Numbers 21:4b-9 is a strange text. In it is written that the Lord God sent poisonous snakes among the Israelite people who were complaining to God and to Moses that they had been better off as slaves in Egypt than they are now in the wilderness eating the manna that the Lord is providing for them each day. Then, when the people repented, the Lord told Moses to make a bronze poisonous snake and set it up on a pole so that if a serpent bit any man he could look at the bronze serpent and live. According to an account in 2 Kings 18:4, the good king of Judah, Hezekiah, broke into pieces the bronze serpent that Moses had made and to which the Israelites had burned incense from the time of Moses until the time of Hezekiah.

Perhaps it would have been more helpful to the readers of John 3:13-17 and certainly to us if the Johannine writers, instead of their reference to the bronze serpent, had written that "everyone who believes that Jesus as the Lamb of God dying on the cross died and dies in their place will have life eternally."

Psalm 98:1-5

These beautiful verses calling upon us to "Sing to the Lord a new song, for God has done marvelous things!" are appropriate for us on Holy Cross Day and on every day. We can give to these words that were intended for Israel a Christian interpretation by understanding them to mean for us that the Lord has won the victory (over death) by vindicating Jesus who had died on the cross by raising him from the dead on Easter morning.

Psalm 78:1-2, 34-38

God is portrayed in this psalm as repeatedly compassionate, forgiving the people of Israel whenever they repented. Though the people were not faithful in keeping the covenant that God graciously had provided for them, God did not utterly destroy them. The same can be said about us.

1 Corinthians 1:18-24

Paul readily understood as he wrote this portion of his correspondence to the followers of Jesus in Corinth that the message about Jesus' death on the cross saving them from their sins is "absurd to those who are being lost." We too might ask, "How can the death of someone else take away the sins of other persons and save them from death?" Jews, Muslims, and most other people who are not themselves Christians, even some persons today who have been brought up as Christians, reason that each person must atone for that person's own sins and, if God wants to forgive them, God can certainly do that, and that God did and does not need to have Jesus die on the cross so that God can forgive sinners who repent.

Nevertheless, for Paul in this text, in the "wisdom" of God, God, through what to the world is the "foolishness" of the proclamation of the cross, considered it to be good to save those who believe. Therefore, Paul and we with Paul proclaim Christ crucified and raised from the dead by the power and the wisdom and the love of God.

John 3:13-17

For those who wrote John 3:13-15, it was necessary that the Johannine Jesus be lifted up on the cross in order that everyone who believes in him may have life eternally. This understanding, expressed here and elsewhere in our New Testament documents and elaborated upon extensively later by the great theologians of the Church, is the basis for the Christian theology of the cross upon which we focus on this Holy Cross Day and throughout the year. It is of the utmost importance that we proclaim this with love and gratitude to God and in the context of love and understanding to the people among whom we serve, especially to the children.

October 31
Reformation Day

This day and these texts, although they are not included in the Revised Common Lectionary, are provided for our consideration here from *Evangelical Lutheran Worship* (Minneapolis: Augsburg Fortress, 2006, 58).

For a biblically based reformation emphasis, reflecting over past reformation efforts in the Church during past centuries and reformation efforts needed in our own time, perhaps we should perceive the writers of the four texts listed here to have been reformer figures in four different situations, each writer self-critical within a different religious milieu. Then perhaps we can use these texts as paradigms for our own reformation work within our own religious milieu, for it would be myopic for any of us to think that there is no need for further reformation efforts within the Church in our time and place.

Psalm 46

This familiar psalm of trust in the Lord God is one of the relatively few eschatological, "no-matter-what-may-happen" psalms included in the Psalter. It is a particularly appropriate source of comfort, therefore, in times of great adversity such as Martin Luther faced during his struggles as a reformer in the sixteenth-century Western Church.

Even though the earth may be returned to its primal chaos, the city of God (Jerusalem) will be secure, not because of the good behavior of its people, but because God is in its midst. As perceived by the psalmist, the Lord God is the one who brings to Jerusalem both the desolations and the peace that will follow after the desolations are complete. The people of the city are merely to be still and to recognize that the Lord is God. Luther gave this psalm of trust a sixteenth-century application as he paraphrased this psalm in his popular song "Ein feste Burg ist unser Gott." It is our responsibility to give the psalm an application in our time and in our place. That is our call.

Jeremiah 31:31-34

The context of this reading is one of restoration after the destruction that the Lord God will bring upon Jerusalem.

The "new covenant" will focus on salvation oriented toward the individual, who will suffer because of that individual's own sin, or benefit because of that individual's obedience to the Lord God, not from the sin of that person's parents or community. This "new covenant" will put into practice the change from the earlier corporate accountability to the newer individual accountability that is explained in much more detail in Ezekiel 18:1-32.

It was not the intention, of course, of those who wrote the words of Jeremiah 31:31-34 to provide a prediction of the Christian New Testament covenant. They anticipated a new covenant with the house of Israel and with the house of Judah, not with some Jews who more than five centuries later would become followers of Jesus and not with many non-Jews who would join the new communities of faith that would evolve into Christianity. Nevertheless, followers of Jesus apparently rather quickly applied this text to themselves and to their new relationship with God through Jesus, and the influence of this text on the development of the Eucharistic words in 1 Corinthians 11:23-26 and in the Synoptic Gospels can be seen. The new covenant concept can have a sixteenth century and a twenty-first-century application as well. It is important, however, that we consider the text first of all in its own context, in which many Israelite people developed interest in individual accountability after their nation and holy city had been destroyed and within the Persian Empire they were influenced by Zoroastrian ideas of the resurrection of the body and of the judgment of each individual person.

Romans 3:19-28

In these verses the Apostle Paul wrote about the limitations of the written revelation for our salvation. In his opinion, the written Torah and Prophetic Tradition provides documentary evidence of our sins, but that in spite of this evidence of our sins we are declared to be forgiven by the grace of God through faith in what God has accomplished in the life, death, and resurrection of Jesus, the Christian Messiah. According to Paul, salvation is a gift of God for followers of Jesus of both Jewish and non-Jewish backgrounds. The gift of salvation is received by the grace of God and accepted for each person through faith in Jesus as the Christ and in what Jesus as the Christ has done and does, not through following the requirements of the Bible as it was known at that time.

Paul's views regarding life and salvation were and still are considered radical and unacceptable in the Jewish context, but they became normative within Christianity as it developed. Of course, many people within the Christian Church, including many Lutheran Christians, contrary to what Paul wrote, continue to attempt to have assurance of salvation by following the requirements of the Bible as we know it, legalistically, rather than by the grace of God accepted through faith in Jesus as the Christ.

John 8:31-36

This traditional Lutheran Reformation Day Gospel reading is an excerpt from a section of bitter anti-Jewish dialogue in John 8. The Johannine Jesus here claims that truth, freedom, and accessibility to God are possible only through him.

As we read this text, we cannot help but ask some basic questions. Could a group of people such as those who were making this claim, with all of their apparent contentiousness, be characterized as free? Could early followers of Martin Luther engaged in bitter polemic with other leaders in the Western Church and in disagreement with other reformers in the Western Church, some of whom were also followers of Martin Luther, be characterized as free? Can Lutheran Christians today who are engaged in bitter polemic against other Christians, some of whom are also Lutheran Christians, be characterized as free? Are the claims of people in such groups that truth, freedom, and accessibility to God are possible only through them convincing, especially to intelligent, thinking fellow Christians? Obviously, our work of reformation is not complete.

How can we be enthusiastically evangelical and boldly self-critical as reformers in our own religious milieu in a way in which the position and stance of the entire Church as the "Body of Christ" in the world of today will be respected and enhanced? Perhaps we should emphasize each day and each year that the inspired and revealed authority of God that motivates us is not only biblical, but is also ecclesiastical, confessional, and personal, and that we are called by God to be self-critical and actively involved in the reformation of the Church in every area of life.

CPSIA information can be obtained at www.ICGtesting.com
Printed in the USA
243734LV00001B/5/P